Mergers & Acquisitions and Partnerships in China

Mergers & Acquisitions and Partnerships in China provides a fast and accessible framework to external growth in China, and is an attempt to accurately describe the main operative conditions and in particular the most common pitfalls for foreign businessmen. The business cases in this book illustrate real business situations, including different outcomes and a thorough analysis of the reasons for success or failure of the case. The authors provide all the necessary tools to better master the negotiation and transaction process, and provide in particular, detailed explanation on the due diligence process and the regulatory framework to help readers successfully lead acquisitions in China.

Written by well-known experts in finance, law, and management, who all have deep business knowledge of China, the book aims to help practitioners, such as law firms, audit and advisory firms, and entrepreneurs to start or grow their businesses in China through successful partnerships, and acquisitions and mergers by explaining how these aspects are regulated by a complex web of laws, regulatory, and political practices in a context where the state plays a key role in the approval of important transactions.

Mergers & Acquisitions and Partnerships in China

Olivier Coispeau
Maverlinn, United Kingdom

Stéphane Luo
INALCO, France & Paris VII University, France

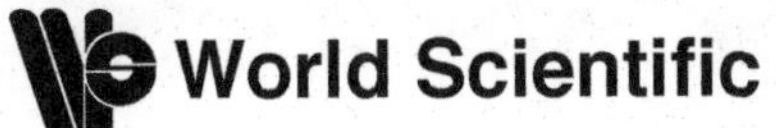

NEW JERSEY • LONDON • SINGAPORE • BEIJING • SHANGHAI • HONG KONG • TAIPEI • CHENNAI

Published by

World Scientific Publishing Co. Pte. Ltd.
5 Toh Tuck Link, Singapore 596224
USA office: 27 Warren Street, Suite 401-402, Hackensack, NJ 07601
UK office: 57 Shelton Street, Covent Garden, London WC2H 9HE

Library of Congress Cataloging-in-Publication Data
Coispeau, Olivier.
Mergers & acquisitions and partnerships in China / Olivier Coispeau, Stéphane Luo.
pages cm
Includes bibliographical references and index.
ISBN 978-9814641029 (hardcover : alk. paper)
1. Consolidation and merger of corporations--China. 2. Partnership--China. I. Luo, Stéphane. II. Title. III. Title: Mergers and acquisitions and partnerships in China.
HD2746.55.C6C65 2015
658.1'620951--dc23

2015004083

British Library Cataloguing-in-Publication Data
A catalogue record for this book is available from the British Library.

In-house Editor: Rajni Gamage

Typeset by Stallion Press
Email: enquiries@stallionpress.com

Printed in Singapore

Preface

To be successful in China over the long run requires developing some widespread, solid, and deep roots in the Chinese business environment. This means working on a detailed and careful preparation as a preliminary step to expansion. The authors are recognized experts in finance, law, and management, and they all have deep business knowledge of China. They provide here a comprehensive and precise analysis of partnerships and mergers & acquistions (M&A) in China.

The book is a multifaceted tool offering a detailed methodology based on the understanding of Chinese culture, the specific conditions for corporate valuations, and also the sometimes fuzzy financial environment. The authors clearly explain how mergers & acquisitions and partnerships in China are strictly regulated by a complex web of laws, and regulatory and political practices, in a context where the state still plays a very key role in the approval of important transactions.

This book is business-oriented and down-to-earth to help practitioners, such as law firms, audit and advisory firms, and entrepreneurs to start or grow their business in China through successful partnerships and acquisitions. The authors provide all the necessary tools to better master the negotiation and transaction process, and provide in particular, detailed explanation of the due diligences process or the regulatory framework. They also gathered with the same concern, to provide the most relevant reference on, the key laws of the People's Republic of China (PRC) to help readers successfully lead acquisitions in this country.

Among the other material provided in the book, seven detailed case studies will be most helpful to the investors contemplating accelerating their growth through M&A or partnerships operations in China.

Lead authors Olivier Coispeau (Strategy, Finance) and Stéphane Luo (Law), and contributing authors Thierry Labarre (Accounting, Tax), Josephine Chow and Stephen Yu (Human Resources), and Frank Zheng (Third Party Due Diligences) are all in their respective fields, recognized experts of China, where they have been working for decades.

The Foreword was kindly written by Professor Seamus Grimes, emeritus professor, Whitaker Institute, National University of Ireland, Galway and Professor Yves Dolais, professor of Chinese Law at the Universities of Paris 2, Aix-Marseille, and Nantes. He is the honorary dean of the Faculty of Law, Economics and Business Studies of Université d'Angers and vice chairman of the French Chinese Association for Economic Law.

Acknowledgments

The authors would like to warmly thank:

Their respective companies Maverlinn, Mazars, Towers Watson, and Keen Risk Solution, through this long-term writing exercise, and formerly RBSC for their support.

The French Chamber of Commerce and Industry of Shanghai for the genesis of this project. Under the stewardship of Annick de Kermadec-Bentzmann, the Shanghai CCI requested a series of articles about M&A in China from the various corporate finance CCI working groups of Shanghai and Beijing. As the idea matured, it became clear that compiling and harmonizing the various contributions, to deliver a more comprehensive piece dedicated to M&A practices in China, would be beneficial to the readership. The initial working group work was later enriched by non-CCI members' contributions to further explore M&A best practices in China.

Alexandra Guillet-Belaud, lawyer, and Alexandra Eva Grasset, legal counsel, formerly at Jones Day who have spared no effort for the preparatory work of this book.

Jan Petersen, for his editing and proofreading work of the French version and Helen Mei who has provided valuable insights on enhancing the first release.

Oriane Zanoli, for assisting in the translation of a significant part of this book in English together with the author, Olivier Coispeau.

All those who would like to remain anonymous and who provided very useful feedback on the first version, and greatly helped in correcting some obvious imperfections and improving the English version.

An early and different version of this work was published in French by SEFI Diffusion under the title: *Partenariats, fusions & acquisitions en Chine* on March 2012 (ISBN 9782895091349).

Contents

About the Authors

Olivier Coispeau

Olivier Coispeau is the co-founder of Maverlinn, a strategy consulting firm specialized in strategic finance and impact innovation projects. As an economist and former investment banker, he has engineered numerous industrial partnerships, and led complex industrial projects in various geographies and M&A transactions for international industry leaders, foundations, and governments, especially in the energy, transportation, and financial institutions sectors. He is also a specialist in industrial strategy and investment, and previously started and co-headed several tech funds in Europe.

Aside from advising on industrial projects, he dedicates the rest of his time working in less-favored areas on responsible leadership. He spent many years in less-favored countries, including China, advising industry leaders on growth acceleration. He has been living in China for over eight years. He has authored and contributed to many publications and he is a frequent guest speaker at finance and strategy forums.

Stéphane Luo

Stéphane Luo is a lawyer at the Paris Bar and specializes in M&A as well as related matters of corporate law, tax law, and contract law for international projects. With over 20 years of field experience, he was an advocate for pre-eminent French and American law firms for more than 15 years. He assisted many companies in large-scale implementation and acquisition projects in China, as well as their follow-up. Stéphane Luo came back to Paris at the end of 2010, in order to support the trend of outbound investment from China to Europe, and continues to put his expertise in service of French and European companies, while dividing his time between France and China.

Stéphane Luo is also a consultant for several law firms and French companies, and teaches Chinese business law at the *Institut National des Langues et Civilisations Orientales* (INALCO) in Paris and University Paris VII.

Thierry Labarre

Thierry Labarre is the senior partner for Mazars in Mainland China. Based in Beijing since 1997, he opened the then-first Chinese Mazars office. This was followed by the establishment of offices in Shanghai (2002) and Guangzhou (2007). He previously worked for Mazars in France as well as in Hong Kong. He has accompanied numerous M&A in China on behalf of companies of all sizes, allowing him to acquire a recognized understanding of the Chinese business environment, particularly of its accounting, fiscal, and financial practices.

Mazars is an international, integrated, and independent organization, specializing in audit, accountancy, tax, legal, and advisory services. Mazars relies on the skills of 13,800 professionals in 72 countries in all the five continents, and is supported by a network of correspondents and JVs in 13 additional countries. Mazars is a founding member of the Praxity alliance (69 independent organizations and 33,400 professionals in 97 countries).

Josephine Chow

Josephine Chow, office practice leader of Towers Wyatt, Taiwan, is the director of the Asia-Pacific M&A services. Towers Watson specializes in human resources consulting. Josephine Chow is also the director of the WorkTaiwan Employee Attitude Research Center. She specializes in employee training and motivation, for both local and multinational companies.

During her career at Towers Watson, Josephine Chow managed several projects related to organization and company transformation, M&A due diligences, post-acquisition integration, compensation mechanisms, talent management, and improvement of performance management tools.

Steven Yu

Steven Yu, principal consultant, is the director of actuarial services of Towers Watson, China. He assists his clients with issues related to actuarial practices and staff remuneration, and has over 13 years of experience in this field. He also provides consulting services to many multinational companies in the area of benefits plan design, as well as post-acquisition integration. Steven Yu is an expert in actuarial valuation, retirement planning, and pension system designs.

Towers Watson is a leading global professional services company that helps organizations improve their performance through human resources management. With 14,000 associates worldwide, Towers Watson offers solutions in the areas of employee benefits, talent management, rewards, and risk and capital management.

Frank Zheng

Frank Zheng is the founder and CEO of Keen Risk Solution, a third-party due diligence company based in Shenzhen. During his career, he has advised many international and Chinese companies on delicate issues related to business reputation. He is a regular invited speaker at business development forums in China.

Keen Risk Solution Co., Ltd. (KRS) is a Chinese professional company specializing in third-party due diligence in China. KRS focuses on in-depth due diligence for M&A risks in Greater China. The firm provides third party intelligence and assistance to negotitation strategy.

Disclaimer

Despite the efforts made by the authors to provide a broad analysis based on updated and quality information, our readers must realize that both the regulation and the business environment may be changing rapidly in a fast-growing economy. Therefore this book shall not substitute consulting seasoned professionals, when considering negotiating a partnership or making an acquisition in Mainland China. Our objective is to help ramp up on the learning curve in providing a general set of tools and analysis. Every case is different, and general principles must be refined and adapted precisely to one's ambitions. One size does not fit all in China, and investing in tailor-made professional business support is probably one of the wisest decisions when starting to establish or accelerate one's presence in China.

Other Publications and Related Contributions by the Same Authors

Réussir en Chine (Tome 1)

Olivier Coispeau contributed a few sections related to M&A in China in this collective guide book. France: Editions Classe Export, December 2012.

Partenariats, Fusions & Acquisitions en Chine

Olivier Coispeau, Stéphane Luo, Thierry Labarre, Joséphine Chow, and Steven Yu (2012). France: SEFI.

Dictionnaire de la Bourse

Olivier Coispeau (2013). France: SEFI (7th edition).

Introduction à l'ingénierie Financière

Olivier Coispeau (1996). *Editions SEFI.*

L'évaluation des Entreprises

Olivier Coispeau and Véronique Bessière (1990). France: SEFI (3rd edition).

Comment Vendre et S'implanter à Shanghai

Stéphane Luo and Olivier Dubuis (1999). France, Center français du commerce extérieur: Thieffry & associés (2nd edition).

Key Abbreviations and Institutions

AIC — Administration for Industry and Commerce
Technically this is a national organization with local departments in every administrative region in China, i.e., generally each province and major city.

AMC — Anti-Monopoly Committee

AMEA — Anti-Monopoly Enforcement Authorities
The AMC and the AMEA are two regulatory institutions established by the Anti-Monopoly Law of 2008 (AML). The AMC is in charge of the formulation and development of guidelines regarding competition, whereas the AMEA, which depends on the AMC, is in charge of their implementation in the market. The AMC is directly under the control of the State Council of the People's Republic of China.

COFTEC — Commission of Foreign Trade and Economy Cooperation
The COFTEC is the regional equivalent of MOFCOM (see this word's definition below). Each municipality or special economic zone has its own COFTEC (e.g., Shanghai COFTEC).

CSRC — China Securities Regulatory Commission
The CSRC is an administration directly placed under the control of the State Council. It regulates the securities and futures market. This administration creates laws and regulations and oversees the delivery, exchange, and payment of stocks, bonds, investment funds, futures contract, and other securities.

FIE — Foreign Invested Enterprise

M&A — Mergers and acquisitions

MAC — Material Adverse Change
The MAC clause usually addresses any events or changes which are initially very difficult to predict, and which affect the financial situation or the ongoing business of a company. Its implementation allows the signatory of a contract, particularly in the context of an acquisition, to renegotiate their commitment to acquire and finance a deal without penalty, between the signing and the closing of the transaction. In the past, MAC clauses were often considered mere boilerplate clauses but have now become essential in an increasingly risky environment.

MNCs — Multinational companies

MOFCOM — Ministry of Commerce of the People's Republic of China
The Chinese Ministry of Commerce, commonly referred to as MOFCOM, is responsible for the formulation of laws, regulations, and treaties on foreign trade, as well as the development of foreign trade in general. The department is mainly involved in import-export, multilateral trade rules, bilateral negotiations, direct foreign investments (FDI), use of foreign investments, external economic cooperation, and consumer protection.

PRC — People's Republic of China

WTO — World Trade Organization
The WTO is the only international organization which deals with rules governing trade between nations. At its heart are the WTO Agreements, negotiated and signed by the bulk of the world's trading nations and ratified in their parliaments. The goal is to help producers of goods and services, and exporters and importers to conduct their activities and thus facilitate international trade.

R&D — Research and Development
Research and development, as defined by the OECD, comprises of creative work undertaken on a systematic basis to increase the stock

of knowledge, including knowledge of man, culture, and society, and the use of this stock of knowledge to devise new applications. They comprise exclusively of fundamental and applied research, as well as experimental development.[1]

SAFE — State Administration of Foreign Exchange
SAFE is the government entity which regulates the organization, operation, and activities of the currency market in China. It oversees the balance of payments and the country's external debt. It is also responsible for managing the foreign currency reserves of the People's Republic of China.

SAIC — State Administration for Industry and Commerce
SAIC is the authority responsible for bills, and drafts legislations related to the organization and administration of industry and commerce in the PRC. It also handles the registration of companies and commercial institutions in the territory, including foreign investments, and issues, then checks, business licenses. SAIC regulates and inspects the quality of the products on the market, food safety, the rights and interests of consumers, brand protection, and commercial irregularities such as corruption or fraud.

SASAC — State-owned Assets Supervision and Administration Commission
SASAC is the government committee which supervises state-owned enterprises (SoEs) in China. While SASAC does not directly manage the SoEs, it appoints their executives, approves M&A, and drafts the laws related to SoEs. At the end of 2010, the SASAC was overseeing 101 public Chinese companies.

SDRC — State Development and Reform Commission
The State Development Planning Commission (SPDC) became the State Development and Reform Commission (SDRC) in 2003. The SDPC was responsible for carrying out China's Five-Year Plans; the SDRC will be conducting research on a range of key macroeconomic topics.

---

[1] Source: INSEE.

Foreword by Seamus Grimes

This text is a major contribution to understanding the mechanics of executing an M&A in China, which is likely to become the most significant emerging market for many foreign companies. It is a detailed, technically comprehensive analysis of a complex process in a business environment that presents particular challenges to foreign investors.

Based on the combined experience of experts in a wide range of business consultancy, with many years of negotiation experience in a culture which has major differences to the West, and in which company models and business practices are still at a relatively early stage of evolution, this text is essential reading for companies contemplating an M&A or other form of partnership in China. The text draws from a wealth of case studies to highlight both the potential opportunities and also the significant pitfalls associated with conducting the various stages of an M&A, from identifying a target company, to researching the specific history of the company, its ownership and potentially hidden legal obligations to existing employees, to ensuring the retention of key management talent, protecting intangible assets and finalizing the deal.

In a business environment where accountancy practices may be non-software-based and sometimes lack transparency, and in which vital legal documentation can be disorganized, in which political factors such as centralized policy may frequently have localized interpretations, the scope for making costly errors are enormous. A lack of appreciation of cultural nuances in the negotiation process, together with language barriers, potentially give rise to serious misunderstandings which can prove fatal for a successful outcome. This text guides the business planners through all the challenging steps of this complex business strategy and will prove to be a major resource in avoiding what could turn out to be very costly errors.

Seamus Grimes
Emeritus Professor
Whitaker Institute
National University of Ireland, Galway
7 February 2015

Foreword by Yves Dolais

Following the successful publication of a first book in French on M&A in China by the same authors, this new enriched work published in English shows that mergers & acquisitions (M&A) and partnerships in China continue to be a major challenge for foreign investors in China as M&A are still a source of both enthusiasm and concern.

Foreign investments in China have long been limited to the creation of industrial subsidiaries and joint ventures with Chinese partners (although some of them were established through usual principles and schemes of M&A). M&A in China are a recent phenomenon which developed in the early 2000s, and have generated a new momentum and enthusiasm for foreign companies dampened by serious concerns illustrated by the renowned failure of Coca-Cola in 2008 in the attempted take-over of Huiyuan, the leading Chinese fruit juice manufacturer.

Every M&A operation in China must therefore be thoroughly prepared in advance.

The M&A market in China still remains below its potential mainly due to regulatory and political uncertainties. Foreign investments in China reached their lowest point in five years in 2012, with foreign acquisitions in China dropping by 28% to USD98.8 billion compared to 2011. The second quarter of 2013 showed a rebound to USD163.2 billion, a level close to the 2008 peak of USD172 billion.

The M&A in China are subject to a complex regulatory, administrative and political framework which is heading towards an increasing control of the Chinese state on M&A projects. M&A in China also call for specific audit requirements.

Since 2006, the legal framework has been reinforced, complicating the process of M&A operations in China. The three main legal texts are the regulation of August 8, 2006 amended in 2009 concerning M&A, the Anti-Monopoly Law which took effect on August 1, 2008, and finally the government circular of February 3, 2011, which created a national security control agency on foreign majority investments stakes in strategic sectors, modelled upon similar existing mechanisms in other countries.

M&A in China are characterized by a mandatory and systematic administrative approval beforehand, based on both legality and opportunity. The difficulties to master the Chinese targets' valuation and to determine the proper acquisition price due to the imprecision of the financial information provided and the constraints related to setting the purchase price, as well as control over the payment of the purchasing price (although the rules have changed since June 2014) are all issues that should be taken into account while conducting M&A operations in China. This emphasizes the importance of mastering very early on the due diligences process and the complex regulatory framework.

This new and fully updated book is a highly anticipated initiative to assist foreign companies in their development projects in China. The interdisciplinary approach of this work provides a helpful and necessary answer to the key questions concerning the challenges and complexity of procedures as well as the risks related to M&A transactions in China.

This book is intended for law firms, auditing and consultancy firms, companies already established in China as well as those contemplating investment in this country. The great merit of the authors is to deliver an extremely detailed and comprehensive study on M&A in China accompanied by numerous business cases and a much needed regulatory appendix.

The authors Olivier Coispeau, Stéphane Luo, Thierry Labarre, Frank Zheng, Josephine Chow, and Steven Yu have all gained an extensive experience in M&A in Asia and China, thus placing this book as an indisputable work of reference.

Yves DOLAIS

Professor of Chinese law,
Universities of Paris 2, Aix Marseille and Nantes
Honorary Dean,
Faculty of Law, Economics and Management of the University of Angers
Vice-President of the French-Chinese Association for Economic Law
8 December 2014

Introduction

Olivier Coispeau

"For China is the greatest mystifying and stupefying fact in the modern world, and that not only because of her age or her geographical greatness. She is the oldest living nation with a continuous culture; she has the largest population; once she was the greatest empire in the world, and she was a conqueror; she gave the world some of its most important inventions; she has a literature, a philosophy, a wisdom of life entirely her own; and in the realms of art, she soared where others merely made an effort to flap their wings."

Lin Yutang

My Country and My People, 1936

Those seeking to conduct business in China or interested by the business life in the People's Republic of China will find this book enlightening. In this respect, M&A and strategic partnerships are both a critical component and an essential factor of growth acceleration. However, strategies are evolving over time, sometimes quickly due to the change of regulatory environment, for good reasons (e.g., legal risk, fiscal impact, flexibility). It is mandatory to closely monitor these changes to find what can be the most appropriate structures for cooperation and growth acceleration. Almost every Fortune 500 company has now built a firm presence in China, seeking to be expanded and consolidated, and SMEs are the fastest growing segment in the foreign business community.

0.1. Success in China Cannot Be the Result of Sheer Luck

After establishing itself as the workshop of the world and the world's leading exporter, China is now seeking value-added products, technology content, international marketing recognition, and powerful brands. In short, Chinese companies need a higher level of sophistication and visibility to meet the needs of their huge domestic market. A stronger presence on the export market under China's home grown brands is also becoming a matter of interest, as China has been for long an Original Equipment Manufacturer (OEM) market with relatively weak international brands. This shall be taken as the status quo.

China is the world's third economic power with a RMB57 trillion GDP in 2013, behind Europe, as a consolidated entity, and the United States, and plans to grow at a yearly 7% to 8%. About 67% of the GDP is generated by eastern coastal and province-level municipalities, with Guangdong, Shandong, and Jiangsu being the stronger contributors. China's economic transformation since 1979 is one of the most striking phenomena in the annals of modern economic history. No other country in modern history has ever generated a comparable 10% yearly average economic growth for more than 30 years (1979–2010), even less so at this scale.

One of the key challenges for the senior management of industry leaders has become the position of their companies on emerging markets and in particular, in China. Building a strong position in China requires significant human and financial investments, and implies successful cooperation with regional and national players.

Virtually unknown in the early '90s, M&A operations and partnerships in China have quickly developed over the last 10 years (however, some early joint ventures were already established under M&A's usual assets deal or equity deal scheme) — after the integration of China into the WTO.

The implantation of the main worldwide market leaders in China has contributed to deeply transforming the Chinese economy, gradually bringing it closer to international practices. Much remains to be done to meet the needs of the largest population in the world, but the catching-up process has started some time ago. For investors and senior management of the world's largest companies, partnerships and M&A remain crucial instruments for quickly ensuring a lasting presence on this huge, complex, and hypercompetitive market. The case section of the book will highlight a number of these defining growth operations (e.g., Hsu Fu Chi, Airbus, Coca-Cola, or Nestlé).

The success experienced by numerous international groups in China is not a mere coincidence. This is certainly the result of financial investments, but even more importantly, of a substantial human investment in leadership. This means vision and high quality execution, time spent overcoming unexpected obstacles, and development of good local interpersonal skills in a complex web of business relationships. Rushing to the Chinese market without being familiar with its specificities is likely to lead to great frustration and pain.

China is the world's oldest and most pervasive bureaucracy,[2] on the way of continuous economic reforms, to build a market economy with socialist characteristics under the stewardship of the Chinese Communist Party. To do business in China takes a lot of patience and perseverance. In China, time is a wise man's best friend. At the same time, foreign businessmen must be ready for action, as windows of opportunity can open much quicker than they can possibly realize, but also shut down. Foreign investors in China must first carefully plan and prepare for entering the Chinese market, before seriously considering any acquisitions or integration with a Chinese company. After due preparation, investors should stick to their vision and move forward swiftly, with flexibility and persistence. The results are not likely to show up overnight but it is likely that endurance will be tested and handsomely rewarded.

In order to be successful, an acquisition, a merger, or a partnership in China requires the mobilization of a compact team of specialists to ensure a rigorous process of identification, acquisition, and integration of the targets. Companies are more successful at M&A when they apply the same focus, consistency, and professionalism to it as they do to other critical disciplines.[3] The stakes and

---

[2] P. Kenna and S. Lacy (1994), *Business China: A Practical Guide to Understanding Chinese Business Culture*. New York, USA: McGraw Hill, p. 8.

[3] C. Ferrer, R. Uhlaner, and A. West, "M&A as Competitive Advantage," Mckinsey & Company, August 2013; available online at www.mckinsey.com/insights/corporate_finance/m_and_a_as_competitive advantage (accessed on December 18, 2014).

risks of any expansion operation must be carefully handled by a team of experts, who are able to guide the acquirer through the different stages of the transaction on China's territory. In such a complex environment, the temptation to skip steps that are considered of little use or too tedious, to take shortcuts, or to act by one's self in order to cut costs is always present. This is a recipe for bitter disappointment, and this attitude is probably the reason behind the high rate of failed acquisitions in China, much higher in fact than in the United States or Europe.

It can be compared to the naive belief that buying a lottery ticket can lead to fortune, without first pondering the odds of losing money in comparison to the chances of winning. Any serious endeavor therefore requires carefully planned negotiations; amateurism is not an option in such an old commercial culture. It is absolutely mandatory to combine finesse, flexibility — in particular in the operation's structuring — determination and lucidity, and a rigorous approach, to ensure the legal and economic viability of the operation. A good knowledge of the Chinese environment and good Chinese business friends are also a must to properly interpret the signals issued by future partners.

0.2. A Chinese Business Footprint Has Become a Strategic Necessity

The emergence of M&A in China can be dated to the early '90s. The economic shift operated by Deng Xiaoping in 1978 initiated the beginning of a new wave of foreign investment in China. The first mid-size foreign investments were made in China by the overseas Chinese in the form of cooperative joint venture, as no real equity based transactions were authorized until 2002. In 2013, M&A transactions in China reached a value of over USD186 billion,[4] showing a 64% annual average growth since 2001 with 1,062 transactions.

[4]"China and Hong Kong M&A Trend Report 2013"; available online at www.mergermarket.com/pdf/ChinaHongKongTrendReport2013.pdf (accessed on December 18, 2014).

Inbound transactions continued to be dwarfed by outbound transactions in transaction number, meaning that China's M&A market is now more active outbound but on smaller-scale operations in average. Inbound M&A deals have oscillated for three years in a corridor of 150 to 200 deals per year. This relatively small number, given the size of the economy, gives a sense of why calibrating and chasing the right opportunity with the proper team in China is important.

Therefore, developing a reasonable growth strategy taking into account the possibility to build and secure a larger footprint on the Chinese market, possibly by acquisition or strategic partnership, is not such an easy assignment.

China has now become the third largest world economy, right behind Europe and the United States, with an annual growth estimated at 10.4% over 2007–2011. As the development goals of the XII Plan assert the ambition to focus on more qualitative growth,

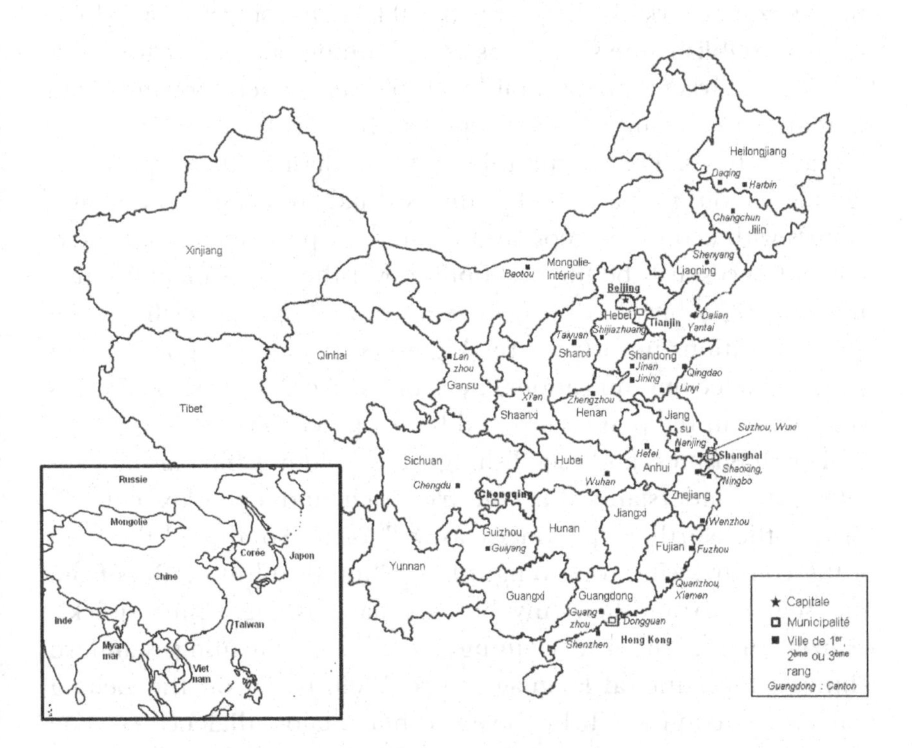

Figure 0.1. Map of China.

China's economy is emphasizing new criteria such as people's welfare, environment preservation, and social harmony. However, this change still translates into a significant growth rate compared to more mature economies. The China economy is now double-sided — one side still emerging, another side converging quickly with mature economies. As a consequence of the size of its domestic market (1.34 billion nationals), the Chinese market is a subject of a sometimes irrational fascination. This gigantic entity represents, compared to most countries, a unique challenge, stemming from its difference, from the multicultural European American environment to its complexity.

Within such a dense territory divided into 23 provinces, five autonomous regions, and four direct municipalities, with a coastline covering approximately 14,500 km (from the Bohai gulf in the North to the Gulf of Tonkin in the South), and waterways such as the Yangzi network extending to 18,000 km, choosing a proper location to establish one's business is a defining success factor. This 9,597 km^2 market is not monolithic. Differences in culture and living standards are strong between regions often crisscrossed by strong migratory flows. This cultural diversity emphasizes the importance of a meticulous preparation for any external growth operation, and it starts with economic geography. The most popular regions today may not necessarily be the best option over the long run, and sometimes taking a bit of risk can be very rewarding, especially as the communications infrastructure (highways, railways, airports, waterways, and telecommunications) develops and quickly connects areas which were in the past considered hardly practicable.

Doing business and establishing a foothold in China also means getting to understand the country's rich and complex culture. Visiting the Northern provinces, as well as the South and the West of the country, will put into light how Chinese culture differs from one region to another. Any businessman visiting China quickly realizes that Mandarin (Putonghua 普通话, meaning standard Chinese, the national language since 1909, based on the Beijing dialect) is completed by seven other major dialects — Yue (Cantonese), Wu (Shanghainese), Minbei (Fuzhou), Minnan

(Hokkien-Taiwanese), Xiang, Gan, and Hakka — as well as hundreds of other ethnic minorities' languages.

Investors who have decided to make their first industrial investment in China may be a little puzzled by cities designated by their rank (first-tier city, second-tier city, etc.). Although these are commonly used, the list of cities belonging to each category may slightly vary according to the sources, as there is no official classification.

Below is an indicative generally accepted ranking of major Chinese cities (in alphabetical order):

Table 0.1. Ranking of China's Major Cities.

First-Tier City	Second-Tier City	Third-Tier City
Beijing	Changsha	Baotu
Chongqing	Chengdu	Changchun
Guangzhou	Dalian	Changzhou
Shanghai	Dongguan	Daqing
Shenzhen	Foshan	Fuzhou
	Hangzhou	Guiyang
	Harbin	Hefei
	Jinan	Jining
	Nanjing	Kunming
	Ningbo	Lianyungang
	Qingdao	Lanzhou
	Quanzhou	Linyi
	Shenyang	Nantong
	Suzhou	Shaoxing
	Tangshan	Shijiazhuang
	Tianjin	Taizhou
	Wuhan	Weifang
	Wuxi	Weizhou
	Yantai	Xiamen
	Zhengzhou	Xi'an
		Xuzhou
		Zhuhai
		Zibo

Clusters of cities, such as the Dongyang, Yiwu, Yongkong, Pujiang, Lanxi, and Jinhua cluster in Zhejiang province, can also create a big surprise when one realizes that what were initially perceived as rather small cities, are in fact a giant urban cluster of population, altogether possibly as big as a tier-one city.

In general, first-tier cities, all located on the coast, are considered the most advanced in terms of economic development, economic infrastructure, communication, and education. The diversity of their economic web creates the right environment to foster a rich, diverse, and multilingual talent pool. The best and sometimes very old Chinese universities will be located in these top cities (e.g., Beita, Tsinghua, Fudan, Jiaotong), and offer a significantly higher standard of life than in the rest of the country.

The advantages of first-tier cities have led to soaring operating costs (e.g., wages,[5] real estate, car licence plates, education, health, energy, etc.). Therefore, an increasing number of companies are turning to second- and third-tier cities, where local governments are truly making huge efforts to attract foreign manufacturers by heavily investing in the modernization of their city infrastructure and offering substantial economic incentives to those who would consider establishing themselves further west.

Many quick and spectacular success stories have been widely commented on in the local and foreign press. One can only admire the rapid pace of the progress made and the results achieved in the last few years. One can also reflect on some of the consequences of such accelerated growth in the long run, such as the changing demography, environmental problems, and the need to reassess Chinese culture and traditions in this development process.

However, it is important to keep in mind that the approach of this great emerging country cannot be justified by a few cases of successful implementations and a collective enthusiasm. Any investor should examine more deeply the key reasons and priorities

---

[5] Wage increase has been ranked as the number one concern in the 2013 AmCham Shanghai member company survey; Davis Basmajian (2013), *Orientation China Guidebook*. Shanghai: AmCham, p. 17.

for establishing a strong presence in China (compared to other geographic options), then prepare the necessary financial and human resources to focus on quickly achieving a number of winning moves to establish one's footprint. Building a business in China can otherwise prove bitter, disappointing, expensive, and unproductive. Most companies are now in China for the Chinese market. The US companies report that their produce for the domestic market is on the rise (up to 60% in 2013), while those in China producing for export markets are steadily declining (17% for US companies in 2012, from 23% in 2010).

Some companies are well known to have been dazzled by the fast growing Chinese market, lacked sufficient preparation, and believed in miracles which never happened. They set objectives aligned with the practices defined by a foreign headquarters located thousands of miles away, as well as unreasonable profitability targets and meagre support to their local team. Such hands off "copy, paste" decisions have almost no chance of being successful in China. Most of those who followed that route have had to rethink their whole strategy regarding the Chinese market, after losing valuable time to competition, money, and sometimes their credibility. It is therefore essential to be ambitious, provide sufficient support to the local team, and build good foundations, but without setting unrealistic expectations. Mushroom growth will always be tempting but revenue bubbles will be unsustainable if the profitability of the operations is not established and sustainable.

Chapter 1

Preparing for an External Growth Operation in China

1.1. Mergers & Acquisitions Specificities in China

(1) Approaching the Chinese market in a rigorous way

The size and dynamics of the Chinese market alone are not a sufficient guarantee of success for an M&A operation or a strategic partnership. Local and international competition is fierce, the legal framework still flexible and sometimes soft, and the business name of the game very clear: maximize profitability and reduce time to recoup investment.

Naïve optimism that business will flow through one's door is not an option, with a few remarkable exceptions (e.g., "dream brands"); nobody is really waiting for your products in this urban jungle, but everybody will be interested to see what you can offer. The emergence of new competitors, possibly from local elites who were yesterday's partners, can be amazingly quick. Industry consolidation strategies must be assessed in the light of China's tremendous capacity to self-generate new entrepreneurs trained in the best universities locally or abroad, and capable to adapt and develop faster than foreigners into the Chinese industrial web. However, this can be a long-term objective for a specific and well-defined product range.

The availability of talent, the growing innovation capacity of the Chinese firms, the intimate knowledge of the economics, the political environment, and the availability of funding — encouraging local initiatives — all induce strong competitive pressures. Price and talent wars often occur to tame competition and result in the disappearance of less resistant competitors, especially when this is coupled with rumors or disclosures of improper products shipped on the market or disappointed teams leaving the firm. Preparing a winning entry strategy takes a bit of detailed and rigorous analysis, to know precisely how to position products and develop one's market share.

Protection of the key "soft" assets — talents, intellectual property (IP) — is often considered a sensitive and problematic issue in China. Damage that can possibly be inflicted on a foreign company due to an unwilling transfer of know-how expertise is huge. Close to the protection of key assets are the risk of internal fraud and the risk of using counterfeit products or releasing improper products[6] on the market, which may lead to serious losses. This requires a constant monitoring of business operations and the way business is done. In China, conflict of interest may be interpreted in a different way than is the West: doing business with someone I know is actually a way to reduce risk.

It is indeed mandatory to be well organized, constantly monitor the way business is done, be surrounded by loyal local allies, and remain very close to on-field operations. Strategies to protect key assets must be designed, especially the more fragile and volatile assets, such as people and intellectual property. This requires being creative, being respectful of the laws, and exploiting every opportunity offered by the existing PRC laws and the local partners' network. Of course, this phenomenon is not limited to China and similar problems can be witnessed in all emerging countries.

---

[6]Shanghai Husi Food Co., a subsidiary of OSI Group, based in Aurora, Illinois, was suspected of using expired meat mixed with fresh meat in producing processed food. It was shut down by local regulators in China. This long-time McDonald's meat supplier was also cut by other fast food chains it supplied. China's Food and Drug Administration ordered nationwide checks of restaurants supplied by Shanghai Husi. Wang Hongyi and Elizabeth Wu, "Tainted Food Scandal Now Focuses on Supply Chain," CHINADAILYUSA, July 24, 2014; available online at usa.chinadaily.com.cn/business/2014-07/24/content_17918628.htm (accessed on September 24, 2014).

It is therefore necessary to carefully plan and monitor the Chinese market's strategic approach, by progressively and relentlessly building a quality position and a foothold. At the same time, as credibility increases, preparing for a well-timed leap is necessary. Progressiveness of the efforts deployed is mandatory and requires a tactical preparation for the key stages of development. Strategically, a company must set ambitious but realistic goals, that take into account the rapid Chinese market growth and the specific appetite of the Chinese market for certain products (e.g., color codes, lucky numbers, positive references to China's culture and traditions).

The establishment of a presence in China as a simple duplication of a presence in Europe or in the US is just a beginner's mistake to avoid. Many management books are full of stories which should have worked on paper in China but finally failed, for obvious reasons uncovered after a more detailed analysis. One foreign automotive manufacturer had difficulties in selling its newly produced car in China. Oddly, it was very successful in other countries, and in theory, well suited for the Chinese market. Someone realized that the car was mostly available in metal green. The most educated people will indeed associate the color with health, prosperity, and harmony, but also with nausea. A more serious concern is that a widespread popular tradition associates green hats in China with infidelity, and it is used as an idiom for a cuckold and tends to make Chinese laugh at it. Therefore, buying a green car is not exactly a symbol bringing "face" to its owner; it is no surprise that such cars were hard to sell without a huge discount in China. In essence, China is a country where experimenting and dialoguing is crucial, and any wise organization must be organized and ready for that.

The stakes associated with a presence in China must be pondered, and the companies willing to do so must realize that important opportunities come with a high level of risk. However, these risks are controllable and manageable, provided that the human investments (advisory, consultancy, training, auditing) and industrial investments are meticulously calculated and methodically implemented, with sufficient flexibility to leave a margin for interpretation to local conditions. Those who prefer to systematically use shortcuts and simplistic approaches will probably face bitter setbacks.

(2) Assessing administrative changes

China's accession to the WTO on December 11, 2001 allowed foreign investors to access many economic sectors previously restricted, thus creating a new wave of international investments. Industrial sectors which were once closed to foreign investors have opened up, although the recent legal evolution has also tightened a few screws, on the grounds of preserving national security. Acquisitions by foreigners of listed companies, following a public take-over bid, have recently been successfully carried out (e.g., acquisition of Supor by Groupe SEB in several steps). However, this reform is still ongoing, and several sectors are still closely monitored or restricted to Chinese majority ownership including media, financial institutions, and airline ticket bookings.

Along with this market reform, China has significantly adapted its state-owned companies created under the communist era to a new market economy with socialist characteristics. This means that China's government did not wish to support loss making or ineffective state-owned companies, and was eager to confront them with the reality of offer and supply on competitive markets.

In specific sectors, the Chinese government pushed companies to merge and better specialize to form integrated conglomerates having the potential to become world leaders. Moreover, the Chinese state is trying to dispose of its interest in these companies and is looking for private investors to manage these assets.

As a result, the number of state-owned companies, as well as the significant number of offers of partnerships and acquisitions of state-owned corporations made available to foreign investors, is decreasing. At the same time, new forms of partnerships based on foreign technology and domestic financial investments are emerging. Still, the numerous constraints on restructuring operations and partnerships concluded within China are such that many operations are still conducted offshore.

Even though China has become a major economic player and has been ranked from time to time as one of the most attractive destinations for foreign investment, the fact remains that it has just emerged from a planned economy derived from a Marxist approach and intends to move towards a socialist market economy, with all the implied possibly unstable changes and rapid adjustments. This transition confers specific characteristics to its relatively young legal environment, particularly in terms of control of foreign investments.

It should be first noted that the restructuring of complex acquisitions and mergers techniques and possibilities, are much less extensive and developed than in mature economies. One must assess what is feasible and under what conditions, before engaging in operations that may ultimately prove to be impossible or awkward in China, for example, due to potentially conflicting political agendas such as protecting "core" national brands.

Control on foreign exchange in China still remains a source of constraints for cross-border restructuring and M&A operations. The gradual internationalization of the renminbi (RMB) is going to change this in the future. But for now, a duality of regimes is applied to Foreign Invested Enterprises (FIE) and purely domestic firms, even though new regulations tend to bridge these two regimes, notably the Company Law and the Enterprise Income Tax Law. Many special texts, particularly in the field of company restructuring and acquisition, continue to provide specific rules depending on whether the investor is Chinese or foreign.[7]

To date, every foreign investment on Chinese territory systematically requires the Chinese authorities' approval. Such approval is

---

[7] For instance, this is the case in one of the texts on acquisition of Chinese domestic entities by a foreign investor (*Acquisition of Domestic Enterprises by Foreign Investors,* as amended on September 8, 2006) or the one with regard to the transfer of shares of listed or state-owned corporations to foreign investors (*Notice on Relevant Issues Concerning Application Procedures for Transfer of State-owned Shares of Listed Companies to Foreign Investors and Enterprises with Foreign Investment,* in force since January 21, 2004; *Using Foreign Investment to Reorganize State-owned Enterprises Tentative Provisions,* effective January 1, 2003).

given at different levels, depending on the size of the envisaged investment and on the industry, which may induce conflicting solutions and requirements depending on whether the relevant authorities are national, provincial, or local, and whether they are in a coastal and economically privileged province, or a more remote and less economically developed district.

Local governments may also have their own interpretation of these laws and regulations. They may even publish implementation guidelines which overlay national laws, which can create complex situations that are always quite delicate to solve and time consuming. Local regulations can be drawn up in terms which may be interpreted differently from the national framework. Convergence towards a viable solution will then be a matter of negotiation and finesse of these texts' interpretation. From this perspective, China is a pragmatic country, and meeting with people and understanding their concerns are very important at each step of the process. The arrival of a new political leadership in China, under the stewardship of Xi Jinping, has also redefined the house rules, and what could be considered acceptable or even normal in the past to grease the wheels is not acceptable any more, associated with corruption and punished.

(3) China still remains a particular environment for M&A

The lack of accounting transparency is too often responsible for creating a difficult environment to assess a potential target. The underlying management of social, fiscal, and environmental liabilities may entail complex issues in an equity deal, implying a transfer of social and fiscal responsibility from the target to the acquirer.

In the past, the obligation to pay in full the acquisition price of a PRC target company within three months was one of the key differences between M&A operations in China and in Western countries, as it increased the Chinese inbound M&A transaction risk profile.

This obligation limited the possible use of safeguard and protection techniques for the acquirer, such as escrow accounts for a part of the buying price or the inclusion of earn out clauses (additional payment depending on milestones). Ultimately, these constraints limited the options available to legally challenge the seller in the event of the discovery of undisclosed liabilities after the closing. The 2014 reform has abolished this restriction and China's M&A practices are converging to the world's best practices.

Acquisition and restructuring strategies can still be delicate to carry out in a fast moving economy and adjusting legal environment. The laws are sometimes drafted in general terms, leaving a lot of room for interpretation. They can be incomplete or even in contradiction with possible interpretations at various administrative levels. It sometimes makes the practice of law look surprisingly flexible when dealing with reference texts. A regular practice of these frequent problems in China, as well as strong interpersonal skills, a good network, and a precise knowledge of what may be a deal breaker will generally indicate whether an external acquisition or partnership is sustainable or not. However, it may take some time to patiently assemble all the pieces of such a jigsaw.

1.2. Typology of Mergers & Acquisitions in China

Before acquiring a Chinese structure, any foreign investor must carefully choose the legal form of the Chinese entity in which its own Chinese target will be incorporated. In addition to the opening of a representation office, which has nowadays become a bit outdated, except for some heavily regulated sectors such as banks, foreign investors can better set up their business in China by using a joint venture (JV) as a host structure, or a wholly foreign-owned enterprise (WFOE or WOFE). Nevertheless, some industrial sectors which have theoretically opened up to foreign investments still remain, in practice, relatively closed. The thresholds typically allowed for these sectors are 50%, 49%, 30%, or even 18% acquisitions (the lowest threshold applies to banking and financial sectors), depending on the level of sensitivity perceived by the local authorities in charge of the related industries.

(1) Joint ventures in China

In the past, joint ventures (JVs) were the only form of legal entity allowing foreign investors to establish a presence in the Chinese market, as they had no choice but to cooperate with one or several Chinese partner(s). Nowadays, joint ventures are only mandatory for a few types of investments and attract investors who really wish to team up with a Chinese partner. If more than 25% of a company is owned by a foreign investor, the entity will legally become a joint venture. Until it was recently revisited on a new basis, this form of relationship was not considered the most convenient one to handle business development, as conflicting strategies between partners and cultural differences could quickly poison the well, and lead to very business-detrimental disputes for both parties. One also does not always realize that sharing capital with local minority partners in a domestic Chinese company could result in a situation of virtual joint venture, with the Chinese party being in the position to significantly influence the course of business by objecting to many important decisions.

In a joint venture, which is a limited liability company, shareholders from the Special Administrative Regions of Hong Kong and Macao, or from Taiwan — even those considered as part of Greater China — are technically identified as foreign shareholders.

Joint ventures have a tendency to be difficult to operate and manage over time, as the partners' ambitions can quickly diverge. Unless everything possible is done to keep the Chinese partner happy, it is wise to consider that such a form of cooperation is temporary and that it is only one of the possible routes to enter the Chinese market. Probably for this very reason, over the past years, the number of JVs has greatly declined in favor of wholly foreign-owned enterprises.

(2) Cooperative joint ventures (CJV) and equity joint ventures (EJV)

Since China joined the WTO in 2001 and the release of relaxed regulations in terms of investment, foreign investors prefer to establish wholly foreign-owned enterprises. JVs have become a small percentage of foreign partnerships and of acquisition or growth vehicles. In particular, cooperative joint ventures (CJV) now account for less than 5% of start-ups. However, as it was previously mentioned, Chinese regulations require that some sectors be accessible to foreign investors only through strategic partnerships (e.g., automotive, unless otherwise stipulated, and financial institutions). WFOEs are therefore not the only answer. In such a case, an appropriate partnership structure must be selected.

Equity joint ventures (EJV) are more widespread than CJV, even though they resemble one another. The process for the authorities to approve the structure (supervisory authorities, type of agreement, tax status, applicable law, and ways to resolve potential disputes) is quite similar for both structures. However, EJV and CJV differentiate themselves in two aspects:

- An EJV is an independent legal structure necessarily endowed with a moral personality. This is not mandatory for a CJV which can thus have lower operating costs. However, the latter form can consequently lack an autonomous legal existence shielding those establishing the structure.
- A CJV is flexible. Profit, risk, and management sharing, as well as the monitoring of financial flows are based on a contractual agreement negotiated between the parties. For an EJV, profit, risk, and management sharing, as well as the monitoring of financial flows are based on the proportional amount of shares held in the capital.

Joint ventures, while not mandatory, may be of interest to foreign investors who are looking for a Chinese partner able to control some key factors of success — networks, brand, land, licenses, and access to key suppliers. This kind of partnership significantly reduces the start-up costs and risks. As part of a CJV, a Chinese industrial can "share" its distribution license in order to access sectors otherwise closed to foreigners.

The same thing is not feasible in an EJV structure, as the so-called license is considered part of the new company's assets (restrictions concerning the accessibility of the sector to foreigners are still in force). The assets involved are, for example, those which have been heavily taxed on transfer or are too complicated to transfer, for administrative reasons. This means that a CJV, although rare in occurrence, can be useful in certain cases, notably for temporary structures put in place for implementing large projects:

- The foreign party in a CJV can bring or rent exclusive technology or equipment. The CJV can then reimburse the partner by a preferred compensation proportional to the income generated.
- Rights are not necessarily proportional to contributions and can be determined at the discretion of the parties. The majority in key decision-making can therefore be flexibly assigned to one party or the other.
- The definition of rights and responsibilities in advance can significantly reduce risks, although the negotiation of this part of the agreement is likely to be long.
- The CJV contract can be modified without having to dissolve the partnership, which allows it to be flexible and responsive to the changes of the environment; the responsibility of the expense items can be contractually assigned to one party or the other.
- The CJV may or may not be a moral person. In the event that it is not, its mechanisms are similar to those of a joint venture. The EJV is always a moral person and has limited liability.

A CJV seems more flexible and advantageous than an EJV, and less risky than a WFOE where everything needs to be built from scratch. However, one must keep in mind that the negotiation of a cooperative partnership can be a long and, sometimes, complex process. Every term of the contract is negotiated separately, which means that the parties can end up disagreeing with each other and be forced to stop the negotiations. Moreover, the particular nature of each CJV requires a specific assessment from the authorities at the time of registration. The fact that the Chinese authorities have to give their approval should be taken into account, in order to avoid substantial administrative delays.

Using a CJV is in general a requirement for foreign players looking to operate in a "closed" or "restricted" sector. For example, in the telecommunication sector, a CJV Chinese partner can lend and share its license with a foreign operator in exchange for fair compensation.

This license being non-transferable to a third party negates the possibility to consider bringing it to an EJV, in which a foreigner is a shareholder. The complex and flexible nature of the CJV clearly underlines the fact that, in order for the agreement to be perfectly negotiated, high quality resources must be contributed to manage what is likely to be a delicate relationship, and therefore enhance the probability of success of such a partnership.

A JV can be created:

- With a mixed capital structure — equity joint venture (EJV) — in which the equity contribution of the partners matches their social and financial rights within the entity.
- Contractually — contractual joint venture (CJV) — in which the amount of equity contribution, social and financial rights, and consequently, dividends, are contractually dissociated. This type of company was first created to manage complex partnerships in specific sectors (e.g., telecommunication or natural resources exploitation) and is now less common in China.

(3) Wholly Foreign-Owned Enterprises (WFOE)

These are limited liability companies created by one or several foreign investors. Over the past few years, foreign investors have favored the FIEs' legal structure.

Table 1.1. Comparison between EJV and CJV.

Majority JV (both)	**EJV**	**CJV**
Ownership of profit and loss	According to capital contributions	According to cooperation contract
Possible distribution of proceeds	Cash according to ownership	Cash subject to JV contract rules
Pros and cons	+ Collaboration contract is clearer + Capacity to issue reserved new shares to partner – Possible valuation problem when increasing capital	+ Flexible collaboration – Disagreement may be more frequent – Longer negotiations with partner – Harder to come to an agreement

They are preferred to JVs, which require the careful management, over a long time, of the relationship with their Chinese partners, with whom interests may finally diverge.

Moreover, in a project where a significant technology transfer is required, the structure of a Wholly Foreign-Owned Enterprise (WFOE) can minimize the risk of disclosure. The management of the WFOE is simplified by the compact structure of its shareholding, which prevents the Chinese and foreign partners from finding themselves in an argument over their sometimes drastically incompatible vision of the future, since this has too often been the cause of numerous JVs' malfunctions in the past.

(4) Foreign-invested joint-stock limited company

These are the only foreign-invested companies that can be listed on the Chinese stock market. JVs or WFOEs, subject to fulfilling certain conditions, will have to be converted into FISC structures before being listed on the Shenzhen- or Shanghai-regulated stock markets. Conditions for establishing a FISC are more restrictive than those required for the creation of a JV or a WFOE, particularly in terms of capital allocation.

(5) Foundations and NGOs

These entities are only accessible through partnerships with Chinese citizens, although the legal framework does not formally set restrictions regarding the nationality of the founder: Foreigners can donate or establish foundations in China, and foreign foundations can establish representative offices in Mainland China.

The first foundation was established in 1981, and the first law concerning foundations, *Regulation of Foundations,* was passed in June 2004 so as to provide a legal framework for the multiplying private foundations. The One Foundation (壹基金) was registered on December 3, 2010, as the first private charitable fundraising organization in China. In 2011, the Amway Charity Foundation (ACF), was the first non-public foundation established by a multinational corporation and supervised by China's Ministry of Civil Affairs.

Foundations are under the responsibility of the Ministry of Civil Affairs. They must have a capital of RMB20 million for national registration and RMB2 million for local registration. The foundations are developing towards the social economy sector.

Under the "dual administration system", only a limited number of NGOs can obtain legal status in China. As a consequence, a large number of NGOs either register as companies or operate unregistered in the grey area. Based on experience, it is even harder for foreign NGOs to register in China, despite the fact that many of them have secure funding. Hopefully, this situation will change in the future.

Foreign NGOs in China generally have three forms of identity:

- Organizations officially registered at the Ministry of Civil Affairs, such as the Half the Sky Foundation.
- Those registered as for-profit organizations, like the Badi Foundation.
- Those neither registered at the Ministry of Civil Affairs nor as for-profit organizations, but working with officially registered Chinese NGOs to carry out projects in China, such as the Library Project.

The emerging but rather closed NGO sector in China has been plagued with many scandals and detrimental rumors. Fundraising is always the number one big problem for nearly all NGOs, as only public foundations can raise funds publicly. Fundraising channels for other foundations and non-profits come from individual or corporate donations, CSR programme funded by companies, and prizes and awards given by the government or other organizations.

In mid-2011, the Red Cross Society of China (RCSC) was exposed by people who claimed that the general manager of Red Cross Commerce was boasting about her luxurious lifestyle, and showing off her fancy cars, expensive handbags, and palatial villa. Posts on Chinese social media raising concerns over how donations were used by the country's state-run organization dealt a major blow to RCSC, which has been struggling to regain trust since the scandal. Donations to the Society dropped by 23.7% in 2012, according to the China Charity and Donation Information Center.[8] Since then, it has become the icon of a dysfunctional NPO sector, which certainly amplified rumors and possibly elaborated misunderstandings.

The Society released a statement in August 2014 saying that new rumors have been circulating, and pledged to improve its transparency. "The incident has triggered a collective outburst of long-time frustration about the Red Cross's murky bureaucracy and questionable governance. And faced with this crisis of trust, the Red Cross Society of China failed to give a reasonable explanation. It will lose its credibility completely if it does not learn lessons from the corruption scandals involving the overspending on meals and other spending irregularities."[9]

In the future, this sector is likely to be much more open to the private sector, including foreign organizations, as "charity organizations [are never forced] to make public their accounts, which provide[s] the leaders [with an] opportunity to carry out corruption. While the Red Cross must clearly open to the public where the donation goes to, our government should reform the charity system."[10] Greater Board independence and stronger governance are likely to be the key measures to enhance the quality of this sector, and create greater and more measurable common goods in China.[11]

---

[8]Su Zhou, "Scandal Woman in Gambling and Sex Probe," *CHINADAILY.COM.CN*, August 5, 2014; available online at http://www.chinadaily.com.cn/china/2014-08/05/content_18247425.htm (accessed on September 24, 2014).

[9]Quoting Yu Jianrong, a Professor at the Chinese Academy of Social Sciences in "Guo Meimei and the Red Cross Scandal," *CHINADAILY.COM.CN*, July 15, 2011; available online at http://www.chinadaily.com.cn/opinion/2011–07/15/content_12912148.htm (accessed on August 6, 2014).

[10]Quoting Hu Xingdou, Economics Professor at Beijing Institute of Technology in "Guo Meimei and the Red Cross Scandal," *CHINADAILY.COM.CN*, July 15, 2011; available online at http://www.chinadaily.com.cn/opinion/2011-07/15/content_12912148.htm (accessed on August 6, 2014).

[11]This finding is supported by a causal relationship between an overall governance index and higher share prices in emerging markets based on a study in Korea by Bernard Black, Hasung Jang, and Woochan Kim (2006), "Does Corporate Governance Affect Firms' Market Values? Evidence from Korea," *The Journal of Law, Economics, and Organization*, 22(2), 366–413.

Partnership with NGOs and social impact innovation companies have become, year after year, an important topic in China, as many MNCs and domestic player need to find trusted and capable partners to help them design and implement their corporate responsibility initiatives on the mainland. Finding trusted teams with relevant experience on social impact projects is key to the success of such partnerships. The recent changes introduced in the China Charity Award, after a billionaire winner was charged with bribing the former minister of railways in dozens of railways projects, is very illustrative of the much needed ongoing reform of this sector: As criteria for the list of candidates were often vague, members of the judging panel voted in line with their feelings or simply favored those candidates who donated the largest amounts, ignoring factors such as the social effect of the candidates' donations and whether the donors sought publicity rather than helping those in need.[12]

1.3. Key Review Items for Mergers & Acquisitions in China

1.3.1. *Foreign Investment Catalogue*

Whatever their structure or form, investments can only be carried out if in compliance with the Foreign Investment Guidelines and the Foreign Investment Catalogue. The Foreign Investment Catalogue was first published in 1995, and then revised in 1997, 2002, 2004, and 2007. Duty free allowances were originally planned, up to the limit of total investment in equipment, and on raw materials for encouraged investments.

Today, the enforceable catalogue allows for three categories of investment: Encouraged, regulated, and restricted (or banned). In the case of regulated investments, additional conditions may be required by the Chinese authorities such as, for example, the presence of a Chinese partner holding more than 50% of the company shares. In sectors where investments are encouraged, investors can

[12] He Dan, "China Award Makes Changes after Winner Involved in Scandal," *CHINADAILY.COM.CN*, August 13, 2014; available online at www.chinadaily.com.cn/cndy/2014-08/13/content_18298431.htm (accessed on September 24, 2014).

benefit from customs advantages (duty-free import of capital goods). It should be noted that while some sectors remain almost inaccessible to foreigners, many others have opened up, notably since the integration of China into the WTO. Similarly, companies based in Hong Kong and Macao are granted some privileges, as well as the possibility to invest in sectors restricted to foreign companies.

As an example, the construction of family houses and villas are not authorized to foreign companies in China, but the construction of tall buildings is possible. This is related to the desire of the Chinese authorities to better manage the scarcity of available land in large cities and encourage the optimization of the space.

1.3.2. *Corporate Object*

The corporate object of foreign investment enterprises (FIEs) is strictly defined by the authorities and usually presented as having a standard business scope: trade of strictly defined goods, production of defined goods, consultancy in specific area of expertise, etc. Extensions are sometimes possible, for example, home decoration retail and interior design consulting, as the two can be closely connected, but any addition must be properly filed to avoid problems if they are not in the object of the firm.

A manufacturing foreign investment enterprise can receive authorization to widen the scope of its corporate object to the trading activities of the products it manufactures. Similarly, a wholesale FIE can widen its corporate object to retail. The request of a consultancy FIE wishing to broaden its business scope to production activities would normally be rejected by the Chinese authorities. The issue of corporate object therefore naturally arises when the target company's object is different from that of the FIE which acquires it. For example, a manufacturing FIE wishes to acquire a Chinese company or another trading FIE, or a consultancy FIE wants to acquire a Chinese company or a trading FIE.

In reality, acquisitions by FIEs of Chinese companies or FIEs whose activities are similar, related, or complementary may be approved or registered without too much difficulty. This also applies to holding companies, which cannot in practice acquire or invest in companies which do not have a similar, related, or complementary corporate object.

1.3.3. *Control on Foreign Exchange (Forex)*

In the Chinese system, all financial transactions, including payments carried out during an M&A operation, are subject to the authority of the State Administration of Foreign Exchange (SAFE). China still has one of the tightest Forex control regimes in the world. Before 1994, almost all transactions involving Forex had to be approved by SAFE.[13] Since then, China has adopted a dual system which has been virtually unchanged for two decades, where prior approval is:

- Not required by SAFE for current transactions such as dividend repatriation or monies payable for international trade.
- Required for capital transactions such as lending money to a Chinese company.

Under the existing regime, capital account transactions also include cross-border guarantees. Specifically, without SAFE approval, a PRC entity, except PRC banks under a quota defined by SAFE, could not provide guarantees to an offshore entity, nor can an offshore entity provide guarantees to a PRC entity. In addition, it was virtually impossible for PRC individuals to obtain SAFE approval to provide guarantees to offshore entities.

In mid-2014, SAFE promoted a new set of rules to support the implementation of China "going global",[14] "to fully utilize

[13]"China Adopts Fundamental Changes in Foreign Exchange Control," *Gibson Dunn*, May 20, 2014, pp. 1–2; available online at http://www.gibsondunn.com/publications/Documents/China-Adopts-Fundamental-Changes-in-Foreign-Exchange-control.pdf (accessed on September 24, 2014).

[14]SAFE, "Transforming Foreign Exchange Administration of Round-trip Investments to Further Facilitate Cross-border Investments and Financing," *State Administration of Foreign Exchange*, August 1, 2014; available online at http://www.safe.gov.cn/wps/portal/!ut/p/c4/04_SB8K8xLLM9MSSzPy8xBz9CP0os3gPZxdnX293QwN_f0tXA08zR9PgYGd3Yx8fE_2CbEdFAM9sw9Y!/?WCM_GLOBAL_CONTEXT=/wps/wcm/connect/safe_web_store/state+administration+of+foreign+exchange/safe+news/b4836a0044f0c86cb4a2be2052fb79ad (accessed on September 24, 2014).

international and domestic resources and markets, to promote the facilitation of cross-border investments and finance, practically serve development of the real economy, and to increase the convertibility of cross-border capital and financial transactions in an orderly manner".

Under these new rules, cross-border guarantees are divided into three categories: (a) Onshore guarantee/offshore lending; (b) offshore guarantee/onshore lending; and (c) other cross-border guarantees.

(a) Onshore guarantee/offshore lending case: The guarantor is a Chinese entity and the beneficiary and guaranteed party are offshore entities, or the case of a loan made by an offshore bank to an offshore borrower. Then, the new rules set that:

- PRC financial institutions, non-financial institutions, and individuals can all provide onshore guarantees in connection with offshore lending. Only filing with or reporting to SAFE (instead of prior mandatory approval) will be required. This is a fundamental change from the current regime.
- PRC financial institutions are no longer subject to any SAFE-issued quotas when providing cross-border guarantees.
- The offshore borrower may not use the proceeds of the offshore loan to engage in businesses outside its normal business scope and the proceeds may not be remitted into China for equity, debt, or other investments.

(b) Offshore guarantee/onshore lending arrangement case: The guarantor is an offshore entity and the beneficiary and the guaranteed party are both PRC entities. For example, a non-Chinese bank gives a guarantee to a Chinese bank lending money to a PRC borrower. Then the new rules set that:

- A Chinese company can obtain a guarantee from an offshore entity for its onshore debts, only if the lender of the onshore debt is a Chinese financial institution. Such onshore debts must be bank loans or binding commitments to make bank loans made by a Chinese financial institution.

- With respect to the debt owed by the Chinese borrower to the offshore guarantor resulting from the enforcement of the offshore guarantee, the amount of such debt may not exceed such borrower's audited net assets for the preceding year.

(c) As for other cross-border guarantee cases: The new rules set that these are not regulated unless otherwise required by SAFE.

The new regime is more restrictive with respect to offshore guarantee/onshore lending than onshore guarantee/offshore lending, which would make it easier from a Forex standpoint to go for outbound than for inbound transactions. This is a major change from China's previous foreign exchange control system, but not such a surprising evolution, as China's huge foreign reserve has become something of a burden to the country's economy and needs to be more easily invested outside of China, as needed.

The new rules which have taken effect on June 1, 2014 are expected to have a profound impact on future cross-border capital flows in China, making inbound transactions possibly less smooth and outbound transactions easier. The latter is likely to have an impact on the activity of China on the international M&A market.

1.3.4. *Success Probability*

The conditions enabling strategic partnerships and M&A contracts to be signed in China have vastly improved due to better organization of the legal environment. However, an estimated 50% of operations still fail after the signing of a letter of intent (LOI), which shows that the market is not fully mature yet.

A partnership or an acquisition in China is still a path fraught with obstacles and pitfalls. Only about 20% of the envisaged M&A projects move ahead of the due diligences stage, i.e., less than half of the international average. Moreover, the process takes on average twice the time to be completed in China than it would need in Western countries, as information is often not properly formatted and possibly scattered in different locations. Patience, excellent judgment capacity, focus on key reasons to invest and concern items, and a certain distance from day-to-day hurdles are mandatory skills for those willing to succeed.

Due to its huge Forex reserves, estimated at USD4 trillion in Q1 2014,[15] China has now started to push its outbound acquisition policy with a cautious and pragmatic approach, showing a mix of ambition and common sense. For Chinese multinational companies, as for the other multinationals operating in China, the external growth process is supported by an economic rationale based on the consolidation of centers of excellence, one of the key restructuring processes in the world of global business and industry, and securing key access to resources — such as minerals, energy sources, and food. The acquisition in May 2013 by Henan Shuanghui (USD6.1 billion revenues) of Smithfield Foods (USD13 billion revenues), the world's largest hog farmer and processor, is one example of the new Chinese ambitions abroad.[16]

While China is still referred to as a "low cost" manufacturing base, practitioners recognize that this is less and less true, especially for large coastline cities. Some industrial sectors, such as textile, have massively relocated out of China to seek cheaper labor force. Establishing a large and profitable business in China can be difficult without significant capital investments. Higher living standards will only reinforce this trend in the future. Investing early on is necessary to apprehend the cultural characteristics and the dynamics of the domestic market before embarking in an acquisition or a complex partnership. As the economy matures, barriers to entry increases and the success rate of development projects is expected to increase significantly. M&A operations in China will continue to grow as China strengthens its position and its integration as a worldwide-leading economy, but one should

[15]Josh Noble, "China's Foreign Exchange Reserves Near Record USD4tn," *Financial Times*, April 15, 2014; accessed online at www.ft.com/cms/s/0/4768bd3c-c461-11e3-8dd4-00144feabdc0.html#axzz3ED. PFK5Q (accessed on September 24, 2014). China reserves are thought to be two-thirds in USD, a quarter in Euros, and the rest in other currencies, especially Yen and Sterling Pound.

[16]"China Goes West 2.0," Maverlinn presentation to IECP Forum, Beijing, January 15, 2014.

Table 1.2. Allocation of M&A Activities by Year and Industry (2010–2013).

	2010	2011	2012	2013
Energy and mining	39%	22%	26%	31%
Finance, investment	15%	12%	11%	15%
Food and beverage	5%	3%		9%
Manufacturing	10%	10%	11%	8%
Information tech.	2%	3%	3%	7%
Real estate	9%	6%	5%	5%
Others	6%	13%	8%	4%
Culture and media	3%			3%
Transportation		5%	4%	3%
Chain retailing	1%		3%	3%
Healthcare	5%	3%	2%	3%
Public service		11%	3%	3%
Internet			11%	2%
Chemical industry	1%	8%	5%	2%
Automobile	4%	2%	2%	2%
Building material		2%	5%	
Total	100%	100%	100%	100%

Source: China Venture Group China M&A Yearly Report.

remember that the number of best targets for acquisitions is likely to be more limited than expected.

1.4. Possible Acquisition Structures

Just like the regional diversity of Chinese cuisine, there are several possible ways to deal with an M&A transaction in China. A typology of the different possible cases will help one quickly understand the advantages and drawbacks, relatively though, by category. This framework is convenient, especially in order to apprehend the degree of complexity of the envisaged operation and prepare for sufficient time and resources.

(1) Using holding companies and regional headquarters

A holding company is a limited liability company whose purpose is usually to consolidate participations from various other companies. Its purpose is to ensure the consistency of the management of the portfolio companies, while allowing controlling shareholders to increase their control over the business.

The number of holding companies in China remains low because of their strict conditions of creation and operation.

- Conditions related to the capital of a holding: At least USD30 million of share capital; reinvestment of earnings and investments.
- Conditions related to a foreign investor stakeholder of the holding company: the investor must own assets of over USD400 million worldwide and have invested at least USD10 million in China, or have established at least 10 FIEs in China with a total investment of over USD30 million.

New regulations encourage the creation of FIEs organized in holding companies, in particular the SAFE Circular 142, which limits the FIEs' possibility to invest their share capital in Chinese firms. This could enhance their development in the view of conducting M&A transactions on Chinese territory.

Current regulations also state that Chinese holding companies can only invest or take a stake in domestic companies. Even though the activities of the holding companies are strictly regulated by these texts, and have a corporate scope limited to consulting and trade activities, holdings can still:

- Provide consulting services to shareholders and to their subsidiaries.
- Centralize the purchase of equipment and raw materials, and assist their subsidiaries with the commercialization of their products.
- Balance foreign currency positions between their subsidiaries.

- Provide technical assistance, personnel training, and human resources management for their subsidiaries.
- Provide guarantees for their subsidiaries.
- Establish R&D center.

After the payment of the minimum capital requirement, holdings can, depending on the Ministry of Trade's approval and their corporate object:

- Sell products manufactured by their subsidiaries.
- Provide shipping and storage services.
- Assemble the products manufactured by its subsidiaries in order to distribute or sell them.
- Provide technical assistance to agents or Chinese distributors for products manufactured by their subsidiaries.
- Provide customer service for products imported in China.
- Distribute wholesale products of foreign investors.
- Act as a broker or wholesaler to distribute the foreign investors' and its subsidiaries' products.
- Export specific products bought in China.

Since February 2004, it is also possible for a multinational firm to establish its holding as a regional headquarters, subject to the fulfilment of several conditions.

Upon approval of the Ministry of Trade, a regional headquarters can then set up financial companies, provide financial services, invest outside of China, and establish leasing companies.

(2) State-owned companies or private companies?

The opinion issued by the Ministry of Commerce on June 3, 2008[17] clearly indicates that the Chinese government encouraged foreign

[17] Opinions of the General Office of the Ministry of Commerce on guiding the national foreign investment absorption work in 2008. Available online at english.mofcom.gov.cn/aarticle/policyrelease/announcement/200804/20080405507111.html (accessed in December 16, 2014).

investors to take part in the restructuring of state-owned companies through targeted acquisitions.

This global restructuring has generated numerous opportunities for foreign investors eager to invest in China. Although these companies are not always well-managed and in good shape, they may have been granted state subsidies in the past; it is not uncommon for their manufacturing (or non-manufacturing) assets to have a significant market value. However, the acquisition of state-owned companies or state assets is subject to a specific procedure and to the control of SASAC (State-owned Assets Supervision and Administration Commission), the commission in charge of the management of state assets and of the appointment of their chief executives.

SASAC approves the mergers & acquisitions of state-owned companies' assets or shares, and supervises the valuation of the related assets. In principle, these assets cannot be sold for less than 90% of the price assessed by a local, independent, accredited Chinese expert. In the event of state-owned assets transfer at such an appraised price, the FIEs do not have to cover the land use rights expenses, insofar as they have already been included in the land use rights transfer price.

However, this type of M&A operations involving state-owned companies or state assets is not without risks. There are two factors to consider: Firstly, procedures are likely to be lengthy and slow, all of which require further approval of the SASAC; secondly, the risks of potential fraud are real (with numerous examples in the past). Indeed, some state-owned companies have been sold to their former chief executives at abnormally low prices; a number of them managed to create substantial corporate value before selling them with a handsome premium to private investors.

Such an approach to fast personal enrichment by misappropriation of state-owned assets has been increasingly severely repressed. In such cases, even the legitimacy of a foreign investment project intending to acquire a Chinese enterprise coming from the transformation of a state-owned enterprise could be challenged. It is therefore of major importance to pay close attention to these issues when starting the process of due diligence and to stay away from dodgy practices.

Private domestic firms owned by Chinese investors may, just like FIEs, within the framework set by the Catalogue of Investments, be acquired by foreign investors. The Chinese-funded companies will then lose their domestic status if the foreign stake is greater than 25%.

(3) Listed or unlisted companies?

The same opinion issued by the Ministry of Commerce on June 3, 2008 states that the IPOs of qualifying Chinese foreign invested companies must be facilitated. This has clearly underlined China's progress towards a market economy. The listing of Chinese companies is quite recent in Mainland China. Indeed, the Shanghai Stock Exchange (上海 证券交易所), historically one of the most important financial places in Asia in the nineteenth and early twentieth century, was suspended in 1949 when the People's Republic of China was founded, and only reopened on November 26, 1990. Since 2010 in particular, with the support from the Central Government, the Shanghai Stock Exchange is working hard on catching up and mobilizing enormous resources to become one of the prominent international financial centers.

The creation of the Shenzhen Stock Exchange (深圳 交易所) in December 1, 1990, resulted in a specialization of the Shanghai market in the listing of large and multinational companies, and of the Shenzhen market in the listing of small and medium-sized companies. These two markets compete with their old time rival, the Hong Kong Stock Exchange, reintegrated in the People's Republic of China, but in a Special Administrative Region (SAR) until 2047. The neighboring Taiwan Stock Exchange started operations in Taipei in 1962: 838 companies were listed on the market in 2013 with a global market capitalization of NTD24,520 billion (RMB5 trillion, €0.6 trillion).

One should notice that compared to the Hong Kong stock market, the daily trading volume on the two Mainland China stock markets (Shanghai and Shenzhen) are at significantly lower

Table 1.3. Capitalization of the Key Stock Markets of Greater China as of 2013.[18]

Stock Markets	Shanghai	Shenzhen	Hong Kong
Capitalization (trillion RMB)	15.1	8.8	18.9
Capitalization (trillion €)	1.8	0.85	2.3
Number of listed companies	953	1,536	1,451
Volume of transactions (day/billion of shares)	11.2	9.1	140.2
Annual growth rate (from 2001 to 2013)/%	15.2	15.3	16.3

levels,[19] meaning that the global liquidity of the markets is not comparable yet. Hong Kong, as a fully internationalized market, has five to 12 times more depth, depending on the year. In general terms, the more liquid a market the more relevant are the traded prices.

The official limited convertibility of the RMB and the lack of sufficient international visibility for domestic companies listed on the Chinese stock market are two factors having quickly pushed many Chinese companies with international ambitions to be listed on offshore financial markets in the US (NASDAQ, NYSE), Hong Kong, or Europe (London, Paris, Frankfurt). However, the implementation in 2006 of new regulations regarding the acquisition of domestic companies by foreign investors, updated in 2009, has significantly limited such practices by requiring CSRC approval for any offshore structured IPOs of Chinese companies, and whose approval has been seldom granted since then. However, some good news came following a difficult time for Chinese companies' IPOs, both in China and outside China, as in September 2014, China's iconic e-commerce giant, Alibaba Group, kicked off its international roadshow to pitch investors prior to its expected record-breaking initial public offering (IPO) on the New York Stock Exchange reported to debut its listing on September 18. The company updated its SEC filing on September 5, with shares

[18]All data obtained from the 2014 Shanghai Stock Exchange Fact Book, 2014 Shenzhen Stock Exchange Fact Book, and 2014 Hong Kong Stock Exchange Fact Book.

[19]The Mainland China stock market conditions are reviewed later in Section 4.1.3.

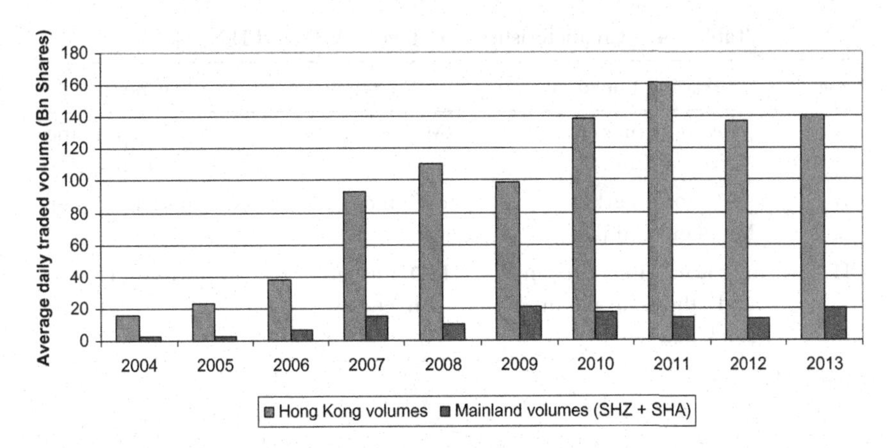

Figure 1.1. Daily Volumes of Shares Traded on the Greater China Key Markets.
Source: Hong Kong Stock Exchange Factbook 2013; Shanghai Stock Exchange Factbook 2013; Shenzhen Stock Exchange Factbook 2013.

expected to be priced at between USD60 and USD66. At this range, Alibaba is valued at USD160 billion, making it the largest IPO ever in the US.[20]

The assets of Chinese companies can be composed of three categories of stocks: A, B (traded on Mainland China markets), and H (traded on foreign markets). Only foreign investors with the Qualified Foreign Institutional Investors status (QFII) can purchase stocks of the A category. Therefore, foreign investors willing to purchase Chinese stocks on the market can only buy, in theory, category B or H stocks.

The different ways for a take-over of a listed company are:

- Acquisition of securities through off-market contracts (most common method).
- Subscription to a reserved capital increase.
- Take-over bid.
- Acquisition of shares on the market (pickup).

[20]Zhang Yuwei, "Alibaba Kicks off IPO Global Roadshow in NY," CHINADAILYUSA, September 9, 2014; available online at usa.chinadaily.com.cn/us/2014-09/09/content_18569706.htm (accessed on September 25, 2014).

Table 1.4. Characteristics of Category A, B, and H Stocks.

Type	Trading Location	Currency	Owners
A	Type A stock market in Mainland China	RMB	Nationals, QFII, and strategic investors
B	Type B stock market in Mainland China	Foreign currency	Nationals, foreigners
H	Hong Kong stock exchange and other international stock markets	HKD, foreign currencies	Authorized investors

Source: Mazars.

In most cases, the buyer will combine several modes of acquisition for the same operation. In addition, the investor will be subject to a lock-up period of 12 months during which he will not be allowed to sell the acquired shares in order to prevent speculative operations by undervalued asset arbitrage.

The Chinese financial law differentiates three types of acquisitions, each type with its own approval and restriction system:

- Financial investment: Corresponding to a stake of less than 5%, for which the regulations related to the acquisition of listed companies do not apply.
- Change of control: Which corresponds to an acquisition of 5% to 30% of a listed company's shares through stock markets.
- Acquisition of a listed company: Which corresponds to a stake higher than or equal to 30% of the company's assets by a legal or natural person or several acting together, carried out by a share deal on the stock market or through the signature of an agreement. This type of acquisition must be followed by a take-over bid open to all existing shareholders, for all or a part of the remaining capital, unless the buyer gets a take-over bid waiver from the CSRC.

Crossing the threshold of 5% equity stake in a Chinese listed company results, on one hand, in the mandatory submission of a written report to the CSRC and to the regulatory commission and, on the other hand, in the notification to the listed company being acquired and to the public within three days of the transaction. In addition, the buyer cannot acquire or sell shares of that company within the three days following the crossing of the threshold. Any subsequent upward or downward threshold crossing (so every 5%) has to follow the same mandatory notification process, and the buyer cannot acquire or sell shares of this company within the two days following the threshold crossing.

Regarding the Foreign Invested Companies Limited by Shares (FICLS), the acquisition process is somewhat specific. Foreign companies seeking to take a stake in a company listed on any Mainland China stock market can only acquire, in principle, class B shares.

However, the rules from December 31, 2005 regulating the administration of strategic investments by foreign investors in listed companies gives the opportunity to foreign companies to acquire, under certain conditions, part of class A shares of a Chinese listed company. This exemption applies to companies willing to invest on the medium- or long-term, including in terms of management know-how and technology.

The foreign investor must be able to provide evidence of the following:

- Good financial shape.
- Internal compliance with principles of good corporate governance.
- Registered capital of at least USD100 million or, in the case of holding companies, that he controls companies whose total combined share capital is greater than or equal to RMB500 million.
- Clean record: No conviction by a supervisory authority in his home country or in China in the previous three years.

The acquisition operation can be structured in multiple steps, but the first move must necessarily deal with at least 10% of the company equity capital. The acquisition of class A shares can be carried out by a contractual share transfer agreement, by subscription to a targeted capital increase, or any other form of acquisition permitted by law.

The operation must respect the constraints related to the acquisition of a stake by foreign investors (see the Foreign Investment Catalogue, restricted industries, etc.). In particular, if the target company is a wholly or partly state-owned company, the target must also comply with the rules on the acquisition of state-owned companies.

In the case of an acquisition by a foreign subsidiary of the buyer, the parent company must provide a guarantee under which it accepts the joint and multiple liabilities of its subsidiary.

The shares acquired are then subject to a lock-up period of three years, during which they cannot be sold. The acquisition of a stake by a foreign strategic investor will automatically change the company status to a Foreign Investment Enterprise, and thus require an application for a FIE certification of approval within 10 days after the closing. When a foreign investor has completed an acquisition under the strategic investment regime, every additional investment in the same listed company will have to be carried out under the same regime.

(4) Companies in liquidation or receivership?

For many years, China's accelerated growth has mainly supported new company creation, but bankruptcies were not a real concern for the Chinese authorities. However, a considerable number of recent bankruptcies, partly related to the 2008–2009 financial crisis and to the campaign against the poor quality of certain Chinese products, have forced, for the first time, the Chinese authorities and the business community to seriously consider the possibility of dealing with bankruptcy and restructuring options.

Since January 15, 2008, based on the principle of national treatment, the State Council has abolished the different existing regulations on the liquidation of Foreign Invested Enterprises in China, and the liquidation process of any Chinese company is now regulated by laws related to corporations and their legal status. However, when a company is not able to pay its debts or when its assets are clearly insufficient to cover its debts, the bankruptcy law applies, allowing the implementation of judiciary recovery, liquidation, or conciliation procedures.

The August 27, 2006 Enterprise Bankruptcy Law enforces since June 1, 2007 a real collective procedure system for companies in struggle, by seeking to balance the creditor's and debtor's interests with, notably, the creation of judiciary conciliation and recovery procedures. This law, which applies to all private, collective, or state-owned companies incorporated in the People's Republic of China, with the exception of Special Administrative Regions (Hong Kong or Macao), now provides a legal framework to the judiciary recovery and liquidation procedures. This framework has led to new opportunities for foreign investors, in terms of restructuring and possibly M&A. Currently, the Chinese authorities are eager to approve more readily, M&A projects, involving take-overs of companies in difficulty and employment protection for the sake of social stability, in order to avoid the some possible social unrest arising from the closure of industrial sites.

The reform of April 2005 on non-tradable shares

At the beginning of the huge wave of privatization of the '90s, the Chinese government had chosen to retain substantial shareholdings in former state-owned companies. In order to do this, rather than dividing the existing capital stock into shares and putting aside part of these shares for themselves, the Chinese authorities chose to maintain the existing capital stock as non-negotiable and to create a new category of shares listed on the financial markets. The two categories of shares have theoretically the same voting rights and return on investment. However, stakes in non-tradable shares can only be sold by following the standard procedure of acquisition of a stake in an unlisted company.

This double capital structure is the source of many unnecessary complexities and problems. It creates significant distortions in the company valuation and an unequal treatment of negotiable securities holders, mostly minority holders exposed to market vagaries, when compared to non-tradable shareholders often privileged but whose shares are subject to a significant discount.

(*Continued*)

(*Continued*)

After several unsuccessful experiences, some of which ended in a relative collapse of the stock market, the Chinese government developed, in 2005, a non-tradable share conversion strategy by which any company can develop a specific program to compensate tradable shareholders (in cash and shares averaging 30% of their stake before reform) in exchange for their agreement on the conversion of the non-tradable shares. The new converted shares are, however, subject to a two year partial lock-up period, during which their holders cannot sell more than 5% of holdings the first and second years.

To encourage listed companies to participate in this reform, the issuance of new shares was suspended from April 2005 to May 2006, and the companies having completed their reform placed priority on the raising of new funds at the end of the moratorium period. This reform continued for several years and was very successful, as a large majority of listed companies implemented conversion plans as early as the summer of 2006. Due to the lock-up period and the voluntary nature of this approach, the first conversions of non-tradable shares actually occurred only in late 2007, and it was planned that half of these conversions would have occurred by early-2010. Therefore, handling these non-tradable shares was a key factor in any stake acquisition project in a listed company.

(5) Share equity deal or naked asset deal?

Foreign investors wishing to conduct external growth projects in China can choose between different styles for acquisition deals: share acquisition (equity), asset acquisition, or mergers. These three types of deals are authorized by Chinese laws and regulations.

The purchase of shares can be conducted directly, that is, the foreign investors will buy shares directly from a Chinese company, or indirectly, that is, via an investment vehicle located abroad (commonly known as SPV [Special Purpose Vehicle]) and which has stakes in the coveted Chinese entity.

In the latter case, the operations are for the most part, conducted within the framework of the law which applies to the offshore investment vehicle. However, even under these circumstances, the Chinese authorities reserve the right to control the operation through the exchange control regulations, especially when the shareholder's investment vehicle is a Chinese citizen. The foreign investor will, in this case, be held liable for the welfare and tax debts to the extent of the shares owned and of the share capital. In return for this transfer of liability (including underlying liabilities), the transaction is more advantageous from a fiscal point of view than in the case of an asset deal. Similarly, the tax benefits that have been conferred to the target company are transferred to the buyer.

The acquisitions of assets can be carried out in China in the following ways:

- The foreign investor creates an FIE which can then acquire another FIE (Case A) or the assets of a domestic company (case B).
- The foreign investor acquires the assets and transfers them to an FIE created *ad hoc* (case C).

Asset transfers are generally more heavily taxed, but they usually represent a lower value, especially due to usual "fire sale values of

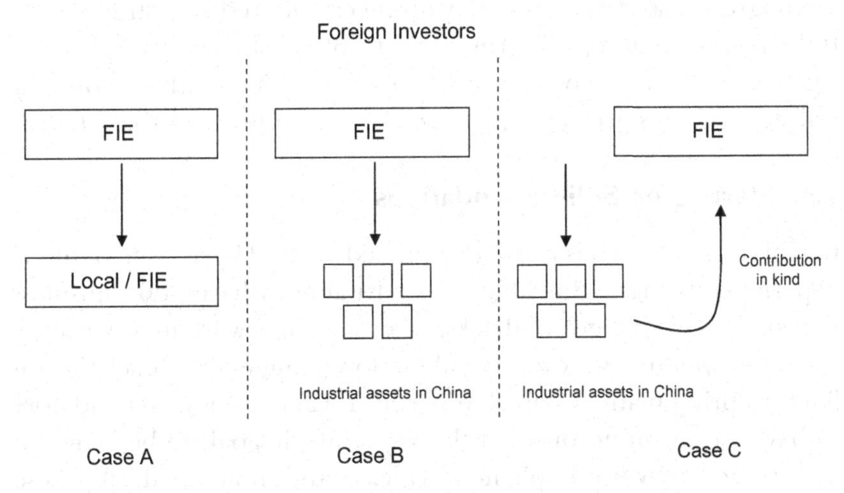

Figure 1.2. Acquisition Options.

equipment" and the difficulty to appraise intangibles, compared to an equity-based transaction. In an asset deal, the taxable basis is usually automatically much lower. However, this entails the loss of the prior tax benefits granted to the target company, although asset deals do limit the risks associated with the transfer of identified or hidden liabilities.

(6) Full ownership, acquisition of a stake, or strategic partnerships? The context of M&A in China these last few years has been impacted by a growing interest of both industrial groups and capital investment funds, China being one of the biggest worldwide growth engines and one of the world's main markets. The industrial landscape in Mainland China is still very fragmented and offers many investment opportunities. These investments can potentially be very profitable, since the Chinese currency appreciation seems almost inevitable over the long term, and China's rapid economic development is supposed to be accompanied by a similar increasing wealth per capita.

Foreign investors have the option to purchase the totality or part of a Chinese company (see the 2009 regulation on the acquisition of domestic companies by foreign investors), or a FIE. However, in a number of specific sectors, the share of capital that can be held by a foreign investor is capped at a level which can vary depending on the degree of strategic sensitivity of the considered industrial sector. If the target becomes a FIE (more than 25% of shares), its legal form will change and become either a JV or a WFOE which will stay unlisted or will start to get prepared for being listed in the future.

1.5. Starting on Solid Foundations

In China, provided it is regularly updated and fed by new encounters, experience is highly valuable. It is advisable to have good business networks to exchange feedbacks, save time, and work in a harmonious atmosphere. An over-confident lone ranger approach is not likely to bring many sustainable results in China. But it is mandatory to have a clear mind on what the key strategic goals to be achieved are, some "how to implement" ideas, and how to distill these objectives to see if the route followed is well-suited to the objectives.

1.5.1. *Defining Goals and Remaining Open-Minded*

The preparation of an external growth project on the Chinese market requires good competitive analysis, and a clear idea about the strategy and resources available to develop business in China. A successful acquisition process tested five years ago to run a deal will not necessarily be the best today. It is therefore necessary to update regularly on best practices:

- Do one's homework, i.e., search recent literature.
- Access seasoned advisors.
- Activate peer networks to exchange views.
- Keep an open mind and continuous learning process.
- Work with a Chinese team.
- Grow a good local network.

Simplistic or rapid reasoning is often a mistake in China; perseverance and realism are key success factors. Partnerships are not meant to last forever, and it is better to define a reasonable term and aim for renewing it, if the parties are satisfied. It is not always possible to find immediately the perfect candidate for an acquisition; several stages of multiple cross-filtering analysis are often required, by simultaneously taking into account the strategic dimension (accessibility), the legal dimension (possibility), and the financial dimension (achievability).

It is recommended to be accompanied by wise, seasoned, and firmly established advisors in order to avoid exhaustion, and to focus on business development as well as think about alternative options in case the main negotiation falls through. Acquisitions in China have evolved, and are more and more professional. The domestic M&A market is very active and not always open to foreigners (who do not have access to all transactions) due to lack of information, or preference for the seller to make business with someone he knows or who has been properly introduced to him ("guanxi"). Foreign investors must be prepared to face serious competition from the beginning of negotiations to the closing of the acquisition, including some possible challenges for the retention of key people and the protection of the target's most valuable intangible assets.

When first coming to the Chinese market, one must keep in mind that good targets from a strategic standpoint are not necessarily good targets from a legal standpoint — for example, in some industries, due diligences may reveal that a significant portion of the turnover or the expenditures are not officially reported in the books, which can sometimes be problematic from a regulatory and risk management point of view. There are as many opportunities as there are challenges, which sometimes can jeopardize and crush an acquisition project.

Business case — Textile manufacturer acquisition

A foreign company was willing to make a possible acquisition of a competitor in the textile manufacturing industry in China. They had some friendly relations with the target and started amicable discussions. A first approach of the seller cautiously started, together with limited reviews. The potential acquirer realized that the Chinese target was three times more profitable than the acquirer's own business, which was a serious problem and very difficult to understand, given industry standards and cost structure. The acquirer managed to perform some limited due diligences, and realized that the target company was bearing a huge and very dated inventory which had never been depreciated.

But that was only one part of the answer; the operational profitability was still extremely high compared to the acquirer's. After some analysis and discussions, the acquirer finally discovered that the target suppliers' invoices were split between Mainland China and Hong Kong. The Hong Kong commissions to suppliers would be paid through a different company, artificially increasing the profitability of the Mainland China business. This scheme was not even made on purpose to cook the books, as it resulted from very old commercial arrangements between the two companies. But after adjusting the target accounts from this situation, the price suggested for the acquisition was not so interesting. Discussions paused, as the acquirer needed to reflect on this, and finally the deal never went through.

1.5.2. *Understanding One's Environment in China*

A successful M&A project in China depends upon a methodical strategic analysis, as well as on a detailed assessment of the target company's managerial, financial, accounting, tax, legal, social, and environmental situation. This preparation starts by first identifying the main potential legal or regulatory difficulties which may affect the M&A project. This prerequisite helps to quickly assess the initial level of technical difficulty for the transaction and avoid losing time on impassable tracks. Among these difficulties, the Foreign Investment Guide and Catalogue can, in some cases, considerably restrict the options available to foreign investors wishing to invest in China, for example, in the media, energy, or finance sector. Similarly, the investor's economic and legal characteristics may result in subjecting the project to further approval processes, e.g., in the context of the Anti-Monopoly Law.

This first outlook of the legal framework will be an essential step in the assessment of the feasibility of the project, and will help define the level of complexity of the intended project.

It will then be followed by strategic and commercial due diligences, and then financial, accounting, tax, social, environmental, and legal due diligences (general points, e.g., legal existence of the company, operating licenses, safety permits).

Due diligences are a term that has now entered the common economic vocabulary, referring to the global audit process of a target company conducted by an investor. They help to map the target surroundings and, more precisely, the risks related to a company at a given time. Their purpose is to check the feasibility of the potential transaction and to ensure that the buyer closes the transaction in the best possible conditions: price negotiation, potential price adjustment, validation of the seller's representations, identification and limitation of warranties, acquisition structure, management of the post-acquisition or restructuring risks, cultural and social integration of the target, and strategy formulation. They are especially important in China, as one is still expected to quickly pay for the full acquisition, and as the ability

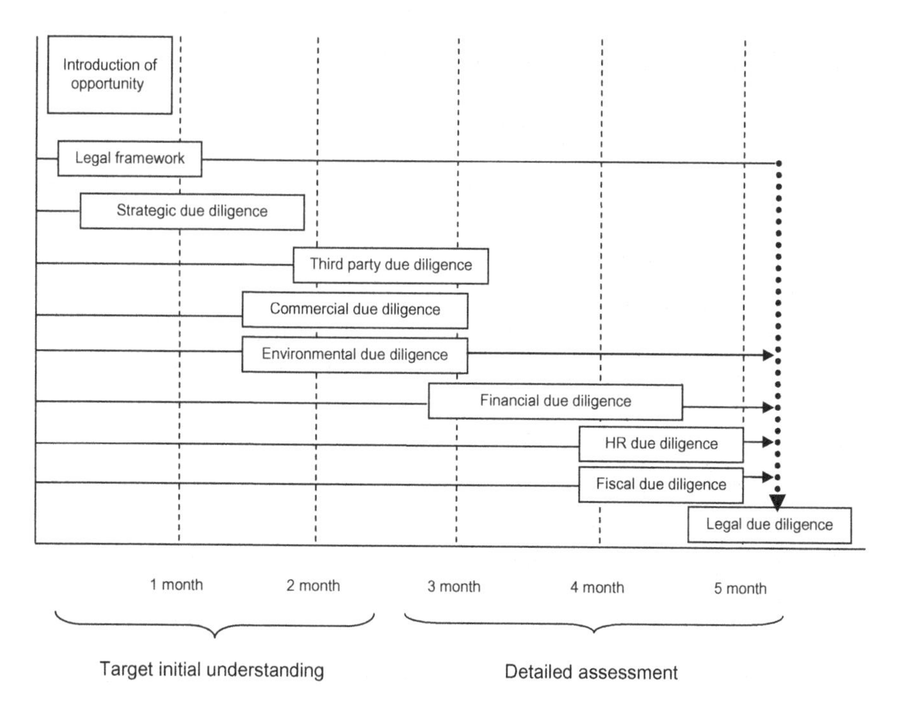

Figure 1.3. Indicative Timetable of Due Diligence in China.

to launch extensive legal action on guarantees may still be limited if a problem occurs.

In order to maximize the usefulness of the extensive audit process, such review must take place before the buyer signs the contract or a binding LOI. At this stage, a confidentiality agreement (non-disclosure agreement [NDA]) and a non-binding LOI are usually requested.

1.5.3. *Starting Negotiations Quickly*

It is customary that the buyer bears the full costs of the due diligences. However, from time to time, Chinese companies may request that the due diligences cost be shared with the seller when they are on the buyer's side.

Table 1.5. Characteristics of the Main Due Diligences (DD).

Step	Topic	Objective
1. Legal preliminary review	Investor	Identification of the main constraints regarding the project (industry, investor profile, competition, etc.)
2. Strategic DD	Market positioning	▪ Internal analysis of the firm and positioning ▪ Market dynamics, growth factors, and competition ▪ Sector dynamics and preliminary strategy assessment ▪ Business plan key drivers (growth, expenditures, investment)
3. Commercial DD	Target	▪ Strategic positioning of target ▪ Commercial potential ▪ Business plan detailed review ▪ Corporate Social Responsibility ▪ Business reputation (ethics, culture)
4. Financial DD	Target	Target financial key figures ▪ Revenues, profitability, debt, risk profile ▪ Cash in hand and debt capacity ▪ Shareholders structure ▪ Listed company details
5. Fiscal DD	Target	▪ Fiscal situation of target ▪ Fiscal liabilities (current, potential)
6. Legal DD	Target	▪ Legal registration in good order ▪ Business is done according to the PRC laws ▪ Social: are social contributions paid ▪ Environment: pollution, safety issues? ▪ Is the business of the target real? ▪ Identification and valuation of the liabilities of the firm

It is good to start by showing the importance of exchanging quality information during the initial discussions, while keeping in mind that the quality of the available information is still often mediocre. Obtaining quality information and actionable analysis will often require significant time and resources.

Chapter 2

Initial Approach of the External Growth Operation

When acquiring a Chinese company, it is a good idea to systematically ask for a seller's due diligence; companies invested by private equity funds will often provide this kind of documentation. This document is becoming a standard for mergers & acquisitions (build-up) and investment by capital investment firms, especially when the memorandum information on the target is very brief. The buyer must then collect critical information on his own in the absence of a data room, and possibly manage the acquirer, who usually dislikes providing detailed information and does not always understand why he should answer so many invasive questions regarding his business.

One should also be wary of a few well organized meetings which can give the impression that the situation is under control: marks of honor, cosy reception, "simplification" of the approach, and close relations to the local authorities. This kind of shortcut is usually dangerous, especially for a foreign acquirer. Common sense and good judgment must however be exercised; empathy and casual conversations on family or hobbies initiated by the seller to break the ice should not be turned down. They are an opportunity to get better acquainted and build the trust between the parties — a prerequisite for fruitful business discussions in China.

2.1. Strategic and Commercial Due Diligences

(1) Justification of the due diligences process

In the acquisition process of a Chinese company, quickly identifying the appropriate target is usually difficult, especially if one does not aim at acquiring the obvious leaders on a market. The language barrier (Chinese spoken languages not only include Mandarin, which is the official language, but also eight major dialects and hundreds of local variants), the multiplicity of actors, the absence of reliable databases,[21] and the lack of centralized data do not necessarily make a strategic analysis simple for an American or a European group. Misunderstandings about the target are also frequent. It is not uncommon for local companies to change names several times. The same applies to firms operating in related sectors, which may have similar or very close names in English and Chinese. Mistakes are thus easily made, and the mobilization of resources used to conduct field audits is essential to have a good quality picture.

Before embarking on an acquisition often following a personal introduction, or through an informal contact at a trade show or a professional forum, it is wise to conduct a rigorous analysis of the competitive environment. The goal is to obtain a set of reliable benchmarks in China. Market mapping techniques and target profiling are almost always used by Chinese businessmen wishing to establish themselves in the US or in Europe. It is not uncommon for prospective foreign buyers to try to save the cost of this step in China, but strategic due diligences must indeed be considered as a mandatory investment. Any strategic due diligence consists of two distinct parts: A global and segmented analysis of the market, as well as of its players and its dynamics; and a close range commercial positioning analysis with the consent of the target, as well as the analysis of its business (distributors, customers, suppliers, and various intermediaries).

It is necessary to fully understand the Chinese decision process and the possibility to quickly retract from their initial position: Numerous

[21] SAIC is making significant efforts to provide accessible, although not fully searchable, business licence directories.

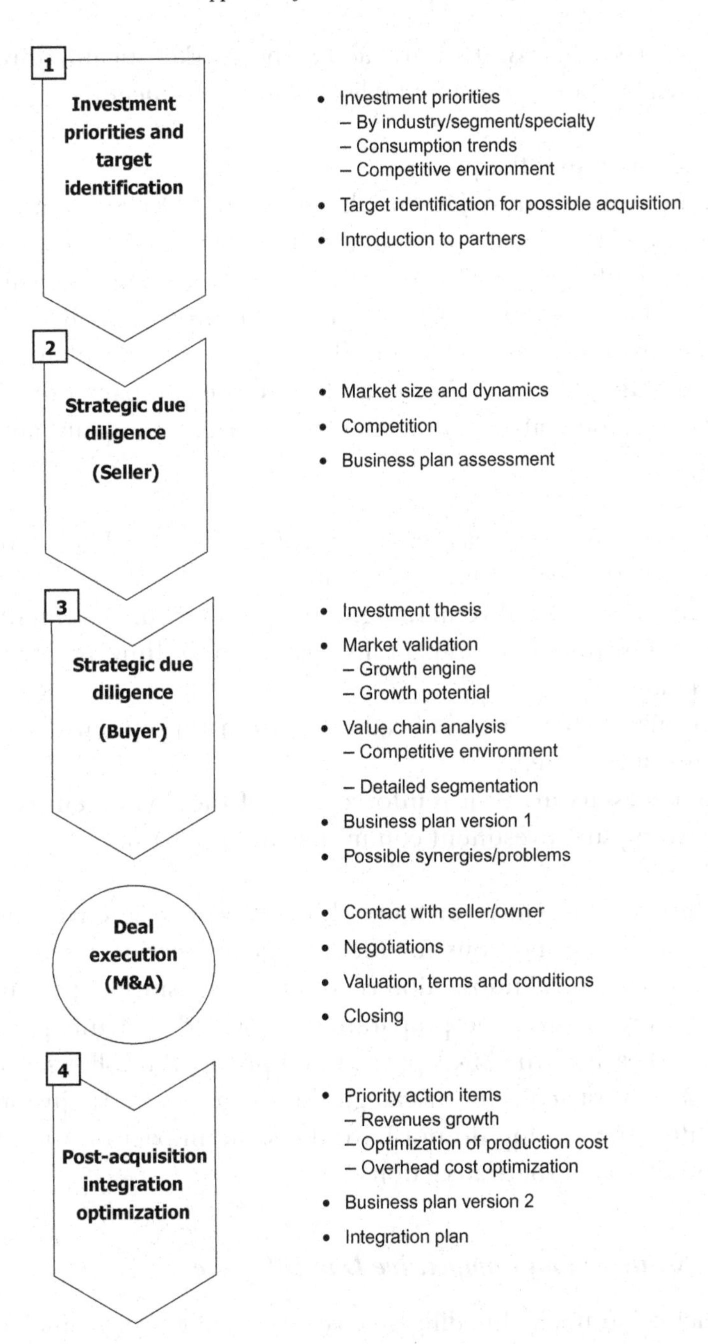

Figure 2.1. Synopsis of an M&A Transaction.

opportunities will arise to learn about the market, mainly through commercial imports or from establishing local production.

(2) Understanding the process
A commercial and strategic due diligence should provide a global view of the competitive positioning of the target or future business (in the case of a partnership) and the market dynamics in which it operates. This is a prerequisite for a more thorough analysis of the main key assumptions underlying the target's business plan, which will later translate into cash flow and therefore company valuation.

The commercial due diligence on a target company aims at identifying:

- Its strengths and weaknesses regarding the breakdown of its turnover (prices, volumes, segments, etc.).
- Its growth potential (emerging, stable, or declining segments).
- The risks that may impact its growth and thus the target's valuation.
- Its future potential growth adjusted from the optimistic assessments of the seller.
- The necessary areas of reinforcement of the investment project regarding the investment committee and the banks.

A highly competitive or more difficult economic environment leads to tighter conditions for M&A projects. In this context, the success of a financial transaction is even more sensitive to the quality of the upstream strategic preparation, provided that this phase is conducted early in the M&A process and provided it follows a rigorous analysis. Post-acquisition strategic due diligences and adjustments made after the signing do not have the same impact on the terms and conditions of the transaction.

2.1.1. *Strategic and Competitive Due Diligence*

Conducting strategic due diligence is a systematic process including research, audit, analysis, and market data processing (filtering) prior to an investment or an acquisition. The main goal for a potential buyer is to gain a detailed understanding of a market, and to assess the possible industrial affinities and business risks. The topics addressed on that occasion include:

- Positioning of the target company on its markets.
- Growth prospects of the markets on which the target evolves.
- Key value proposition for customers of the target company.
- Competitors' apparent strategies and the risk of potential newcomers.
- Resources allowing the development of this position in the future (business plan).

A strategic due diligence (SDD) process is a representation of the key factors of the environment in which a business is located or in which it wishes to develop. This dynamic representation is important in order to understand who the market players are on a given segment and geographical area. This process aims at providing a taxonomy of the players, to find out their ambitions as well as their means and prioritize them. This process can be easily outsourced.

The next step is to create a dynamic representation of the market, in order to apprehend the global strategy and then take action. In terms of tactical analysis, this representation leads to a selection and prioritization of the different ways to conduct a business development operation on a given market: increased competitive pressure, changes in the marketing mix, or, more drastically, external growth operation by "elimination of a competitor", or, more subtly, acquisition of channels (distribution, image builders (brand), or skills (technology, know-how)).

2.1.2. *Methodology and Key Success Factors*

The strategic due diligences must lead to a good and detailed understanding of the following elements:

- Product offer and the positioning of the company.
- Current market, its growth, and competitors.

- Industry dynamics as a prerequisite to defining a strategy.
- Key assumptions of the business plan (sales, margins).

A clear distinction must be made between the market due diligences — where only the revenue generation process is validated — and the commercial due diligences. The latter allow the validation of the complete business plan over several years, including the sales development, the changes in structural costs, and the allocation of fixed and variable costs. This validation is the cornerstone of any investment process.

A market due diligence focuses on the analysis of the supply and demand structure, as well as on the analysis of the competitive dynamics. This due diligence requires information typically including:

- The company: its profile including history, nature, and organization.
- The products: range, marketing mix, and suppliers.
- The market: customer segmentation, competitors.

2.1.3. *The Due Diligence Process*

Collecting data, analyzing the target situation, and writing a brief impactful summary highlighting the key findings of the investigation are the three stages of the due diligence process.

2.1.3.1. *Data collection*

Data collection is primarily based on four sources of information, which are then cross-analyzed and reconciled for key findings, gaps, or mistakes:

- Interviews with the management of the target company.
- Interviews with industry experts, professional associations, industry peers, and market observers.
- Stakeholder surveys: staff, customers, suppliers, and distributors.
- Analysis of specialized databases related to the sectors and companies.

Data collection is used to support the analysis of the target company, which focuses on four points:

- Internal vision of the company.
- Market and competition.
- Perceived strategy.
- Business plan.

Each point studied has an independent source of data, which must be confirmed and cross checked:

- Information concerning the internal vision of the target company is generally supplied by the seller after signing a mutual confidentiality agreement.
- Most information about the market of the target company and its competitors come from experts' advices and interviews, as well as synthesis and studies of external markets. These research companies use large teams on the field and in commercial events, such as international fairs and exhibitions.
- The study of the industrial strategy integrates the information collected on the market from competitors, suppliers, and customers to validate the market size and determine growth opportunities.
- The business plan summarizes all the information received by integrating them in a structured financial framework designed to show the profitability of the considered project.

Once the data collection is completed, the market analysis and mapping of the market will show accurately where the company stands in its competitive environment.

2.1.3.2. *Analytical Stage*

This phase provides an update on the key aspects to take into account when assessing the positioning of the company in its markets, including:

- The internal vision of the company.
- The market growth and its various constituent segments.

- The competitive dynamics and the industrial strategy allowing to define what the company wishes to accomplish in this market.
- The business plan, that is to say, the financial expression of the defined strategy (necessary investments and expected return on investment).

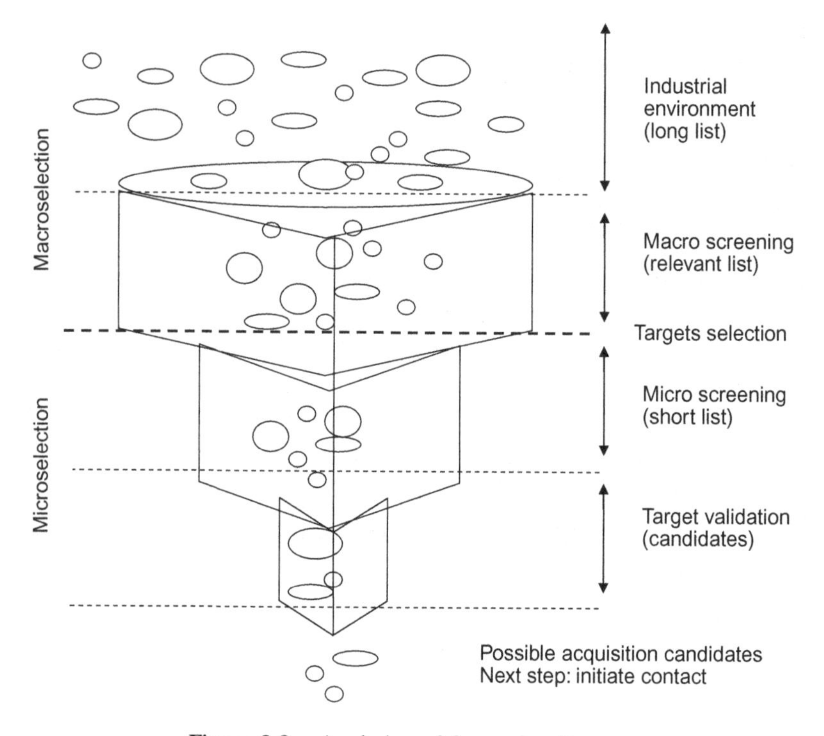

Figure 2.2. Analysis and Screening Process.

2.1.3.2.1. Approach of the Target Company

The goal is to identify and analyze the essential operational characteristics of the target company, and to quickly determine its degree of economic compatibility with the buyer. This compatibility analysis will be conducted through:

- Its market position.
- Its asset portfolio.

- Its organization by division and market segments.
- Its industrial culture.

This analysis also provides an overview of the internal organization of the company, its financial performance, its product portfolio, or the junction of its value chain.

2.1.3.2.2. Competitive Analysis

The goal is to acquire an accurate understanding of the market dynamics and the performance of the target competitors on the Chinese market. This section aims at studying:

- The strengths and weaknesses, and opportunities and threats by product, division, or segment.
- The organization by business line.
- The corporate culture.
- The key success factors, the market share.
- The competitors' profile.

The analysis must be fine-tuned through interviews with industry players and industry experts, on market trends and competitive positions of the key players. The analysis will therefore help summarize the trends and size of the market, the market share, and the competitors' profile.

2.1.3.2.3. Strategic Position of the Company

The segment analysis regarding volumes and growth, product positioning, the impact of research and innovation on future supply, and the organic and external growth opportunities will be subject to a rigorous analysis using strategic analysis tools. The purpose is to create a dynamic representation of the product and product family portfolio, and opportunities for organic growth (new products intensity, leverage on existing products, substitution risk) and external growth (M&A, strategic partnerships), in order to assess the target's full potential. It also helps to identify the key issues the buyer must immediately work on right after the acquisition (e.g., technology transfer in order to solve quality problems, integration of the products in a broader range).

2.1.3.3. *Building a Business Plan*

The financial business plan consolidates all the information received during the previous stages in order to verify the profitability of the target and its valuation over a period of several years. It is a financial model of the company, enabling the simulation of several scenarios depending on the variation of key market parameters (prices, volumes, costs). The business plan is built on the analysis of sales growth by market segment, by product, by nature of costs (classification of the fixed or variable costs, direct or otherwise), by calibration of structural costs, and by comparative analysis of the sector margin structure.

Any business plan presented by the seller will always be challenged during negotiations if the underlying assumptions are not adequately substantiated. In China, it is not unusual to encounter a situation where no business plan is provided, where the acquisition is proposed "as such" and on the basis of often inaccurate accounting.[22]

Once the analysis is over, it is possible to work on a simulation of the company's performance in the future. This will make it possible to evaluate the sales development, to measure the specific impact of certain business activities, and to better understand the plausible growth of structural costs, the liquidity constraints, or the evolution of global profitability. This step is essential, as the business plan is the cornerstone of the valuation of a company, using a discounted cash flow method which remains an essential and reliable decision tool for the acquirer.

The global process, notably the information sources, must be accurately documented in the due diligence report, which will also

[22] Refer to Chapter 3, Section 3.2 — Accounting Risk Management.

be used to better negotiate the purchase price. This report could be opposed by other analysis carried out by the vendor. It is therefore advisable to have a good quality and professional piece.

2.1.4. *Due Diligences Are a Key Success Factor of External Growth Operations*

The success of a due diligence process relies on four main key factors of success:

- **Communication** — which consists of engaging in a proactive dialogue with the parties involved and managing the expectations based on time, budget, and information restrictions that can sometimes be encountered. The due diligence process engages the parties in an ongoing dialogue, in order to understand and overcome possible difficulties and the possible options to solve the problem within a tight time schedule.
- **Management commitment** — whose purpose is to ensure a continuous work process and staff motivation, even, in some cases, when the market analysis is difficult: For example, in the case of a narrow, technical, fragmented market segment on which the available information is almost non-existent — which is common in China with technical products.
- **Information management** — which requires excellent organization for the process to be completed. The research must start quickly, including the expert interviews and the written requests for information. This process requires close monitoring, frequent follow-ups, check-ups, and a rapid consolidation of the requested information to ensure that the market picture is accurate and dynamic. The experts will suggest other approaches if too many difficulties are encountered to cover the whole market in a short period of time (for example, selection of a representative sample in a smaller area).
- **Schedule and resources management**, and a clear vision of the expected results — It requires an ordered plan, a detailed schedule, and a great rigor in the monitoring of the work in process.

Due diligence specialists can deliver case critical and precise conclusions in only a matter of weeks. They maintain permanent contact with the client through the organization of steering committees and customer seminars. Many companies choose an outside advisor to conduct the strategic due diligences and save time.

The first investment decision of the executive management is, therefore, to recruit the needed resources. The transaction team must be staffed by a compact and capable team of top professionals. Their mission is to reduce the uncertainty regarding the industrial options, so that the acquirer focuses his efforts on the strategic decisions once the options are properly presented, analyzed, and evaluated. When this phase is over, the strategic due diligences are then completed post-acquisition by operational efficiency audits and change management audits.

2.2. Technical Feasibility of the Operation

Once the target, and the strategic and trade-related issues of the deal are identified, and the initial feasibility validated, it is necessary to avoid wasting time and lead the way for an extensive but reasonable audit of the target. These audits are managed by specialized teams and include gathering, analyzing, and making the synthesis by priority and degree of importance of accounting, tax, and legal issues presented to the teams by the seller at the request of the buyer's advisors. The good thing in hiring seasoned local teams is that, what may seem inconceivable for green foreign auditors will certainly not be unheard of for good professionals. This will also come with a prompt assessment of the severity of the problem and possible remedies to the situation.

Building an indicative schedule

Due diligences are a standard part of M&A transactions in developed countries, but are sometimes difficult to conduct in emerging countries where the information is less structured and fragmented.

To ensure an active collaboration of the seller with the process, one must clearly explain the reasons behind these due diligences to

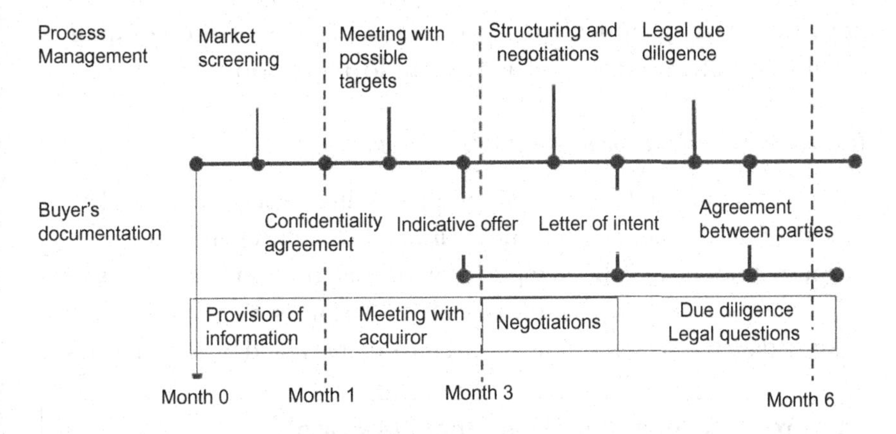

Figure 2.3. Due Diligence Process.

the Chinese target companies who may find this process unjustly intrusive, and react strongly to requests perceived as being too numerous and disruptive. This difference of appreciation by the Chinese party should be taken into account in the estimate of the time required to implement the corresponding procedures. These procedures generally start with an explanatory and confidence-building phase, where the buyer and his external advisors explain the goals and the development of the process, in particular the signature, if necessary, of confidentiality agreements, in order for the assignment to progress as smoothly as possible. Even after this, it is not uncommon for the target company's management to be surprised by the level of detail of the required information and the work conducted. This process must be managed with business sense and diplomacy, so as to avoid a negative reaction and an outright rejection from the Chinese party possibly unaccustomed to such requests.

It is still relatively rare in China to have the selling party set up a structured and exhaustive data room containing the information necessary for auditors and lawyers within the context of their due diligences. The baseline information will often have to be significantly modified by the due diligence team itself in order to be reconstructed in a usable form. For example, a classic is the difficulty to get the details of sales or margin by customer, by distribution network, or by product, or a complete overview of the company's employee status (exact number of employment contracts).

Process the available or unavailable information

In case the available information proves insufficient, a spreadsheet model of all the target's activities will need to be prepared in order to properly understand the key performance factors. Similarly, it is sometimes necessary to hire professional investigators to reconstruct the missing data by cross-checking it with information held by third parties.

A word of caution: The Peter Humphrey case[23]

In 2013, on the sidelines of a corruption scandal involving British pharmaceutical firm GlaxoSmithKlein (GSK) operations in China, Peter Humphrey, a foreign private investigator and long-term resident of China, was detained and later sentenced by Chinese authorities to two years and six months, with a fine of 200,000 Yuan (USD 32,500), and to be deported after serving the jail term. His wife was given two years and fined 150,000 Yuan. Both were sentenced for illegally obtaining private information on Chinese citizens, including paying for ID and phone numbers, car and home ownership records, and details of cross-border travel of individuals as well as their family members. The court also warned that any illegal investigation, even if disguised as something else, will never be allowed.

This appears to be part of a wider crackdown by authorities on information (including access to company records, journalism, and social media) that could potentially destabilize the delicate Chinese public opinion, at a time when an unprecedented campaign to curb corruption at all levels of Chinese society is being implemented. Investigators will therefore need to be very careful to source information only from legal ways.

[23]Wei Tian, "Foreigners Jailed for Obtaining Private Data," *CHINADAILYUSA*, August 9, 2014; available online at usa.chinadaily.com.cn/china/2014-08/09/content_18279040.htm (accessed on September 30, 2014).

Such information would need to be analyzed and verified, several times if necessary, through interviews with the management of the target company. This requires time, a good access to and a great availability of the management and accounting teams, and a seamless communication with these teams (beyond the "on the field" due diligence period). This communication requirement can sometimes put a lot of stress on the confidentiality of the ongoing discussions regarding other employees or even third parties. The relationship of trust that the consultants will have created with the management and accounting team, and their level of collaboration, will often be decisive regarding the success of the operation. This relationship will then continue during the post-acquisition integration phase, for which some milestones must quietly be put in place as early on as the due diligence stage.

In the case of financial and accounting due diligences, it is important to note that some Chinese companies still use manual accounting and book keeping, that is to say, without an accounting software. All activities are reported by the accountants in a double entry paper accounting book. In this case, the due diligences audits will have to be adjusted accordingly. Unless all the manual entries feed an accounting software, this will limit the statistical analysis possibilities and increase the time necessary to undertake the usual assessments.

Even when accounting is computerized, it is often limited to the strict minimum necessary to issue financial statements under the form required for tax returns by the tax bureau. In small-sized companies, accounting is rarely a real management tool or an information system. Moreover, the technical level of the accounting team is often uneven. As a result, the accounting data are often unreliable and the time necessary to audit them is longer than in the West. Similarly, the majority of the target company's legal information (key contracts, invoices, list and personnel situation, licenses and permits required for the target's activity, etc.) is rarely organized in a systematic way, and it is common for the lawyer in charge to receive a few archive boxes full of disorderly documents by way of the data room. One can dream of impeccable electronic data rooms as the next frontier for M&A in China.

Some may have even questioned the usefulness of the due diligence process in China, where transparency is not a prerequisite and where the apparent situation often covers a very different reality. So why not save the cost of tax and legal due diligences, and only conduct a summary accounting due diligences?

Assets present on the balance sheet but non-existent in reality, share capital never or partially paid-up, factories built on land for agricultural purposes or leased illegally, illegal workers, tax and social liabilities, event fake contracts, etc. — these are mere examples of fairly common situations that the due diligences can highlight.

2.2.1. *Tax and Financial Due Diligences*

The tax and financial due diligences are instrumental in closing a successful acquisition transaction in China. As in other jurisdictions, their goals include:

- Checking the validity of the accounts presented by the seller, this is to say, of the purchased (or transferred) assets and of the liabilities assumed.
- Assessing the quality of financial statements used as a basis for the transaction.
- Understanding in detail the key operating elements of the activity purchased to assess if past performance would likely be recurring in the post-deal environment.

  Although the elements analyzed would vary depending on the specificities of each deal, this may include, for example, the details of sales by client type, distribution channel, potential seasonality, volume, price differentials, etc.; the cost and variability of the different production factors, etc.
- Assessing the quality of the financial forecasts (business plan) provided by the seller (or better, jointly prepared by the buyer's and the seller's teams).
- Identifying risks generated by the business in the past, to which the future owner would be exposed to and, particularly, identifying as upstream as possible, risks that would be significant enough

to put in question the principle of the acquisition itself; that is to say, deal breakers beyond which an alternative solution, generally the creation *ex nihilo* of a brand from a new wholly foreign invested enterprise, should be preferred to taking over an existing firm. In this case one should expect some significant hurdles including time spent for the creation of the structure, recruitment and staff training, and development of the distribution network.

Investors should be aware of the necessity of such an approach which minimizes the risk of unpleasant surprises post-acquisition. In China, it is all the more important to gather a detailed understanding of the business to be taken over, given that legal actions against the seller are generally difficult to implement. Although acquisition contracts can include liability guarantees or price adjustment clauses in order to take into account elements that the seller did not disclose and that could diminish the value of the company, the effective implementation of these clauses is rarely easy. This is a consequence of the limitations of the Chinese legal system, as well as of the thinly-veiled protectionism that local Chinese authorities lean towards when foreign investors are part of a deal. In addition, some situations exclude post-deal price adjustments by design, notably when the activities taken over belong to a state-owned company in difficulty.

The restatement of financial statements is the first step of the financial due diligences, and allows to work with numbers similar to those that would result from the use of accounting standards familiar to the buyer.

2.2.1.1. *Identification of Non-Prescriptive Elements*

It is important to identify non-recurring or atypical items which contributed to operating results and cash flows of the company in previous years in order to exclude them during the preparation of the business plan post-acquisition. This identification will be based on a very detailed analytical review of the financial statements, ideally on a monthly basis, and on specific checks of accounting data samples concerning risky financial components and items.

2.2.1.2. *Identifying Relationships with Related Companies*

It is particularly necessary to ensure that the transactions with companies related to the target company (including typically family relationships for private businesses, but also more informal arrangements between state-owned enterprises or parts of large conglomerates) are carried out at market price in order to draw the appropriate conclusions on the actual profitability of the target. Moreover, if the target is dependent on related companies for the supply of certain key products or services, it is important to identify and document these relationships through contracts so that the company can benefit from them post-acquisition.

In the same vein, it is necessary to clearly identify expenses, which are either:

- Paid by the company for the benefit of management and therefore are, in effect, additional compensation with tax and social implications that should be clarified.
- Paid directly by the shareholder or one of its related structures and which therefore do not appear directly in the financial statements of the target company, but are actually required for its operations and which, in this case, are understated operating costs.

2.2.1.3. *Anti-Competitive Practices*

The auditor will seek to identify any commission that may be paid to win new business, and which often materializes as the reimbursement and endorsement of invoices submitted by the recipient of the commission, without having any direct link with the business of the company. If such practices are identified beyond the immediate impact on the profitability of the corresponding business, the foreign investor will have to choose whether or not he wishes to perpetuate them according to his own legal restrictions, as well as the level of risk he is willing to assume.

It is on this type of issues that the ethics and reliability of the target's current management, together with the values and the corporate culture of the acquirer, can be better assessed in order to determine the future compatibility of the two parties and, therefore, the viability of the acquisition project. In many cases, maintaining the existing management is often necessary and they must be convinced to accept the governance practices and framework implemented by the new investor, as well as the degree of transparency he requires (periodic audits, communicating operating tools, etc.).

2.2.1.4. *Tax Issues*

The issues covered by the tax due diligence particularly addresses:

- The understanding of taxes applicable to the business.
- The assessment of the target's tax returns and actual tax payments in the past.
- The identification of potential tax risks associated with understated taxes.
- The search for possible ways to optimize the taxation of the business, the structuring of the contemplated transaction, or the subsequent disposal, which should be anticipated as much as possible, notably in the case of an acquisition by an investment fund.

The main difficulties encountered are related to:

- Delays or deficiencies in the declaration and payment of tax on the basis of some "creative" accounting.
- "Arrangements" with the tax offices to pay taxes based on a flat or lower-than-should-be rate.

Cases of non-compliance with the applicable regulations will have be carefully analyzed to determine:

- The late penalties and interests which may be payable in the event of a tax audit.
- The probability of occurrence of such an audit and of a challenge of the previous declaratory basis.

- The opportunity to report and proactively correct the identified problems with the tax authorities.
- The gradual or immediate change of the procedures in order to avoid this situation in the future.

Customs issues should also be studied during this stage of due diligences using a similar pattern. Furthermore, special attention should be paid to the transactions with related companies, pre- or post-acquisition, insofar as the tax office may challenge the transfer prices used in the absence of relevant documentation regarding their adequacy to normal market prices. Finally, it should be noted that in tax matters, the administration can audit the last three fiscal years. However, in cases of presumptive fraud, the administration can go back indefinitely. Old practices can thus entail a significant risk for the new investor, and it is recommended to go back as far as possible when conducting the tax due diligences on prior years.

2.2.1.5. *Social Issues*

As for tax matters, it will be necessary to check compliance with applicable laws and regulations, including for example, the existence of an employment contract, the employees' age, their seniority, the minimum wage, the regulation on overtime payment, the social security contributions, the withholding of individual income tax, or the identification of existing "early retirement" pension plans and such, which could hamper the profitability of the business. Health and safety issues will also need to be considered at this stage to ensure the production process complies with local regulations.

Some local firms will have reached non-documented "agreements" with authorities to cover specific non-compliance issues in the above matters. Thanks in large part to social media, industrial accidents (workshop explosions, fires, asbestos and radon contamination, exposure to other hazardous chemicals, etc.) are now widely reported and Chinese authorities are applying tough sanctions on people deemed responsible. In addition, if alerted, local media and global non-governmental organizations will scrutinize Chinese operations, and demand transparency and implementation of global best practices. Verbal agreements with the officers in charge of collecting social security contributions or conducting safety inspections (such as the fire department for example) will not protect the company if the agreement is later challenged after the change of ownership.

Finally, notably for industrial operations, the environmental footprint of the business on its environment will be defined: air emissions, waste water, solid waste, soil and groundwater contamination, disposals and other pollution, etc. Industries most at risk to such issues include the chemical, food, pharmaceutical, metallurgical, toy, automotive, and electronics industries, amongst others. Some professional firms specialize in environmental due diligences, and will help identify and quantify potential environmental liabilities as well as areas of non-compliance with local regulatory prescriptions.

The cost of changing operational processes to regain compliance with both local regulations and buyer's policies and best practices will have to be assessed as early as possible and included in the post-deal business plan.

Requirements of specific Corporate Social Responsibility (CSR) reporting frameworks will also need to be anticipated to ensure internal and external communication needs will be met.

More generally, a detailed communication plan will be prepared around the proposed M&A operation. In China, it will include government relations actions targeted towards local authorities and, if needed, depending on the size and visibility of the deal, media and public relations to ensure that the operation is perceived favorably in an increasingly nationalistic context, where foreigners are less welcome than during the first phase of China's opening up. Other actions must also be contemplated in the buyer's home country to alleviate potential concerns around technology transfers, job losses, etc. Professional public relation (PR) firms will be selected based on their understanding of the local culture, context, and public opinion drivers in both China and the buyer's home market, as well as their experience with communication tools adapted to each targeted public (media, national and local authorities, staff, general public, NGOs, etc.).

Contingency plans will be prepared to react quickly and appropriately if the confidentiality of the deal is compromised before completion.

2.2.1.6. *Identification of the Acquired Assets*

In the event that the purchaser only acquires certain assets of a Chinese company, it will be necessary to identify and separate the assets taken over from the rest of the assets kept by the seller. This "carve-out" generally requires a complete audit of the seller's accounts, including the non-transferred assets, in order to check that all the transferred assets have been identified. This often leads to communication issues with the seller, who may have difficulties understanding the necessity of such an intrusive scope of investigation. Diplomacy and common sense will have to be used to explain the chosen criteria and sign mutual non-disclosure/confidentiality agreements to make everybody comfortable.

Generally, the due diligences that need to be performed in the event of an asset deal are comparable to those applicable to a transaction on securities (share deal) to the extent that, beyond the simple valuation of the transferred assets and liabilities, it is important to understand the former operating conditions of the business and, specifically, to estimate what they may be in the future.

2.2.1.7. *Insurance Coverage*

It is important to ensure that the insurance policies taken out are appropriate, both in terms of asset protection (adequacy of the insured amounts with the accounting values), and with respect to liability and operating loss if that situation arises. This is often overlooked by Chinese business owners (for example, fire, accident) and the cost of implementing additional policies has to be anticipated.

2.2.1.8. *Identifying Internal Audit Weaknesses*

Although it is not usually an issue capable of derailing the acquisition process, it is important to take advantage of the due diligence work to identify the main weaknesses in internal controls in order to be able to reinforce policies and procedures once the acquisition is finalized.

The most common weaknesses are generally due to:

- An insufficient separation of duties.
- An insufficient documentation of the supplier selection process (request for proposals, tendering process, etc.) leading to possible over-invoicing fraud schemes.
- An inadequate monitoring of physical flows (receipts, shipments, cycle counting, etc.).
- The management's tendency to "bypass" control frameworks in place and create shortcuts for faster delivery.

2.2.1.9. *Synthesis on Issues Related to the Financial and Tax Due Diligences*

The list of issues above is not exhaustive. In this domain, the accounting creativity of Chinese entrepreneurs is remarkable and each assignment leads to new discoveries. In this context, it is not rare to see companies presenting:

- Tax returns reporting losses to reduce the tax payable.
- "Management" accounts presented to the foreign investor and showing significant profits. Although these "profits" are shown through the due diligence process to be actually recurring losses, the identification of easily implementable synergies (introduction of a new technology, opening of a new export market, production and/or distribution rationalization, etc.) justifies the acquisition.

However, it is interesting to note that the problems encountered (identified adjustments, risks and uncertainties, etc.) are rarely of a very technical nature. They are more "basic" issues, such as incorrect bank reconciliations, cut-off issues, etc. which, if comparisons are made with acquisitions carried out in the West, can have a significant impact for foreign investors. This is of course a consequence of the relative simplicity of many of the production, service, and distribution operations in China on which most of the acquisition process is centered, as well as the regulatory environment, especially concerning finance (controlled exchange rate regime, near absence of derivative contracts, etc.). But this mostly reveals, with some exceptions, the immaturity of many Chinese companies and thus, implicitly, the importance of synergies and the productivity gains a Western management approach can bring to the table.

2.2.2. *Legal Due Diligence*

Its purpose is to ensure that the intended transaction is possible regarding the legal situation of the target company, or to assess the conditions under which the transaction will have to be concluded to ensure a maximum legal certainty. In many cases, it also allows to identify problems and risks that will constitute additional elements or arguments in the price negotiation and the valuation of the target company.

The legal aspects of the due diligence mainly include collecting regulatory, legal, and social information, as well as writing a due diligence report gathering the collected information and addressing the legal issues or problems that have or will arise during the transaction. Collecting information in China is often a long and difficult process, particularly because of the lack of bookkeeping and transparency in accounting according to customary international rules, but also due to the absence of a national register for corporations and archives. There is a certain belief that information means negotiating leverage and that it is therefore best to avoid disclosing information and documents about the target company — the Chinese being excellent negotiators. As restructuring and M&A transactions are quite new in China, one should not neglect the relative inexperience of the sellers — before the '90s, the terms merger and/or acquisition were almost unknown in Chinese laws. But the relative inexperience of the sellers can also result in an opportunity for the buyer to show the benefits of the partnership, as the target company may be less prepared for the analysis resulting from the due diligence investigation and for the contemplated acquisition project.

A Chinese seller is reluctant, in practice, to sign confidentiality agreements and legally binding contractual clauses concerning indemnities and mechanisms, ensuring the good progress of the due diligence process as well as the seller's cooperation and the truthfulness of the information. In Europe, for example, the seller is bound by a transparency and diligence obligation towards the buyer, who may then embark on the acquisition project on the basis of a less detailed investigation; but such a legal obligation does not exist in China. In addition, either the certainty of completion or the payment of an indemnification in case of contractual breach of one's commitment remains difficult to enforce.

The documents supplied by the seller must be confirmed and completed by information and documents that Chinese authorities are allowed to communicate, notably to lawyers. Similarly, there are third party investigation companies located in China and in Hong Kong that can double check these documents or highlight some facts which can be singled out for additional checks by the legal team in charge of conducting the due diligence. The extent of the due diligence depends on the context, the size and nature of the contemplated operation, the business activities of the target company, and the strategic ambition of the project. There is therefore, in principle, no standard "one-size-fits-all" list, but the following elements will necessarily be addressed in such audits.

2.2.2.1. *Organization*

The following include:

- History and structure of the company.
- Financial capital requirements: accounting and legal existence of the contributions.
- Licenses and permits required for the activity, and expiration dates.

2.2.2.2. *Assets*

The following include:

- Tangible assets: legal title and identification.
- Land use rights (a particularly sensitive issue difficult to control in China).
- Intellectual property/intangible assets: The payment of right for the use of software is still very uncertain and may result in penalties.

2.2.2.3. *Key Contracts*

- Key contracts: Who are the end customers? Will they go through intermediaries not controlled by the buyer?
- Employee/employment contracts/human resources: One must systematically check that the payroll and pensions have been paid; furthermore, keeping employees that may need to be laid off later should be avoided.

2.2.2.4. *Finance and Contingent Liabilities*

- Loans to "partner" companies that may become unrecoverable once the management changes.
- Forex: compliance with the applicable procedures.
- Taxes: adequate reporting, filing, and payment.
- Officially filed accounts — it is common for accounting to be multiple (internal and external).
- Environmental issues: Do extensive audits related to this subject because of stricter regulation; ask for monitoring reports.
- Litigation and administrative proceedings/interests, penalties, and damages.

2.3. How to Structure the Deal from the Beginning?

In China, more than in any other country, the upstream preparation of an M&A campaign and the preparation for the integration are really key success factors. This is due to, on one hand, the relative novelty of these acquisition issues, and on the other hand, the specific overlapping of guarantees, and financial, tax, and legal topics. A good organization will allow the buyer's management to focus essentially on business development rather than on solving annoying technical problems after the deal is closed. Thereby, a fourfold structure should be established before negotiating guarantees and financial, tax, and legal elements.

2.3.1. *Tax Structuring*

2.3.1.1. *Asset or Share Deal?*

Depending on circumstances, the purchaser may wish to acquire either the shares or the assets of the target company. From a tax perspective, this choice will have a significant impact on the negotiations because the tax cost for the seller will be very different, as illustrated by the following Tables 2.1 and 2.2.

Therefore, the difference between those two basic schemes should be taken into account during the negotiations, considering that the tax cost and the additional delays in the case of an asset deal must be included in the price to pay to overcome the risk of contingent liabilities related to a possible repurchase of shares.

2.3.1.2. *Interposition of a Holding Company*

The tax structuring of an acquisition can lead to interposing a holding company, created especially for this purpose, between the target and the acquirer. The potential tax advantage, apart from other legal or financial rationales, comes from locating this holding in a country or territory benefiting from preferential withholding tax rates due to specific tax treaties with China. These rates usually apply to dividends, interests, or royalties.

A classic example is to acquire more than 25% of the equity of a Chinese company through a holding entity located in Hong Kong, thereby securing a 5% withholding tax rate on dividends paid, compared to a 10% withholding tax rate for a non-treaty country. This is however, subject to specific requirements, notably in terms of substance

Table 2.1. Tax and Tax Base Calculations on Asset Transfers in China.

Tax	Business Tax	Capital Gains Tax	VAT	Clawback and Import VAT	Stamp Duty	Deed Tax
Rate	5%	25%	17% on inventory transfers	Rate determined by Customs	0.05%	3% to 5%
Tax base	Intangible assets transfers	Disposal of land and building use rights	Up to 2% on the transfer of equipments or used vehicles	Disposal of non-taxable goods in a five year limit after import	Effective on contracts	Purchase of land or property use rights
Payable by	Seller	Seller	Seller	Seller	Both parties	Buyer

Source: Mazars.

Table 2.2. Tax on Equity Deals.

Tax	Corporate Income Tax	Stamp Duty
Rate	25%	0.05%
Tax base	Taxation on the capital gain of the transfer	Effective on contracts
Imputation	Charged to the seller	Charged to both parties

Source: Mazars.

in the Hong Kong entity, and therefore must be carefully considered with the help of a professional advisor.

Another reason that can justify the interposition of a holding company lies in the allocation of revenue and expenses between China and the holding. The typical set-up is as follows:

- The holding company, located in a low-tax area (such as Hong Kong for example), is in charge of high value-added activities (e.g., marketing and international distribution, global supply chain management, etc.).
- The activities taxed in China, such as manufacturing, are activities generating a lower added value.

Provided all functions along the chain of value, as well as the risks and rewards generated by the business, are properly allocated between each entity, such structuring may be acceptable. However, it should be noted that the Chinese tax authorities are implementing increasingly stringent tax audits on transfer prices. Therefore, transfer prices between the holding and the Chinese company will have to be carefully documented to support that they reflect fair market values.

2.3.1.3. *Acquisition of an Offshore Holding*

Transfer price considerations must also be carefully assessed when acquiring offshore companies holding Chinese assets. In the same set-up as described above, the seller may have a manufacturing

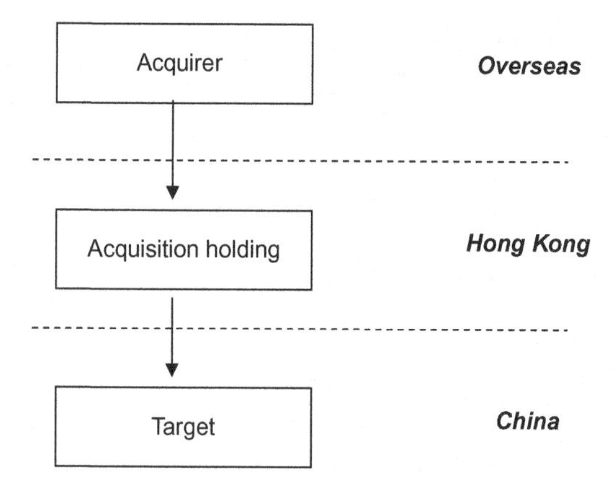

Figure 2.4. Interposition of an Acquisition Holding.

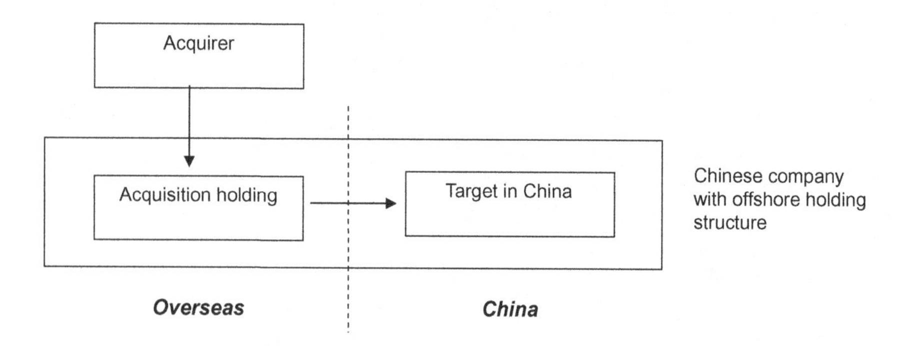

Figure 2.5. Interposition of Offshore Holding.

subsidiary in China and a holding company located offshore for trading purposes. If transfer prices do not reflect fair market values, the buyer may inherit the corresponding tax exposure.

It is not uncommon to see sellers transferring their shares below the fair market value to a location where there is no tax on capital gains to prepare for a later sale to the buyer at their real price. Alternatively, the seller may offer that the payment of the Chinese acquisition be made to a sister company of the group located offshore. Both schemes may subject the buyer to tax exposure if the corresponding tax has not been paid.

2.3.1.4. *Taxation of Holding Companies*

Holding companies are subject to the same taxes as other companies and, notably, to:

- The corporate tax based on their income at the standard rate of 25%.
- VAT on sales of goods and following the VAT reform started in 2012, provision of a number of services, including to its subsidiaries.

However, it should be noted that:

- Dividends received by the holding company from its subsidiaries in China are not taken into account when calculating the corporation tax.
- This is compensated by the fact that the portion of overhead costs corresponding to the subsidiaries management expenses is not deductible. This portion is calculated on a pro rata basis between the income generated by investment and the operating income.

2.3.1.5. *Tax Treatment of Mergers & Acquisitions*

The general framework applicable to mergers & acquisitions is the one applicable to the purchases and sales of shares. It provides for investments to be valued at their fair value at the date of the transaction. The gain or loss generated by the transaction will be taxable at the rate applicable to the entity selling its shares.

However, some tax circulars issued in 2009 and 2010 specify under which conditions the taxation of the gain or loss from a restructuring operation may be temporarily deferred:

- The restructuring is motivated by a valid business reason and not only by a tax benefit.
- The transaction involves at least 75% of the assets or capital of the entity.

- At least 85% of the transaction is paid in shares.
- Business continuity for at least 12 months after the restructuring.
- Continuity of ownership by the shareholder for at least 12 months after the restructuring.

Although the above conditions are quite restrictive, the scope of their application is very broad, as it includes changes in legal status, debt restructuring, and acquisition of share capital or assets, as well as mergers and divestitures. If conditions are met, the restructuring will benefit from a temporary corporation tax exemption except for the part of the operation that is not paid in shares, for which the gain or loss will be calculated on the difference between the fair value and the historical tax base in proportion to the part paid in cash compared to the total fair value. However, it should be noted that a cross-border restructuring transaction will only qualify for the above regime in three very specific cases:

- A non-resident company transferring the shares of a Chinese company to a wholly-owned non-resident subsidiary.
- A non-resident company transferring the shares of a Chinese company to a wholly-owned Chinese subsidiary.
- A Chinese company using shares or assets to invest in a wholly-owned non-resident subsidiary.

Finally, the periods of tax exemption and reduction that a company involved in the reorganization can claim, as well as the deferrable losses, can generally be transferred to the new entity resulting from the merger. However, in this case, there has to be a separate calculation of the taxable income of the company's business that previously benefited from the deferrable tax benefit (or loss), in order to demonstrate that this benefit (or loss) is in fact only charged to the results of the business that has historically generated it as if there had been no merger. For example, it will not be possible, when merging a structurally loss-making company with a structurally profitable company, to impute the carried forward losses of the first to the future profits of the profitable company. Carried forward losses can only be used if the business generating them becomes profitable within the new entity up to the five years during which they can be carried forward.

Moreover, it is possible to defer the application of the VAT and the business tax in the event of the transfer of a complete branch of activity (by opposition to individual assets and liabilities).

2.3.1.6. *Post-Acquisition Tax Integration*

In China, there is no tax integration regime allowing a group of companies to offset the gains of some entities with the losses of others. However, a company that has several branches may choose to consolidate the calculation of the corporate tax at the registered address of its head office. Nevertheless, payment must be split among the tax administrations of each branch based on the pro rata of the payroll, assets, and sales of each site. The other taxes (VAT, business tax, etc.) are paid at the registered address of each site.

2.3.2. *Financial Structuring*

Chinese law distinguishes the share capital from the total investment made by the company. The decree implementing the law regarding joint ventures, modified in 2001, defines the total investment amount as "the sum of the funds used to raise capital and the working capital". The "provisional regulation on the ratio between the share capital and the total share investment of equity venture" (1987) requires that the amount of share capital of a foreign invested enterprise, including WFOE, be at least equal to a certain percentage of the total investment. When a foreign invested enterprise increases its total investment, the regulation requires that the legal ratios above also be applied to the share capital. This theoretical ratio is used to define the FIE's debt capacity in foreign currencies or in RMB with a foreign currency guarantees. For example, a company whose total planned investment (not necessarily carried out) is €100,000 will have a minimum share capital of

Table 2.3. Total Investment/Share Capital Ratio.

Total Amount of the Planned Investment	Mandatory Proportion in Share Capital
Equal or less than USD3 million	At least 70%
Between USD3 and USD10 million (included) Exception: If the total investment is lower than USD4.2 million, the share capital has to at least be equal to USD2.1 million	At least 50%
Between USD10 and USD30 million (included) Exception: If the total investment is lower than USD12.5 million, the share capital has to at least be equal to USD5 million	At least 40%
More than USD30 million Exception: If the total investment is lower than USD36 million, the share capital has to at least be equal to USD12 million	At least 33.33%

Source: Ministry of Commerce People's Republic of China (MOFCOM) official website; available online at english.mofcom.gov.cn (accessed on September 30, 2014).

€70,000 and a €30,000 debt capacity. However, in this same example, the company can borrow beyond this limit locally in RMB, provided that one can find a bank willing to make such a loan.

Loans granted in foreign currencies (or currency guarantees) by foreign financial institutions or by the FIE's parent company must receive approval from SAFE, which will allow the opening of a special account on which the loan will be paid out and most of all will enable the conversion of the loan in foreign currency and its reimbursement. In the absence of registration, the permission to convert foreign currencies to RMB in order to repay the loan would be rejected by SAFE, as would the conversion of the debt into capital.

Accordingly, the financial structuring will seek to avoid overestimating the total investment and thus the share capital, whose reduction may be difficult and time consuming. On the other hand, an underestimation of the necessary resources (too cautious a business plan) will require a capital increase, which is less risky. However, the process of such an increase is time consuming and can cause the company considerable difficulties if it no longer has enough cash for its day-to-day operations. Moreover, an appropriate financial structuring by the granting of a shareholder loan will allow repatriating the extra cash by paying back this loan. Note that the amount of deductible interest is limited. A third pillar of financial structuring is to define, prior to the acquisition, a reasonable royalty system (service, technical training, royalties). It will also repatriate cash in addition to the two first items.

2.3.3. *Legal Structuring*

2.3.3.1. *Mergers & Acquisitions*

Mergers, i.e., mergers of equal as we typically know them in the West can occur in China but are relatively rare, probably due to the fact that the market economy in China is still young, and also because of the discrepancies in the application of the regulations in the event of mergers involving entities located in different Chinese provinces. In substance, the texts basically recognize two types of mergers: merger by absorption or merger by creation of a new entity.

At the moment, Chinese regulations do not allow cross-border mergers. It is not possible to directly merge an entity located abroad and an entity located in Mainland China, even if the Chinese entity is a FIE. Therefore, the only mergers allowed in China are those between FIEs, or between a FIE and a wholly owned domestic enterprise.

2.3.3.2. *Share or Asset Acquisition?*

From a legal perspective, an asset acquisition allows, in China as in elsewhere, to focus on the very substance of such an acquisition and to limit the risks to the full ownership of assets and liabilities. Assets deals are used as a protection from contingent liabilities and risks associated with the full purchase of legal entities, in the absence of an up-and-running regime of representations and warranties. The assets are either both acquired and transferred to a FIE or acquired by a FIE created for the operation. Beyond the tax impact for the seller, the risk that he may become a competitor is significant. It should be noted that some assets benefit from preferential tax regimes conditioned to their non-transfer. This should be checked during the due diligences.

The acquisition of a company's shares allows acquiring a business, comprising, in particular, customers and certifications or licenses which sometimes take a long time to obtain. On the other hand, there was an uncertainty as to the existence and the valuation of possible liabilities and as to the reality of some assets. Now, the payment of the acquisition price can be freely scheduled and agreed between the parties.[24] The importance of the various due diligences is thus emphasized, as it can help reduce the risk together with an adequate payment structure.

It is also standard practice to include a material adverse change clause so as to be protected in the acquisition price against unexpected last-minute financial counter performances.

Finally, regarding the share acquisition, some special cases that may occur should be noted:

- Licenses are not always transferable (e.g., exploration rights) or only under certain conditions, which must be specifically negotiated.
- In the case of an acquisition of a group of companies, it may be necessary to carve-out the activities foreigners are not authorized to conduct before the transaction is completed.

2.3.3.3. *Investment Vehicles*

Five criteria can be used to choose the legal form of the investment vehicle:

- Economic efficiency in order to penetrate the Chinese market (networks, licenses) and possibly to ensure the involvement of a Chinese partner.

---

[24]A circular of MOFCOM, dated June 17, 2014, has abolished the obligation to pay no later than three months after the transaction completion. For futher details, access relevant circular at MOFCOM official website, http.//english.mofcom.gov.cn/.

Table 2.4. Comparison of the Different Acquisition Structures in China.

	Foreign Company	**Foreign Invested Enterprise**	**Chinese Holding**
Application of the M&A regulations (2006)	Yes	Yes	No, except for targets operating in a restricted sector
Nature of the acquired company	FIE	FIE	Domestic company
Exchange controls	Amount subject to the approval of MOFCOM and SAFE	Amount limited to the FIE's total investment + conversion of the share capital subject to the approval of SAFE	Using the share capital in foreign currency to acquire shares is prohibited, except where otherwise regulated
Payment currency	Foreign currency	Foreign currency	RMB — income from the activity on the territory or income from the sale of an existing stake
Merger monitoring procedure	Subject to the review under the new anti-trust legislation		
Corporate status of the buyer	Subject to the qualification criteria applied to foreign companies in some industries	Possible approval for activities related to its investments	Subject to qualification criteria applied to domestic companies in some industries
Possible reuse of the investment vehicle for multiple acquisitions	Yes	Yes	Share acquisitions strictly monitored. No clear restrictions on asset acquisitions
Divesture-Approbation	Subject to MOFCOM's approval	Subject to MOFCOM's approval	No
Divesture-Tax	Withholding tax of 10%	Corporation tax of 25%	Corporation tax of 25%
Mandatory reserve	Only applicable to the target company	Two level of reserves: the holding and its subsidiaries	Two level of reserves: the FIE and the domestic company

- Minimization of the risk concerning the assessment of the acquisition and tolerance regarding this risk.
- Audit of the structure, particularly with regard to the changes of its financing (if joint venture partner).
- Retention of intellectual property.
- Tax efficiency (offshore holding) during the operation and at the closing.

2.3.3.4. *Acquisition via an Offshore Structure*

The offshore structure, particularly in a jurisdiction without tax on capital gains such as Hong Kong, is frequently preferred for a potential equity change of ownership in the form of an IPO or the sales of shares to a new buyer (trade sale or private placement). Indeed, no license will be required in China: This operation will be locally exempt from taxation on capital gains. Finally, confidentiality will be better secured offshore since in China no equity change is possible without approval of Chinese authorities, which leads to the risk of information disclosure.

In the specific case of an acquisition of assets paid offshore, sometimes suggested by the seller (for tax reasons) or the buyer (for guarantees reasons), two problems arise if the asset has mainly been paid offshore:

- The buyer brings the price "into" the Chinese company and can therefore not amortize it.
- The purchaser must, in addition to its offshore payment, capitalize the Chinese company who will buy the assets.

2.3.4. *Structuring Guarantees*

Until early 2014, guarantees in China had to be structured specifically. The applicable regulation was characterized by the absence of a safety net for the buyer. In the past, it was stipulated that the payment of the acquisition price should be made within the three months (up to one year if MOFCOM provided an exceptional authorization to do so) following the moment the operating license is issued, which was clearly a limiting factor to possible uncertainties on the quality of the target. Fortunately, a recent circular of MOFCOM has abolished the restriction on the timing of acquisition price payment.

The buyer's primary protection (guarantees) regarding asset and liability risks are common practice in China but cover a more limited spectrum than in the West. They can be very awkward if any compensation is supposed to be paid out of China due to Forex regulation. Conditions have improved recently, since the price can be freely defined by contract between the parties. Legal recourses, particularly following the acquisition of a state-owned company, could be inefficient and only lead to sterile and costly discussions. A Chinese seller setting up guarantees abroad was an impossible situation in practice, as the transfer of assets abroad, just as the exchange of shares with a listed foreign entity, requires the approval of MOFCOM.

One of the simple solutions to structure warranties is to make sure that the seller will indemnify the target directly, not the buyer, which is situated outside of China. However, this solution has some limitation, as such monies are considered a taxable income (25%).

More tailor-made solutions can be structured in the form of consulting contracts in China or abroad between the acquirer and the seller for the post-acquisition phase. The terms and conditions of such a contract can be modulated according to the occurrence of unexpected events, such as new liabilities or lower asset valuation. However, one must be careful with this type of arrangement and make sure they comply with the relevant legal and fiscal regulations.

Finally, it is not possible to create more than one class of shares (common and preferential) to adjust the conversion value on the results of the company. Therefore, it is tempting to imagine an acquisition in several stages, for example, a 51% take-over of the target's share capital, an option to purchase the rest at a given time, and an adjusted price based on the results.

This method, which makes it possible to modulate the risk and payment terms, has two drawbacks:

- The re-value of the company, following the acquisition of the first 51% of the company, can be analyzed as the payment of an additional price.
- The sale of the other 49%, even in the context of pre-contractual commitments, may be challenged by the partner. This situation can turn into an open conflict with the Chinese partner, which would inevitably be very damaging to business. And at the end of the day, it is likely to be very difficult to force him to sell the remaining shares.

Consequently, it is absolutely essential for any and all M&A or strategic partnership projects in China to minimize risks through serious due diligences procedures, and to remember that post-transactions remedies are more likely to be much more expensive than curing the problems upfront.

Chapter 3

Managing Acquisitions Risks

3.1. Third Party Due Diligence

3.1.1. *Trust Is What Is Really at Stake*

Relationships and really knowing your partner are a requirement in China before concluding any meaningful transaction, as one needs to clearly understand if the owner and the management of a target or strategic partner can be a trustable party to deal with. The quality of business practices of a target must be clearly assessed and rated, and this goes as far as the business reputation and professional ethics of its leaders. Compared to the West, this discovery stage must come quite early in the negotiation process to avoid wasting time and money in a possibly disappointing acquisition process.

The case of a US-based video company requesting some help to understand why its strategic supplier partner, a Chinese traffic lens manufacturer, kept delaying a shipment critical to their production is very illustrative of this situation. The reason given by the supplier was a shortage of raw materials. In addition, the customer also has had some substantial quality issues with the supplier, which was displaying an extensive product line, certifications, factory photos, and a strange residential-looking address. Upon recalling the supplier's main calling line, someone who seemed to be a wife in the midst of house work picked up the phone.

After further discussions with the supplier, it was discovered that he was actually not manufacturing the lens but was some sort of unofficial reseller of low quality products. This dodgy intermediary was in fact buying rejected lenses from a source within the actual lens manufacturer's facility, which was finally identified. He then sold them to various companies as top quality ones, at a seemingly good price, compared to first grade products. This US firm admitted that it had never performed any detailed audit on its partner or visited its production facilities. It was just attracted by a good price and a nice product presentation.[25]

Everything is certainly not expected to be perfect, but clear yellow and red lines must be drawn, especially when it comes to illegal business, chronic lack of integrity, and dodgy business practices. If the revenues model historically depends on corrupt or dodgy practices, it is wiser aborting the deal if there is no clear ethical path to acceptable profitability. Chinese companies have been pointed out, but the foreign subsidiaries of some international companies have been equally identified, promoting the most unethical practices for the sake of growing their business faster, sometimes under the stewardship of their local foreign leadership.

If the seller is targeted for corruption and "voluntary cooperation with authorities", things are likely to be complicated in the context of an acquisition and risks are not only reputational but also legal. In a best case scenario, this will result in cleaning liabilities and possible loss of all corrupt revenues. In a worst case scenario, even if an investor acted in good faith in acquiring or joint venturing, future transactions and operations could be administratively barred or

[25] This case is extracted from an article written by Chris Wingo, Managing Director of Sage Consultants, in the *Shanghai Amcham Orientation China Guidebook*, 2014, p. 100.

frozen.[26] No reasonable foreign company is really a candidate for this in China, given the hassle and the time expected to be wasted.

3.1.2. *The Third Party Due Diligence Framework*

Third party due diligence usually involves legal data mining under the surface of publicly available information, first in better structuring publicly available literature, and second in excavating non-publicly available information, including field observations.

The reason for such analysis is that some successful businessmen can be clever in overstating the value of their business, interfere with the judgment of the acquirer, run bad reputation or even illegal business, hide serious conflict of interest, or create seemingly incomprehensible obstacles to solving some simple questions.

The third party analysis methodology is based on the framework and methods of competitive intelligence. Running a 360 degrees full dimensional due diligence method in an environment where the information is scarce and not always reliable is critical in order to have a better understanding of whom an acquirer is dealing with, and vice versa. This methodology aims at identifying and understanding inbound and outbound flows related to the object of analysis: goods flows, staff flows, capital flows, and information flows. The process can extract key information from discreet interviews of former staff, suppliers, customers, or related parties under the premises of not alerting the target.

The accounting books may be cooked in a clever way, senior management may be cleverly twisted and very good at hiding their misbehavior and corrupt practices, but a converging and consistent pattern of information from stakeholders (e.g., suppliers, staff, civil servants) is likely to reveal gross inconsistencies and shed a different and crude light on the case.

---

[26] Peter Neumann, "Best Practice," presentation at the M&A Conference: Marry in Haste, Repent at Leisure, European Chamber of Commerce, Shanghai, China, July 16, 2014.

Table 3.1. Some of the Key Third Party Investigation Questions.

1	**Corporate history** Evolution of the target company
2	**Management profile** Key management principals and background
3	**Reputation and level of integrity** Determine if the company is reliable and honest
4	**Status with authorities** Has the company been investigated/suspected by authorities?
5	**Social environment** Prominent business, political, or criminal connections
6	**Litigations and blacklists** Company's involvement in litigations or serious business practices
7	**Unethical/illegal business practices** Has the company been accused of illegal business practices?
8	**Business style and values** What are the key drivers and values of the company?
9	**Corporate social responsibility** Is the company acting in a responsible way?

In emerging countries and fragmented environments, it is advisable to move the third party due diligence early to get a three-dimensional picture of the process and use it as a deal breaker for the transaction. In case early discoveries are incompatible with the acquirer's culture, it is better to quickly stop the negotiations. Indeed, this small upstream precaution is likely to bear a very high yield for the rest of the process.

3.1.3. *Running Third Party Due Diligence*

As a good start to the basic investigations of a legal third party due diligence, four aspects can be considered as a priority to better know a target:

(a) Company's operations.
(b) Company's decision-making management.
(c) Local politics, investment policies, and business environment.

(d) Possible interference from competitors and interested related parties (conflict of interest).

The key research items for each section will involve answering the following questions:

(1) The company operations

- What is the actual operating situation of the company? Is the company's general business environment good and comprehensible?
- Are its production and operating activities on track? Is there any kind of risk factor or negative rumor that influences its normal operations?
- What is the target company's position, ranking, and reputation in the industry?
- What is the target company's status and reputation in the city and the community?
- Is the target involved in any serious litigation, labor, or environmental disputes?
- Is the target having a routinely unethical attitude with its staff, e.g., use of blackmail, salary retention, extortion of signature for working contract amendment, extension of work permits or visa (for workers from another region or foreigners)?

(2) The company's management

- Background, resume, and professional qualifications of its legal representative, shareholders, and major executives.
- Respective duties within the company, and operation and management style of the legal representative, shareholders, and major executives.
- Reputation of the legal representative and main executives in the industry (e.g., are they known to be prone to openly flaunt their wealth and extravagance, or on the opposite side, donate significant amounts of their own money to charitable causes?).

- Criminal records, litigation records, and all kinds of disputes over obligations of the legal representative and executives.
- Any special political background or relationship of the legal representative and executives with any organized crime.

(3) Local policies and legal environment

- How are the public and private policy attitudes of the local government towards the M&A?
- Whether the local political situation is stable, and whether the change of principal officials of the government will influence the implementation of the agreements concluded.
- Are there any public or invisible barriers in the local government?
- How is the operational efficiency of the local government? Is there any obvious custom of unspoken rules?

(4) Possible interference from competitors and interested related parties

- Attitudes and possible interference means of the competitors in the industry towards the M&A (e.g., inciting political boycotts, calling for safety or antitrust investigation, etc.)
- Attitudes and the possibility and possible ways of interference of the employees from the acquired party towards the M&A.
- Attitudes and the possibility and possible ways of interference of the local major environmental protection and labor groups towards the M&A.

The investigation items of these four aspects basically cover the actual operating situation and executives' possible ethical risks of the acquired enterprise, possible reactions of the competitors and other interested parties, and even the macroscopic political and security risks. This goes much beyond the limitation of traditional due diligences, which are mainly confined to the legal and financial areas, and lead to the prospective forecast on some risk factors that have relatively direct influence on the success of the transaction. These risk factors include: the acquired company's actual operation status, problems concerning environmental protection and labor disputes, and possible boycotts from interested parties. The objective is to anticipate and be in a position to defuse the possible risks in advance.

3.1.4. *Extracting the Best from Third Party Due Diligence*

Usually, traditional due diligence starts before the official start or during the operation of the M&A activity. However, third party due diligence is completely assigned by the acquirer to be either operated before the official start of the M&A or during the screening of the acquisition target. With a comprehensive screening of the enterprises that meet the preliminary requirements of the acquisition in specific industries, potential buyers are allowed to have an initial understanding of the value and risks of the acquisition targets without disturbing the targets and other benefits-related parties. Therefore, this can not only play a role of keeping secret and concealing intentions in the early stages, but also help to gain more time and room for manoeuvre, so as to develop a more realistic and economical M&A plan.

Achievements of third party due diligence combined with behavioral analysis tools provide strong strategy support for the transaction talks

In an important significant negotiation, if one party knows exactly about the real situation and negotiation plans of the other party prior to the negotiation, this can undoubtedly represent a significant advantage during the negotiation and the former party can take the initiative of leading the negotiation.

- Third party investigation firms can legally collect in-depth information on the acquiree's current actual operation situation, level of cash flow, and various risk points, and cross check this information with publicly available data.

- They can also work on profiling the negotiators, collecting in advance the personal educational and professional background information, personality traits, and negotiating records or styles in previous negotiations of the acquired party's leading executives and negotiation team members. This may help to establish files of key target personnel, and predict several possible negotiation schemes and the bottom line of the opponent negotiation team when combining with the analysis on the opponent's real situation before the negotiation.
- Behavioral science pattern analysis can later provide a relatively precise inference on the specific negotiation strategies and tactics used by the opponents, making the other party's move more predictable.

Monitoring the intentions and behavior of the acquired company's interests-related parties and providing early warning against possible crises

In the beginning and process of the acquisition or partnership negotiation, and after the deal has been signed, the possible hostility from the acquired company's employees, competitors, media, environmental protection groups, labor groups, and other NGOs is likely to bring different degrees of risks to the transaction, jeopardize a smooth integration, and eventually destroy the value of the acquisition. It is advisable to start early in the acquisition process with a good understanding of the following:

- The investigation scope of the third party due diligence will cover beforehand the attitudes and trends of the acquiring party itself, its competitors, and other interested related parties in the transaction. Their possible reactions can be predicted and judged through professional analysis so as to help the negotiating team get corresponding measures ready in advance.
- The interests-related parties' may have a different attitude on the transaction and behavioral changes will be more or less reflected in the local media, internet forums, and communication groups, and the third party investigation firms under the

framework of comprehensive risk control can make appropriate analysis on the hostilities and resisting behaviors that are being brewed, and grade the threats via the public opinion monitoring software and professional analysts.

- For those real and credible boycott threats, the third party investigation firms will learn more about the background, determination, and competence of their initiators and main participants, as well as the disposal process of past similar local incidents, so as to provide first-hand reference basis for the acquiring party to take appropriate measures.

It can be expected that with the growing number of M&A activities and the increasing complexity of the M&A environment, third party due diligence based on competitive intelligence will not only further provide investors with more support, but will also be known by more business investment sectors, private equity funds, and multinational consulting firms, and help the increasingly diversified M&A subjects find and seize opportunities, and foresee and monitor risks.

3.2. Accounting Risk Management

3.2.1. *Pre-Assessment*

Under the 2006 regulations, the value of assets and the transfer price of shares must be evaluated by a certified audit firm complying with the Chinese accounting standards. The sale or transfer of company shares at a price well below the assessed asset value is not authorized, although the assessment criteria are not explicit (Article 14).

In the event of restructuring, it is possible, under certain conditions, to make intra-corporate divestitures at historical values, especially for the assessment of the corresponding taxable income.

The valuation methods most frequently used are, for equity deals, the net asset value, and for asset deals, the net book value, the market value, or the replacement cost, depending on the nature of the asset. However, it is important to keep in mind that in the case of an acquisition of shares or assets of:

- A private company — the price is set as a result of the negotiation between the parties.
- A state-owned company (SoE) — the price cannot, in principle, be less than 10% of the price set by the audit firm during their valuation process, unless special approval and/or the price agreed upon results from a public bidding process organized locally (via the mandatory publication of the acquisition project).

3.2.2. *Common Accounting Restatements*

3.2.2.1. *Applicable Frame of Reference*

Chinese companies must prepare their accounts according to the Chinese accounting standards called "Accounting System for Business Enterprises (ASBEs)".[27] There are two versions of ASBEs:

- One for listed and state-owned companies, as well as banks and insurance companies ("new Chinese accounting standards").
- One for the other companies ("old Chinese accounting standards").

The new Chinese accounting standards, adopted in 2006 and in force since 2007, are very similar to the international standards (International Financial Reporting Standards or IFRS), with which a process of convergence is promoted by the Chinese authorities.

Although some differences remain between the new Chinese accounting standards and IFRS, it is unlikely for them to impact most M&A operations, given the fact that they are relatively technical and specific by nature. These Chinese standards have recently

[27] Some very specific sectors, such as non-profit organizations, have accounting standards that differ from the ASBE or specific application guidelines that should be taken into account.

been accepted by the European authorities for IPOs on regulated European markets.

Examples of residual differences between the new Chinese accounting standards and the IFRS

- According to Chinese standards, accruals for impairment cannot be reverted (according to IFRS, only impairments related to goodwill cannot be reverted).
- Borrowing costs have to be capitalized (this is an option under IFRS).
- Biological assets are stated at historical cost (instead of at fair value in IFRS).

The legacy Chinese accounting standards applicable to private companies, which still represent a significant part of the targeted M&A projects, differ significantly from the IFRS. It is important to recognize the fact that these standards are also applicable to foreign invested enterprises,[28] particularly those created by the acquisition. However, the main difficulty of the financial due diligences does not so much come from identifying the differences between the Chinese and international accounting standards than from the compliance to these standards, whether they are Chinese or international. Indeed it should be noted that in China, most private non-foreign invested companies are not subject to an annual mandatory audit. The accounting practices actually used by Chinese companies can therefore differ quite materially from theoretical principles, and the quality of the financial statements can be extremely mediocre. In practice, this is often the case.

[28] Ultimately, it is planned to extend the use of the new Chinese accounting standards to all large sized companies, but the corresponding reform has not yet been initiated.

Furthermore, even when an audit has been carried out by a local firm at the request of the target company or the Tax Bureau, the quality of the audit performed is still often inferior to what it would be in the West and the audited accounts generally remain unreliable.

3.2.2.2. *Accounting Practices in China*

The reasons for such a gap between the accounting practices observed on the ground and the theoretically applicable accounting standards include:

- The weight of history: Historically, the Chinese accounting model introduced by New China (from 1949) stemmed from the "funds accounting" inspired by the Soviet model in which the aim was not to measure a profit or a loss for the shareholder (which did not make sense in a economy where all means of production were state-owned), but to allow the monitoring of assets and resources utilization as part of an administered economy. Although the conceptual framework has evolved since China opened up to international trade in the late '80s, there is still a bias towards a "cash-basis" accounting, in which sales are recorded only when the payment has been effectively cashed in and the expenses only when they have been cashed out, at the expense of an "accrual-basis" accounting.
- The impact of tax regulations: Traditionally, financial statements are mostly prepared only to meet the requests of tax authorities. Tax returns are based on the results calculated according to tax regulations which are, in China as elsewhere, different from those derived from accounting standards. For simplification purposes, Chinese companies often use these tax rules in their financial statements.

Examples of differences between accounting principles and tax rules

- The need for an official invoice (fapiao, issued under the supervision of the Tax Bureau) for an expense to be deductible. But in China, this official invoice is generally issued only at the time of the payment, which reinforces the bias towards a cash-basis accounting.
- Accruals are not deductible (there again, bias towards a cash-basis accounting).
- Asset amortization is deductible only if their calculation is based on the (relatively long) amortization periods prescribed by the tax regulations (for example, five years for IT equipment) and if a residual value at the end of life of the asset of 3% to 5% is taken into account.
- Provisions for asset impairment (inventories, receivables, etc.), as well as asset write-offs are deductible only after a case-by-case prior approval by the authorities. Most companies will not even request such an approval to avoid a possible tax audit.
- Provisions for risks are not deductible.
- Deductibility of start-up expenses is spread over the five years following the start of the activity.

- Cautious business owners: Chinese business owners have often had a tendency to minimize the profit of their company from a tax optimization perspective, obviously with the aim to minimize the taxes to be paid, in a context where the governmental tax audit tools have long been notoriously insufficient, and where the deep roots of the business owners in their communities (village, district, province, etc.) have sometimes made arrangements with tax authorities possible; but also because they operate in a complex legal environment which has continuously evolved since China has opened to foreign investment. This situation has favored a significant lack of transparency of financial statements.

It also pushes for a business model essentially based on short-term cash generation, sometimes to the detriment of the quality of its long-term growth and the relevance of its accounting presentation.

- The rapid growth of most companies, which has often outpaced the business monitoring systems, often weakly or not computerized at all.

Therefore, it is common to have to deal with target companies which either have a double accounting system (one for tax authorities and another for the business owner), or a significant difference between the official accounting records and the reality, or even both at the same time! The key will then be to identify, as exhaustively as possible, the existing issues, and to sort between those that can potentially jeopardize the acquisition project and those that will only have to be taken into account in the acquisition price or in the integration plan and post-acquisition upgrade.

3.2.2.3. *Main Issues Encountered*

Issues commonly encountered during a financial due diligence of Chinese companies are described, following the same order as the financial statements. The aim is not to list all the tasks to be undertaken in a due diligence process, but to insist on certain Chinese specificities.

3.2.2.3.1. Balance Sheet

Cash and deposits: Bank reconciliation is sometimes used to hide transactions whose accounting could become problematic, for example, payments for which an official invoice ("fapiao") is not available. The detailed analysis of reconciliation entries is imperative, as well as confirming the accounts balances directly with the bank managing these accounts. The involvement of an audit firm registered in China, and thus entitled to do so, is preferred for confidentiality reasons. Moreover, bank confirmation should allow identification of amounts which would be unavailable because they are blocked by the bank to cover existing commitments, including discounted notes payable, for example. Similarly, it is recommended to proceed, if possible, to a physical cash inventory, as it is not uncommon to discover cash advances already paid to employees which are only accounted for when expense reports and corresponding official invoices are presented.

Many Chinese business owners have set up, in parallel with the official cash and deposits, a "slush fund" system. It is fed in various ways: For example, sales of scraps and rejects not accounted for in the official books, or sales payments for which customers have not requested an official invoice ("fapiao"), and which are therefore easier to avoid recording in the official books. This "slush fund" will enable, for example, payment of some additional compensation to the management, omitting the individual income tax withholding normally owed by the employer, or to pay suppliers who are not able, for various reasons, to provide official invoices.

In some cases, the cash flows going through these unrecorded accounts represent a significant part of the total activity. It is then important to precisely understand and analyze those flows in order to assess the actual profitability of the business. Everything then depends upon how tight the internal control procedures designed to track these parallel cash flows are. At best, the corresponding cash is deposited in a dedicated bank account, often in one of the accountants' names, which facilitates its monitoring. In the worst case scenario, everything is paid in cash with insufficient or even non-existing documentation and it is difficult to measure the corresponding impact. Such a practice is generally not sustainable when the target company has become a foreign invested enterprise, which is subject to a level of scrutiny significantly higher than the one to which most Chinese companies are subjected. Besides, these Chinese companies are in a much better situation to find arrangements with the authorities, if needed. The business model will have to be reworked to include the additional costs arising from stopping such practices, in particular with regard to taxes.

Receivables: It is not uncommon that receivables, even very old ones, are not depreciated, or insufficiently so, because of the tax rules stated above. It will therefore be needed to obtain (or in most cases, to recreate) an aging balance statement allowing for a recoverability assessment on a statistical basis, which has to be complemented by a line-by-line analysis for significant account balances. In practice, one of the difficulties encountered in China is that a certain number of companies do not pay their suppliers invoice-by-invoice, but pay a lump sum amount from time-to-time. That lump sum is deducted from the existing invoices, without being matched to specific invoices. Therefore, the accounts are often difficult to analyze in detail. This frequent lack of account reconciliation can make it difficult to identify outstanding customer claims (deductions for missing items, quality issues, etc.).

Other receivables: This item can often be used to record disbursements that the absence of official invoices ("fapiao") did not allow to consider as a legitimate expense. It is therefore important to understand the nature of the corresponding amounts, as well as their collectability. The cash advances and loans made, either to the business owner's family or to other partner companies, must be analyzed, knowing that in theory, Chinese regulations allow loans only through financial institutions and that cash advances, sometimes informal and without any contracts, could be difficult for the new investor to recover if any problem should arise. Similarly, non-compliant loans from the business owner's family and friends are usually accounted as other liabilities.

Inventory and work in progress: For industrial and distribution activities, it will be absolutely necessary to organize an exhaustive physical inventory to check the existence of the corresponding assets. This process will have to be repeated once the acquisition takes place.

In terms of valuation and depreciation, the main issues encountered concern:

- The lack of depreciation for obsolete, damaged, or slow-moving inventories.
- Understanding the different elements of production costs integrated into inventories.
- Not taking into account lower-than-normative activity levels in the calculation of the production costs.

Property, plant, and equipment: The main difficulties encountered are about:

- The physical inventory of fixed assets (their existence).
- The identification of unused, obsolete, damaged, or unnecessary (within the context of the buyer's business plan) assets.
- Checking the historical acquisition costs and the beneficial ownership of the fixed assets. This helps identify possible revaluations practiced in China in the past, and which will need to be analyzed in order to assess if they were relevant. The full payment of the main fixed assets will also have to be examined, to identify possible mortgages or other securities on assets not yet completely paid.
- Harmonizing the depreciation methods by eliminating, in most cases, the residual values used only for tax purposes, and by bringing back the depreciation periods to the ones usually used in the activity in question.

Auditors should work hand in hand with the buyer's technical teams, who are in a better position to validate the condition of the manufacturing site, in order to identify assets that may not have been properly valued.

Checking the beneficial ownership rights of assets is critical, in particular for state-owned companies which may have experienced many previous mergers in their chaotic past. It is not uncommon to find assets recorded in the accounts of target companies belonging in fact to a third party and used without a contract or compensation. This situation can change immediately after the take-over by the foreign investor, who is generally more solvent and not part of the informal, yet complex, network of relationships and mutual favors in which companies operate in China.

Land use rights: As they generally involve significant amounts, the legality of the title deeds and the full payment of the corresponding amounts, including the related duties and taxes, should be checked, together with the professionals in charge of the legal due diligence.

Intangible assets: The main problem regarding trademarks, patents, etc., lies (in addition to the control of ownership rights, historical cost, and correct amortization, as we have seen for tangible assets) in the possibility of setting up an impairment test based on a generally unreliable historical evolution and on inevitably optimistic projections, often poorly documented, if not far-fetched.

Capital: Check that the share capital was actually paid. Even if a verification report was issued by an auditor, it is common to see some business owners temporarily "lend" the amount of the capital for the time of the audit and then return it back to themselves immediately after. Private Chinese companies suffer from a very limited credit access and are, in many cases, very inadequately capitalized. Foreign investment, if properly structured, that is to say if the money brought in by the buyer does not only benefit the seller but also, at least in part, the business, should allow the company to have the resources necessary for its development.

Debts: The main issue as far as liabilities are concerned is their exhaustiveness. The search for unrecorded liabilities will be based, to the greatest extent possible, on a review of subsequent payments and on a good understanding of the business model of the target company.

Provisions for risks and liabilities: are among the provisions that are rarely recorded in China and for which it will be necessary to estimate the impact and include:

- Provision for warranties.
- Provision for sales return.
- Specific commitments within the context of an "early retirement" pension plan.

Off balance sheet liabilities: Private Chinese companies often have difficulties obtaining bank loans. In some cases, a bank will only accept to extend a loan if another company stands as guarantor for this loan. Therefore, it is not uncommon for companies to arrange cross guarantees: Company A acts as a guarantee for company B, which can then have access to a bank credit; but at the same time, company B acts as a guarantee for company A, which can then also borrow from the bank. Attention must be paid to identify such practices, which can put the company at risk if said guarantee is called by the bank.

3.1.2.3.2. Profit and Loss Statement

Cut-off issues: Because the tax deductibility is linked to the issuance date of the official invoices ("fapiao") instead of the actual transaction date, this is a crucial point on which adjustments are almost always necessary, in order to present the situation and the results of the target company in line with Western accounting practices. Turnover is often accounted for only upon issuance of the official invoice ("fapiao").

The issuance of the invoice is not necessarily related to the time of the delivery. This is important as taxes, in particular turnover taxes, are paid when the official invoice is issued. If this invoice remains unpaid by the customer, the corresponding loss will generally not be deductible. Therefore, the supplier will always wish to delay issuing the invoice until its customer's payment, while the latter will want the issuance to be as soon as possible, in order to benefit from the deductibility of the corresponding expense. In practice, the time of issuance depends on the "balance of power" between the customer and the supplier:

- Either at the time of the payment by the customer.
- Either at the request of the customer; the request may be completely unrelated to the delivery and sometimes before it.

The assessment of the financial impact of delays, between the actual delivery of provision of service and its recording, will depend on the quality of the financial management systems of the target company. Similarly, it is important to check if accruals for wages are correct, and if they are paid at the beginning of the following month; as well as to check the accruals for a possible 13th month or bonuses; and more generally to check all the elements whose payment is not made on a monthly basis. Tax returns are due every month in China and it is generally the frequency in which the accounting activities are cycled. Payments not following the same timing are likely not to be properly apprehended.

Case Study

When all goes wrong: The Caterpillar story[29]

Caterpillar, the world's leading manufacturer of construction and mining equipment, has been active in China for over 30 years. In June 2012, it finalized the purchase of ERA, a Hong Kong listed manufacturer of underground coal mining equipment, through its wholly owned subsidiary in China, Siwei, for USD677 million.

In January 2013, Caterpillar announced that an internal investigation had uncovered "deliberate, multi-year, coordinated accounting misconduct" at Siwei, leading to a non-cash goodwill impairment charge of USD580 million — over 85% of the deal value.

---

[29] See the full Caterpillar case in Chapter 6, Case Study Two.

A review of documents that followed the disclosures point to the following lessons:

(a) Do not lose your common sense, and take the due diligence process seriously

Caterpillar's management appeared to have been so eager to close the deal that it ignored or dismissed various pre-acquisition "red flags" that should have been taken into account, at least in the proposed valuation of the deal, including:

- Siwei had material cash flow issues.
- Siwei had above one year of customer receivables on its balance sheet.
- Its inventory also represented over one year of sales.
- Key operating licences were missing.
- Financial targets were repeatedly missed.
- Overtime salary to workers were not paid.

From court documents, it seems that due diligence results were not even discussed formally at Caterpillar's Board level.

(b) Be careful of perceptions

It is possible that the following factors led to less stringent scrutiny of the due diligence results than what a transaction of that magnitude would require:

- Close ties to local authorities in the very sensitive mining sector.
- Sense of urgency in gaining significant market share in the world's second largest economy.
- Sense of comfort from the presence of foreigners with significant experience in China, and credentials among the directors and controlling shareholders of the target.
- Sense of security due to the fact that the company was publicly traded in Hong Kong with audited financial statements.

(c) Expect the unexpected and plan accordingly, as not everything will be revealed through the due diligence process

According to Caterpillar, the alleged accounting fraud (including a second set of accounting books) had been going on for several years, but was only discovered in November 2012, five months after completion of the deal, when discrepancies were identified between accounting records and physical inventory counts. Investigations identified improper cost allocation and revenue recognition practices resulting in overstated profit.

3.3. Human Resources Risk Management

Mergers & acquisitions (M&A) can be successful but can also lead towards big failures. Many M&A did not achieve the synergy and generate the return as originally planned. One of the main reasons for failure is that many companies are not prepared to meet the human resources (HR) challenges that M&A introduce. Although the merging companies usually give lots of importance to financial matters, HR issues are often the neglected ones. The top three M&A success factors for a smooth integration seem to be the following[30]:

1. Formidable leadership.
2. Well planned communication.
3. Early management of people issues.

The HR issues are particularly important for M&A in China, as talent attraction and retention has constantly been ranked as the number one HR challenge in the past several years. All pre-merger financial analysis and forecasts will be of little practical value if the HR issues are not handled appropriately and large turnover of talents occurs during the M&A process.

---

[30]According to a global survey of experience acquirers conducted by Towers Watson worldwide in 2013. See "Retaining Talent after a Transaction: Lessons from Organizations That Do It Well," *Towers Watson*, October 2012; available online at www.towerswatson.com/en/Insights/IC-Types/Survey-Research-Results/2012/10/retaining-talent-after-a-transaction-lessons-from-organizations-that-do-it-well (accessed on February 4, 2015).

HR issues occur at all stages of M&A activity; this includes the identification of targets, due diligence, negotiation and signing, transition planning and management, and post-merger integration.

3.3.1. *Human Resources Due Diligence Stage*

As stated above, the importance of HR is often underestimated, and assessing people risks is often thought of as "soft", but a failure to do so could result in a large amount of "hard" financial losses. The main focus of HR due diligence is to identify five risk areas of HR aspects, i.e., compliance risk, financial risk, talent risk, cultural risk, and operation risk in undertaking M&A activity in China. Findings from HR due diligence also help the senior management of the acquiring company to prepare for the deal negotiation, transition planning and management, and post-merger integration.

3.3.1.1. *Compliance Risk*

On January 1, 2008, the new Labor Contract Law of China (LCL) went into effect. The LCL is designed to provide more protection to employees' rights and reduce labor abuses in manufacturing and many other industries. While more protections are provided to the employees, the employment cost increased for most companies. The LCL came as a "perfect storm" to many companies, as the effect of the cost increase was compounded by the global economic downturn in 2008 and 2009. While there are many clauses to the LCL, foreign investment in China needs to pay special attention to the following:

(1) A written contract is required for every employee

The requirement to sign either a fixed-term or open-ended contract with each employee makes China closer to many European countries. If an employee has worked for a company for over 10 years or has signed a fixed-term contract twice, he or she needs to be offered an open-ended contract. To enforce the signing of written contracts with all employees, the LCL allows the employees to claim double salary for the period they work without written contracts. While the employees can resign at will with no penalty, the employers are to a large extent bounded by the contract terms and layoffs before the contract term ends have become more complicated than before.

(2) Severance payment requirement for layoffs is clearly defined
The LCL defines minimum severance payment requirement for employers if they wish to terminate employment of employees under fixed-term or open-ended contracts. In general, the severance payment amount is one month for each year of service, subject to certain limits. Employers should also pay special attention to the procedures to terminate contracts and layoffs, due to business reasons such as economic downturn or M&A. Government filings may be required and employees under certain situations (e.g., pregnancy, disability, etc.) are protected.

(3) Roles of labor unions are enhanced
The LCL requires each company to form a union or an employee representative group. The union or employee representative group will have more power, since the LCL requires that they be consulted for any changes in employment terms and benefits. Though the union is not given the veto power under the LCL, its enhanced role makes China one step closer to the European countries.

In any M&A in China, when the target is identified and initial contact is made, an HR due diligence needs to investigate and identify any compliance risks. A thorough review of the HR policy and employee handbook is needed to make sure that all the policies, particularly the three items mentioned above, are in compliance with the LCL. The HR due diligence also needs to check supporting documents for evidence that all the contracts are signed, severance payments are made for involuntary terminations, and other relevant policies are followed. If any incompliance is discovered (e.g., written contracts are missing for a group of employees), the potential government penalty needs to be estimated and the necessary steps to rectify the issues in the future need to be documented for management reference.

3.3.1.2. *Financial Risk*

It is essential to quantify the financial risks associated with the labor cost during the HR due diligence process as it is one of the most important pieces of information for the management when they evaluate the potential acquisition target. Summarized below are some key items for the labor cost.

(1) Employee compensation and benefits
The cost of compensation and benefits is a significant part of the overall labor cost. In China, the guaranteed portion of the total compensation in many domestic companies and state-owned enterprises (SoEs) includes not only the basic salary, but also various types of allowances for meals, transportation, shift differentials, mobile communication, etc. The allowances are sometimes referred to as the "grey income", and the amount is often big compared to the basic salary. A guaranteed bonus of one-month basic salary is often paid to the employees at the end of the year and is typically referred to as the "13th month pay". The variable portion of the total compensation is often linked to the performance of the company and the employees, which is similar to the practice of European or US companies.

However, the variable pay is often a large percentage of the total compensation in domestic companies and SoEs. While the average pay mix (ratio of guaranteed pay to variable pay) among European and US companies is around 80/20, it is common among domestic companies and SoEs in China to have a pay mix of 50/50. Therefore, discovering the "grey income" and the bonus payout practice is an important task in the HR due diligence in China.

Regarding employee benefits, it is important for foreign companies to know that many SoEs in China offer legacy pension benefits and post-retirement supplemental medical benefits to their employees. A monthly pension of €100 per employee can easily translate into tens of millions of Euros on companies' balance sheets. An actuarial valuation needs to be performed to understand the financial impact of these benefits programs on companies' future cash flows and annual reports under the US GAAP or the International Financial Reporting Standard (IFRS). Since the liabilities associated with pension and post-retirement medical benefits are often so big, they directly affect the financial health evaluation of the target company. Actuaries need to be called upon to quantify this risk at an early stage of the HR due diligence.

(2) Social security contributions
All companies in China are required to make statutory social security contributions for their employees. The statutory contributions are made for retirement, medical, unemployment, occupational injury, maternity, and government housing fund. The required contribution percentages vary by different cities and locations, and could be up to 40% to 50% of the payroll for employees whose salaries are less than three times the city average. What one often discovers during the HR due diligence are the missing social security contributions and/or miscalculation of the contribution amount by using the incorrect salary base. For example, although it is required that employees' total compensation amount should be used to calculate the social security contribution, some companies incorrectly used basic salary for the calculation. The acquiring company needs to estimate not only the correct future social security contribution amount for the employees of the target company, but also the social security underpayment it needs to pay back in the future. Any underpayment of social security is also a liability that needs to be addressed during the deal negotiation.

(3) Severance payment
As discussed previously, the Labor Contract Law of China sets minimum severance payment requirement for employers if they wish to terminate employment of employees under fixed-term or open-ended contracts. If the acquiring company considers a Reduction in Force (RIF) after the merger, it should budget a reserve for the severance payment. To make the employee communication as smooth as possible and not to raise any unnecessary publicity during RIF, many companies offer more generous severance payment

amounts than what is required under the LCL. Therefore, a reserve for the severance payment should be calculated during the HR due diligence. In some cases, if the reserve is large, it should be recorded on the company's financial statement as a liability in accordance with IFRS or US GAAP.

(4) Executive benefits

The contracts of senior executives often contain change-in-control clauses that give them fairly significant compensation in case they lose their positions in the company due to the M&A. These clauses are also called the "golden parachute" in the US. In China, the magnitude of this type of compensation is much smaller than that in Europe or in the US. However, executive benefits such as stock options, retention bonus, and deferred compensation are protected, and thus the acquiring company should have a good estimate of executive benefits costs during the HR due diligence.

3.3.1.3. *Talent Retention Risk*

No matter how attractive an M&A deal looks on paper, it will not be successful if the key talents of the acquired company cannot be retained, and the people issues around the M&A cannot be properly addressed and resolved. The M&A often makes people feel uncertain about the future direction of the company, their job security, as well as their future career growth with the new company. Consequently, some people, particularly those key talents with skills, knowledge, and high market value, may consider leaving and pursuing opportunities with other companies. The potential turnover of key talents would not only disrupt the continuity of the post-merger business operation, but also present big challengs to HR to recruit and train new people to fill those vacancies. The financial implication could be significant.

It is important to identify the talent retention risk during the pre-deal HR due diligence. There needs to be a talent assessment process to identify who the talents are and what the cost will be to replace them should they decide to leave. If financial incentives are needed to retain those talents, a cost estimate should be conducted to budget the right amount of retention bonus. For the acquiring companies, the more they know about the talent retention risk of the target company, the better they will be prepared to set the talent retention strategy after the deal is closed.

3.3.1.4. *Cultural Risk*

When multinational companies acquire local companies in China, they will most likely encounter cultural differences and conflicts. When West meets East, there will be national cultural differences and organizational cultural differences. Some of the key issues that can arise in due diligence, in respect of cultural aspects of HR and labor relations, are as follows:

- If there are ongoing bad relations with employee representatives, strikes, or other employee actions that are likely to occur over the following several months before and after the acquisition.
- Poor relations with employee representatives could lead to difficulties in implementing future changes and/or resentment and hostility towards the new owners of the company.
- Outstanding claims may exist with respect to disputes with employees and employer representatives. The acquiring company will need to handle that after the merger.
- When the target company's culture or way of doing things is very different to those of the acquiring company, significant disruption may occur if the acquiring company wishes to impose its approach to business on the target company.

An informal assessment of the cultural gap needs to be conducted as part of the pre-deal due diligence. If possible, interviews with target companies' executives and M&A team members will be very helpful to understand the current situation, and to prepare for the cultural integration after the merger.

3.3.1.5. *Operation Risk*

The HR due diligence should also cover the review of the HR policies and procedures to uncover any potential operation risks, which are often closely related to the compliance risks, as mentioned previously. The due diligence should review the HR recruitment procedure, labor contract signing and renewal, exit procedure, overtime application procedure, and annual leave application procedure, etc. If the procedures are not clearly documented and followed in practice, a dispute may occur and sometimes may result in negative publicity and law suits. These risks need to be identified during the HR due diligence.

3.3.1.6. *Case Study*

In late 2008, a large multinational company headquartered in Beijing decided to acquire a business unit of a US company located in Shanghai. It is a typical asset deal where all the technologies, equipments, workers, and managers of this business unit will become part of the acquiring company after the deal is closed. The names of the two companies still cannot be disclosed. During the acquisition process, many HR issues arose, and many lessons can be learned from the process.

Firstly, the HR due diligence was not conducted before the decision was made to acquire the target company. Just a few months before the deal was closed, the senior management of the acquiring company discovered the following:

- In an asset deal, all employees of the target company will need to terminate their current labor contracts and sign new ones with the acquiring company on or before the closing day. Based on China's Labor Contract Law, the severance payment clause will be triggered due to the early termination of current labor contracts, even though the acquiring company's intention is to keep all the employees after the acquisition.

- Since many employees of the target company have fairly long service with the company, the estimated total severance payout would be a few million US dollars. This has come as a surprise to the acquiring company, as this expense was neither brought up during the deal negotiation nor budgeted as part of the post-deal labor cost.
- Since the acquiring company has never communicated to the target company's employees about the pending acquisition, there are many speculations and rumors about the future of the new company. Many senior or mid-level managers, and over half of the skilled workers, are considering finding employment opportunities with other companies.
- The potential large turnover of skilled workers will have a significant impact on the business operation. Even if the company conducts aggressive recruitment of new talents, the production could be severely disrupted because it takes at least six months to train the new employees.

All the issues mentioned above largely resulted from the lack of due diligence before the M&A decision was made, and lack of preparation with respect to employee communication and post-merger integration. Formulating a strategy to prevent the merger from falling apart even before the deal becomes effective was much needed, and a set of remedial action plans including, but not limited to, the following was defined:

- Collect the employee data and calculate the total severance payment amount that the acquiring company may have to pay.
- Identify the key employees that the new company will need to retain after the merger and design a retention program for them.
- Communicate with the employees about their future with the new company, the visions from the senior management, and the background of the acquiring company. The communication can be through emails, group meetings, all employee meetings, etc.

- Prepare the new contracts which guarantee the recognition of past services for all purposes, including benefits and severance.
- Design an incentive plan to encourage employees of the target company to commit to the new company and sign the new contracts before "Day 1".

After these actions were taken, the merger went a lot smoother than originally anticipated. Even though there were still employees who left the company, most of them chose to sign the contract with the new company, and the business operations were not disrupted.

Key success factors

Below are several suggestions to all HR professionals who may be involved in M&A in China:

- Understand the M&A objectives, approach, and target company background.
- Think from the perspective of future integration.
- Focus on both the financial and human resources issues.
- Thorough and speedy HR due diligence is important.
- Keep the target identification and due diligence confidential.
- Establish an M&A project team.
- Involve third party consultants and professionals in the due diligence process.
- Plan ahead with a detailed action plan.

3.3.2. *Post-Merger Integration*

Upon the completion of due diligence and confirmation of the target company being in line with the overall business development strategy and intention for M&A, companies should initiate integration planning while preparing for its board and governmental agency approval. Studies have shown that 50% of companies suffer decreased productivity in the 4–8 months period preceding integration. This is one of the most undesirable situations for any company.

Therefore, it is important to have a carefully designed integration plan to ensure that operations and business remain unaffected. The efficiency in which companies can resolve their "staff" related issues during the integration process is a key component for a successful M&A.

3.3.2.1. *Talent Retention and Management*

Whatever the goal of a merger or acquisition — whether it is to accelerate growth or to gain access to advanced technologies and management know-how — the success of the deal will depend largely on having experienced professionals, with the organization's vision in mind to guide it on its way. Acquiring companies overseas is not like building new factories in a foreign country, where you can start from scratch. In most cases, the target company will have an existing culture and processes that need to be integrated into the new entity. So having experienced management who can handle these delicate issues becomes of great importance, especially for companies in the knowledge industry.

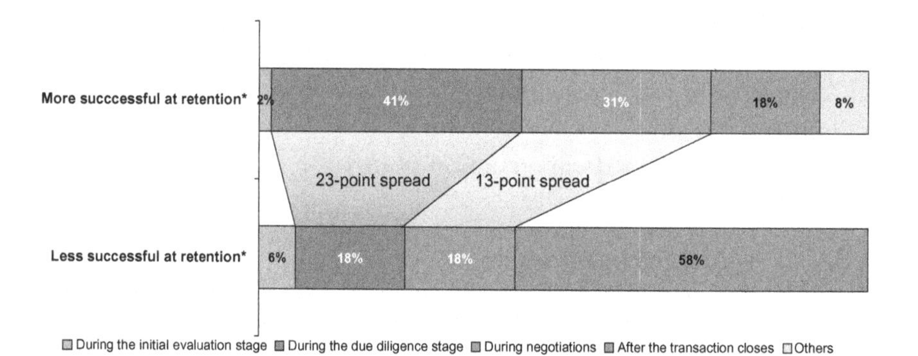

Figure 3.1. Successful Companies Identify Employees Early in the Process.

* "Successful at retention" is defined as those rating their retention agreements high or mostly effective at retaining employees during an acquisition, and retaining all or nearly all of their employees through the retention period in past acquisitions.

Source: 2012 Towers Watson M&A Employee Retention Survey, Towers Watson website: www.towerswatson.com.

Recent research has found that in successful deals, key talent retention is identified early in the deal cycle.

In light of this finding, it is quite troubling to note that Asian employers identify talent to retain later in the life cycle of a deal than do their global counterparts. Given the importance of key talent retention in the success of a deal, this could have the potential to put Asia-Pacific employers at a significant disadvantage.

In March 2011, China-based Australia Dairy Corporation announced it would acquire stakes in Hyproca Dairy, marking the first M&A deal between a Chinese dairy corporation and a foreign milk powder enterprise. Learning that many employees at Hyproca Dairy intended to resign, Chen Yuanrong, chief executive officer of Australia Dairy, promised them not to change the original management model, not to transfer Chinese employees over, and not to close down the factory after the acquisition. Together with the rollout of an incentive program to provide employees with stock options, the Chinese company successfully retained certain key employees, which helped to smooth over this often turbulent transitional M&A stage.

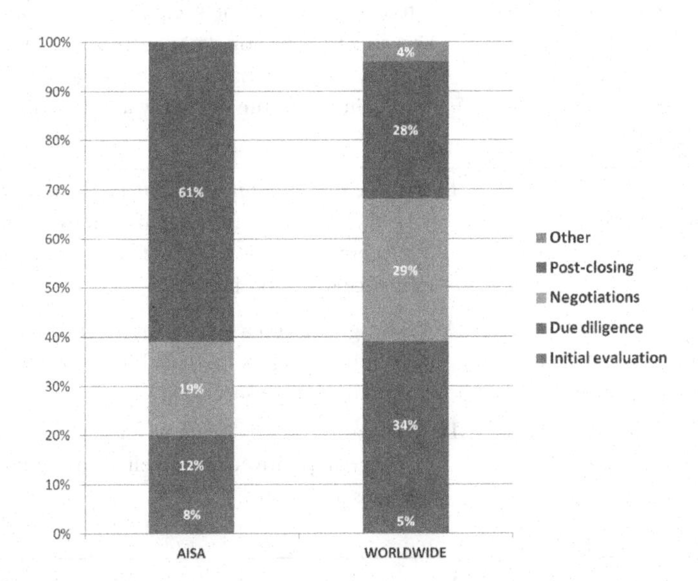

Figure 3.2. Stage at Which Global Acquirers Identify Talent to Retain.

Source: Towers Watson website: www.towerswatson.com.

The following principles seem to be key conditions to maximize retention after a deal:

- Identify retention candidates early. This means at or before due diligence, when feasible.
- Combine monetary incentives with relationship-building activities.
- Establish principles to guide deal-related decisions — and adhere to these principles.

When it comes to retention, after the key talent to be retained has been identified, the following six steps are recommended.

Table 3.2. Six Steps to Build an Effective Talent Retention Programme.

Short-term	
Step 1: Short-term retention plan	A competitive talent retention plan to retain key talent in the critical 1–3 years of the new company can be a strong start, and avoid transaction-related turnover.
Step 2: Link to executive contracts	Tie separation clauses and relevant compensation into executive contracts, e.g., confidentiality, non-solicitation, non-compete, change-in-control clauses, etc. This may serve the purpose of protecting both the company and individuals.
Medium-term	
Step 3: Design organizational structure and new job roles	Design the new organizational structure and job roles that articulate the responsibilities of each management position, level of autonomy, and influence to the business.
Step 4: New long-term incentive plan	At this stage, design a long-term incentive plan to align top managers' personal interests with the company's future success.
Step 5: New reward system	Design a new reward system to ensure external market competitiveness as well as internal business alignment.
Long-term	
Step 6: Development opportunities	Prepare clear career development road-maps for key talents that match with the company's business strategy and drivers of the M&A deal.

It is always important to bear in mind what the deal drivers are when planning retention, e.g., if the deal driver is to acquire advanced technology, then R&D people would be critical to retain, and if acquiring a brand is the main purpose for a deal, then marketing, customer services, and sales force are the key talents to retain, etc. Of course, senior management is normally on top of companies' retention lists, as they play the important role of stabilising the workforce, ensuring business continues as usual, and maintaining key customer relationships. However, some companies may consider excluding individuals from this group who opposed the deal, as they may be reluctant to change and become obstacles to the new company's vision and goals.

3.3.2.2. *Compensation and Benefits Integration*

The differences in compensation and benefits system, structure, and standards may surface during the due diligence process. As employees will have questions and doubts with regard to their future compensation and benefits, which may affect their willingness to stay with the new company, compensation and benefits integration is also a vital step during M&A integration. The most important aspect of compensation and benefits integration is legality, eradicating and amending the unlawful practices. Chinese labor laws and social insurance provisions differ from city to city; therefore, it is important to have a comprehensive understanding of the local legal practices. Additionally, local practices regarding reward strategy and design should be taken into consideration. Besides mandatory benefits, the three most prevalent supplementary benefits in China are medical benefits, housing benefits, and education programs.

However, an increasing number of companies are now starting to utilize flexible benefit programs as a tool in benefit harmonization, as flexible benefit is an ideal way to balance the differences in benefits between the merged company and its former entities.

To maintain market competitiveness, it is vital to attain a comprehensive study and understanding of compensation and benefits structure in China through local market research and surveys.

3.3.2.3. *Culture Integration*

Corporate culture such as leadership and management style, decision-making process, and human resources programs will affect the company's overall business operations. The integration phase will include the fusion of existing cultures from the two companies, creating a single culture that is fitting for the new company. This may result in a new culture or the disappearance of one of the two. There are three steps during this process: (1) exemption, (2) change and promotion, and (3) re-exemption.

Exemption refers to the letting go of the culture of the target company and holding the new company's business strategy as a starting point. Combining the existing cultures that are beneficial towards the strategic development of the new company, and the addition of some new elements, are essential in the formation of the new company's corporate culture. Upon verification of the new company culture, well-targeted communication events will help the employees understand and embrace the new culture and, at the same time, change their past mindsets and behaviors. The final step, "re-exemption", is to fortify the new culture through mechanical designs which will ensure that employees' behaviors are aligned with the new culture. During this process, everyone will face challenges while making the adjustments. Thus, it is important for employees to respect each other's past company cultures.

In addition to corporate culture, international M&A requires special attention to national culture and cultural differences. For instance, the differences between Western and Eastern companies can easily be revealed through organizational behavior; Western companies are performance-oriented, while Eastern companies are seniority-oriented; Western companies emphasize vigilance and planning, while Eastern companies emphasize flexibility and response. The key to a successful cultural integration is mutual understanding and mutual respect. Therefore, foreign companies conducting M&A in China should always hold a certain level of understanding and respect for the local culture. Well-designed team building activities may enhance the familiarity of employees from both sides and foster cultural integration.

3.3.2.4. *Communication*

When word about an M&A transaction first gets out, employees are often affected by a strong sense of insecurity and their minds get filled with questions, starting from "why is the company undergoing M&A?", to "me" questions, such as: "Will I be able to keep my job?", "Will this affect my job?", "Who will be my boss?", "Will there be adjustments to my compensation and benefits?", etc. All sorts of rumors and unreliable information may be passed around at this time, causing the demoralization of employees, which allows competitors the chance to recruit away companies' elite employees. Communication is indeed a priority during the integration process in order to avoid undesired reaction and unexpected loss of employees. Effective communications should be combined with integration strategy goals, with messages emphasizing: the joint future rather than the past, impact on individuals, integration timeline, and consistent communication. Communication may be conducted via internal videos, e-mails/announcement, FAQs, group sessions, or face-to-face meetings between managerial and subordinating staff. In addition, organizations should include a two-way communication structure and establish a channel in which employees can seek answers for all their questions. Sincere face-to-face communication is the only effective method of providing security and confidence.

3.3.2.5. *Case Study*

A major global company had acquired a Chinese company to enter the booming China market. This global company encountered several obstacles at the integration stage:

- The global company's heritage is a countryside-based manufacturing company, and the Chinese company's heritage was a sales-driven organization with functional reporting lines. The corporate culture differences were not only felt at the top but also affected all associates.
- Top management argued that there was no clear direction of the new company, and that associates did not know where they were going or how to work together.

- The global company had no clue how to harmonize total rewards programs, including salary, incentive, and benefits.
- The global company wanted to make employees stay focused, ensuring the performance of the new company, despite the undercurrents of changes.

When implementing solutions for a smooth integration in order to achieve M&A synergy, the action plans and the process should include, but not be limited to, the following:

- Interview executives to understand the current situation and future direction, and clarify the new organization's business and talent strategies as principles, in order to develop implementation solutions.
- Design and conduct a two-day workshop for the management team to diagnose current cultural differences, define the desired culture, identify blockages for goals achievement, set an action plan to overcome blockages, and energize the management team. Best practices of mission and vision statements were shared to help clarify the new organization's strategy.
- Create a senior management team-building program. Multiple methods were used to help top leaders think more strategically and foster team development in a relaxed environment, such as off-site workshops including group-awareness exercises, constructive games, experience sharing, group discussion, etc.
- Develop reward strategy based on the new business direction and HQ guidelines, and define key elements of the new total reward philosophy, i.e., target market, competitive positioning.
- Design new reward programs aligned with the reward strategy, including the cost implications of adopting the new programs. New reward programs include a broadband structure, base salary structures, retirement and vesting benefits, and terms and conditions of employment.
- Benchmark with market peer groups to ensure competitiveness of the new programs and watch for the extent of internal inequities.

- Develop the communication strategy and plans to solve employees' "me" issues and deliver consistent key messages. Activities can include identification of stakeholders, development of key messages, communications channels/vehicles/timing, grouping of audiences, and scenario planning. Materials created were Frequently Asked Questions (FAQs), slide presentation, memos, talking points, etc.

After the actions were taken, the top management team established trusted relationships through team-building activities, sharing their past experience and desired working styles, and company culture clarification. Compensation and benefits programs reflect the core values of the new company. Key talents stayed with the company and employees stayed focus on delivering good performance during the integration, due to timely and qualitative rewards (compensation and benefits), and consistent communication during the integration phase.

3.3.2.6. *Key Success Factors*

Key elements to successful human capital integration in M&A in China include:

- Establish clear post-merger metrics and targets early, and monitor progress frequently.
- Expect that organizational and cultural issues will present the greatest difficulties.
- Engage top management and foster broad participation in post-merger integration to retain key talent.
- Dedicate project managers and teams to lead post-merger integration.
- Act quickly on major revenue-related post-merger activities.
- Communicate with customers and employees as soon as possible after deal announcement.
- Develop integration plan that takes care of both financial and human capital aspects of the business.

- Have a clear direction for the new business strategy.
- Integrate total rewards linked with the overall business strategy.

3.3.3. *Conclusion*

Despite many challenges, M&A deals between Chinese and Western companies are going ahead at an unprecedented pace. While the process might not always be easy, the effort will prove worthwhile. Any investment made in overcoming those challenges can go a long way towards stabilizing the organization and sustaining high levels of key talent engagement and performance in the future.

Multinational companies' overseas expansion is not easy. Barriers can be put up due to the "national security" excuse by foreign governments. Even if the proposed M&A deal is approved by the local government, the employees, the press, and labor unions in the overseas country may remain sceptical. There may be no quick solution to these challenges. While the problem can be addressed by putting in place good global governance processes and policies, a well-developed human resource system, and a strong company and employer brand, these are solutions that can only bear fruit in the long run.

Fortunately, the economic slowdown has made companies more open to inbound as well as outbound investment from Asia-Pacific, and gives global enterprises a greater chance of being able to expand overseas through M&A.

3.4. Risk Management Summary

Risk management is a constant concern for the general management of foreign companies in China. Identifying trustable potential local partners in one targeted market segment is possibly the most important first step of an acquisition. It is also critical to be prepared to some degree of flexibility, as the legal and regulatory framework is constantly evolving, both nationally and locally. Some interpretation of the current regulation can create gray areas and uncertainties and consequently, difficulties. Conducting M&A as well as negotiating partnerships in this context entail numerous strategic, financial, and legal risks, which can nevertheless be limited by adequate and determined preparation.

3.4.1. *Implementing Guarantees (Asset/Liability, Earn Out Clauses, Purchase Price in Escrow)*

Very often in Europe or in the United States, part of the sale price is reserved (in escrow) pending the fulfilment of certain transfer conditions, or to ensure that there are no material surprises after the transfer of property and after the purchase of all the shares. The possibility for the purchaser and the seller to retain all or part of the purchase/sale price in an escrow account placed in the hands of a trusted third party (attorney, bank, etc.) used to be difficult in China. This was mostly a consequence of the requirement for the buyer to pay the full acquisition price within three months (up to one year if MOFCOM provided an exceptional authorization to do so). This obligation officially set up by the "Provisions on Mergers and Acquisitions of Domestic Enterprises by Foreign Investors" is now void but was strictly enforced in the past.

Asset and liability guarantees can be inserted into contracts in order to protect the buyer and secure the considered transaction. They can be classified into three categories:

- Balance sheet guarantees (assets and liabilities).
- The price revision clauses (or clause of collateral value).
- Guarantees of profitability.

The balance-sheet guarantees: Historically, the liability guarantees were among the first clauses used by practitioners. They are designed for any increase in social, environmental, and tax liabilities issued before a specific date (the date of the transfer in most cases, but it may be another date), which would become visible after this date to be carried by the seller. Asset guarantees mirror liability guarantees and are designed for any material decrease of the value of the corporate asset before a specific date (the date of the transfer in most cases, but it may be another date), which would become visible after this date to be carried by the seller.

A combination of these two clauses is often used. The seller agrees to take care of all undisclosed liabilities or decrease of value of the basket of assets, but it still remains difficult in China to demand and enforce that the owner of a company commits to anything beyond the selling price. The section dedicated to guarantees structuring introduces different possible "solutions" to address this situation in China.

Adjustment clauses: Adjustment clauses of the transfer price in favor of the acquirer is designed as a protection against crashing valuation, as a consequence of assets depreciation, discovery of new liabilities or risky potential liabilities, or the occurrence of any penalizing event likely to affect the value of the company during a certain period following the acquisition.

It is common practice not to distinguish between them in China. They are often embedded in "catch-all" balance sheet guarantees, but they are in fact inherently different. Balance sheet guarantees are considered a compensation for the loss of market value of some assets and not an adjustment of the selling price, based on the revision of the future prospects of the target. Most importantly, they can extend beyond the selling price. This is not the case of adjustment clauses of the transfer price, which are necessarily limited to the transfer price.

Profitability clauses: Are designed to ensure that the accounting profit of the current fiscal year and/or fiscal years subsequent to the transfer will be at least equal to a specified published amount. Otherwise, the seller will have to pay back an amount equal to the difference between the agreed upon result and the actual result. These clauses are especially useful in the context of partial equity participation, when the seller continues to hold shares and takes care of all, or part, of the company's management.

In the past, given the obligation to pay the price within a maximum time frame, the earn out clauses were difficult to implement for payments made in China. Now, the suppression of the obligation to pay the full amount of the acquisition in three months of the closing has opened new possibilities to implement earn-out clauses; in addition, they still remain possible when part of the transfer is made offshore. The earn out or price supplement clauses are clauses through which the parties agree that, in addition to a fixed price collectable upon completion of the transfer, part of the price will be paid later on an agreed upon date based on the results of the company during the months following the transfer. Once again, these clauses often go along with the seller staying in the target company, at least until the end of the agreed upon period for the payment of the price supplement (in order to fight against unfair competition).

Moreover, the pledge on shares is authorized by Chinese regulations and can also be a useful guarantee in restructuring and M&A deals. The pledge on shares must be registered with SAFE after approval by Chinese authorities (AIC, MOFCOM). SAIC has published measures for the registration of pledge on shares applicable from October 1, 2008, defining notably that the pledgee and the debtors were to jointly apply for registration, modification, cancellation, or revocation/removal of the pledge on shares. In practice, this new measure will create many difficulties if the debtor and the pledgee refuse to partner for the registration. Pledge on shares, which were already uncommon due to the complexity of the approval and registration procedures, may become increasingly rare. This results from the absence of a mechanism allowing the parties to lift the guarantee and the pledge on shares if one of the parties disagrees.

3.4.2. *Struggling Against Possible Unfair Competition*

Unfair competition remains a major concern in China during M&A. It is always possible for the seller to create a new parallel competing structure, directly or indirectly, and thus empty gradually (or suddenly) the contents of the sold company (customers, key employees, etc.), therefore seriously damaging the transaction valuation.

The Anti-Unfair Competition Law contains few measures allowing effective action against such practices, which still remain too widespread. The non-competition clauses in contracts can consequently be very useful, if not vital, as well as setting up asset and liability guarantee mechanisms, and price revision or supplement mechanisms to the extent possible.

Keeping the seller involved in the management of the target company can also be a way to dissuade him from creating a competing structure, especially if he is offered a profit sharing scheme. In other cases, on the contrary, notably in the event of a subsequent technology transfer, it can be in the buyer's interest to avoid involving the seller in the company management. In all cases, protection of intellectual and industrial property should be a well-documented aspect of the transaction.

3.4.3. *The Closing*

The closing follows the signing by the parties of the binding documentation and it is the final stage of the negotiation process, and results in the realization of the transaction, and in principle, in the transfer of the related rights and obligations. However, in China, the complete success of the transaction will always be subject to the approval, or *nihil obstat*, of the Chinese authorities and the subsequent procurement of a new operating license, notably in case of a share deal. The introduction of the Anti-Monopoly Law on August 1, 2008 has created the need to include the notion of pre-closing in Chinese law.

This concept could develop in cases where the competition authority will have set conditions to the transaction, and in such a case they can all be fulfilled only after the proposed transaction or part of it takes place (e.g., subsequent disposal of a sector of activity):

- Completion of prerequisites and suspensive/resolutive conditions (one must be wary of Material Adverse Change (MAC) clauses,[31] and refer to the theory of lack of foresight).

---

[31] The Material Adverse Change clause has been designed to provide protection from having to perform a contract after a significant negative event occurs, and should not be confused with the Force Majeure clause.

- Corporate formalities.
- Administrative authorizations.
- Transfer of contracts.
- Transfer of intellectual property.
- Transfer of legal responsibilities.

Chapter 4

Negotiating Effectively

4.1. Valuation Methods with Chinese Characteristics?

The laws of gravity, just like the general laws of finance do apply to China, as elsewhere in this world. The valuation of a company for sale is based on the quasi "Newtonian" principle, that the seller must be financially compensated at a satisfactory level for him, to induce him to sell the asset he has built[32] and, symmetrically, that the buyer must be able to justify that the acquisition economically creates value for him at a measurable time and for a defined monetary return. Any other consideration moving away from these principles would be hard to justify, even if sometimes very persuasive efforts are made to try to prove the opposite. In China, this has to be put in the cultural context of local negotiations, and therefore the formal and cultural aspects are decisive factors.

It is thus not surprising that the valuation of Chinese companies is based on methodological tools comparable to those available in the West, even if the emerging characteristics of the Chinese economy introduces some additional complexity to set a good toolbox. Emerging markets differ from developed markets in areas such as

[32] The owner of Huiyuan, a Chinese fruit juice company listed in Hong Kong and targeted by Coca-Cola in 2008, explained that he has raised his company like a son but was planning to sell it as a "hog" (a graphic expression in Chinese meaning to maximize one's profit).

accounting transparency, liquidity, corruption, volatility, governance, taxes, and transaction costs. These differences will likely affect firm valuation. Faced with such a level of complexity to retrieve information, contrasting risk approaches and models with different core components, practitioners often resort to using classic mainstream models in day-to-day valuations; such models originating from mature markets and being adjusted for risk and local factors.

The Western valuation tools are generally well-known and understood by Chinese businessmen, although some, for tactical reasons, prefer to avoid using them. As in any negotiation, the interest of the seller is to maximize his gains, while that of the buyer is to maximize his return on investment. In China, one has to remember that, given the speed of the development of the economy, the profitability is more looked at on a short-term basis. The profitability of an acquisition must be quickly demonstrated. This point has to be insisted upon during valuations and negotiations. Based on this simple observation, the following discussions will be greatly simplified.

Financial and accounting due diligences can help identify adjustments that must be made to the accounts and/or the business plan, submitted by the buyer to reach the final transaction price. The initial valuation of the target according to international standard methods and after the due diligence results help to rationalize negotiations, and lead to a well-articulated price acceptable for both parties. However, it will not be always possible to have a reasonable discussion if the seller has set its own walk-away price on completely different criteria, for example, on a transaction concluded many years ago at a possible unreasonable price or valuation reached by another company that he will compare with, even if the comparison is hardly possible.

The value of the assets of a Chinese company is often not visible at first glance, and this may be confusing and should be kept in mind. An example is provided by a Chinese company manufacturing medical toothpaste and incidentally a small line of cleaning products using traditional Chinese medical ingredients. The valuation of the whole business was totally disconnected from market values. The market characteristics and the international valuation of the actors left no doubt on the likely valuation spread for such a company. Uninformed investors simply did not know that the company had, at a certain time, invested at very favorable conditions in a small bank that was about to be listed or sold to a larger one. The exceptional value of this hidden financial asset represented in fact most of the real value of the company, and therefore the valuation of the most visible part of the business was irrelevant. Such examples are not rare in China.

Chinese business owners are sometimes inclined to base the transaction price on a perceived value of their company, even if this is not always justified by a well-articulated and rational financial valuation. After sharing information and mutually accepting compromises, negotiations between the parties will usually lead to a more acceptable solution.

In an emerging country, the decision to become a financial or industrial partner in a project depends on its perceived level of risk and its expected profitability, which can be highly ambiguous. Emerging markets in general have a more unstable legal environment and weaker corporate governance institutions; financial markets tend to price assets in emerging markets at a discount with respect to comparable assets in developed markets. On the other hand, since controlling shareholders in emerging markets can expect to receive more private benefits from control, at the expense of non-controlling shareholders, they will in general value the benefits of control more than controlling shareholders in developed markets.[33]

M&A projects on emerging markets are like the purchase of precious stones on the black market: You do not buy because it is cheap. This motivation, independent of ethical considerations related to the origin of such gems, is not enough to justify a transaction. The incentive to buy is simply that it has to be profitable, but a more refined analysis leads to discount this expected profit with a level of ethical risk, which may ultimately destroy your company if one's unethical or irresponsible behavior is exposed, with possible consequences. There are only good or bad deals, and "good"

[33] Robert F. Bruner *et al.* (2002). "Introduction to 'Valuation in Emerging Markets.'" *Emerging Markets Review*, 3, 310–324.

Table 4.1. Complexity Level of the Transaction.

Transaction complexity — Target score card					
	Restricted				*Open*
Industry	1	2	3	4	5
	OEM				*Iconic*
Brand	1	2	3	4	5
	Weak				*Strong*
Mutual trust, ethics	1	2	3	4	5
	Weak				*Strong*
Leadership	1	2	3	4	5
	SoE				Private
Ownership	1	2	3	4	5
	Majority				*Minority*
Deal structure	1	2	3	4	5
	Equity				*Assets*
Deal type	1	2	3	4	5
	Weak				*Strong*
Integration ease	1	2	3	4	5
	Weak				*Strong*
Financials	1	2	3	4	5
	High				*Low*
Potential liabilities	1	2	3	4	5
Total score	**10**	**20**	**30**	**40**	**50**

deals are possible or not in a defined ethical framework: Do we accept or not to buy (cheap) conflict-related diamonds[34]; do we

[34] These African diamonds fuel the many wars waged by rebels against the governments. Extracted from mines located in countries where wars are raging, they are sold illegally through underground networks to supply the rebel groups which exploit them with weapons.

take the risk to violate the embargo on a certain country to conduct more business, for example; do we close our eyes on the pollution of the river because it can be dealt with controlling authorities? This is simply unreasonable, as this is likely to be uncovered sooner than later.

The level of complexity of a transaction in China can be assessed using a relatively simple multiple entry table.

There are many layers of complexity between these poles, depending on the economic situation and legal structure of the target company.

The three main types of valuations are the same in China as in Europe:

- Comparable market data (listed companies, transactions).
- Discounted future cash flows method.
- Real options.

There are several reference books in Europe and the US on general company valuation, but this book focuses on emerging countries where classic models must be adapted as market conditions are often imperfect. A brief reminder of the basic valuation methods is presented in this chapter, but our objective is not to go into the details of each of them. The aim is rather to highlight some of the specific features of valuating companies in China and in other emerging markets.

As mentioned in the section dedicated to environmental and accounting due diligences, the starting point of any valuation is the availability and quality of the financial and senior management information. The possible lack of information is a recurring problem for all emerging markets.

It must be noted that on average, the size of the company to be valued is noticeably smaller than in Europe due to the large number of fragmented industrial players in China and the size of regional markets. This does not mean that all Chinese companies are small, but the size of the target companies available to foreigners is on average smaller than what can be acquired in Europe or the United States.

The valuation of companies in China is based on the understanding of two types of factors:

- The specificities of the Chinese market.
- Adapting the usual methods of business valuation to China.

In China, practitioners are usually not very comfortable with the methodology of real and financial options, and struggle to model the options embedded in the real assets. Thinking in terms of real options is highly complex, and the domestic market is still not very developed for derivative products. Real options also have a tendency to be intertwined and reproduce, each one creating new options, resulting in strings of complex options on options. The specific conditions in China's fast moving economy can be expected to only amplify these problems.

4.1.1. *The Chinese Market Influences the Key Aspects of the Target Valuation*

The understanding of what is possible to be assessed (legal and economic), and the access to a sufficient quality level of information, are critical to the use of any valuation model. This applies to all emerging markets for which the pair growth/risk requires a much more thorough analysis than mature markets.

4.1.1.1. *Defining the Range of Possibilities: Majority, Minority, Unauthorized Transactions*

The regulatory framework that applies to a given target in a specific industry is the starting point of the valuation of an acquisition in China. For example, it is not possible for a foreigner to invest in some strategic sectors (e.g., military electronics) and to acquire majority stakes in certain areas (e.g., financial institutions). It is therefore necessary to refer to the Catalogue of Foreign Investment. When the investment is only authorized as a joint venture or as a minority stake in a Chinese company, valuation criteria ought to take into account the lack of control premium and the quality of governance.[35] The liquidity and the timeline of the return on investment must necessarily be carefully considered. Chinese negotiators sometimes indicate that their valuation includes a market entry premium; it can hardly be justified now, in a global and increasingly open economy.

Obtaining the necessary licenses and approvals implies taking some level of risk. It adds to the operational uncertainty a possible increase of the cost of the acquisition.

The acquisition of state-owned enterprises (SoE) requires the involvement of professional evaluators approved by the Chinese authorities. The purpose is to prevent overvaluation and the underpricing of state assets. The used methodology is often based on the reassessed net asset value. With a few exceptions, intangible assets are often valued at a low level and are subject to a separate negotiation between the parties. China is an old agrarian and trading nation used to dealing with the concept of value added on physical goods rather than sophisticated intangibles. Some time is still needed to see the evolution, but no doubt this perception is now changing rapidly.

In the case of a partnership, a good structuring of the governance will enable the foreign investor to have (or not) control over the cash flows generated by the joint company. The control of the cash flow and the type of governance defined between the parties will have a direct impact on the valuation of the partnership. A detailed modelling of various scenarios is often required to understand the consequence of selecting one governance option over another.

---

[35] Chong-Eng Bai *et al.* (2002), "Corporate Governance and Firm Valuation in China"; available online at SSRN: http://ssrn.com/abstract=361660 or http://dx.doi.org/10.2139/ssrn.361660 (accessed on October 2, 2014).

4.1.1.2. *Analysis of the Target's Market*

The historical and expected growth rate of the generic markets in which the target company is operating must be properly defined by segment and product. For any valuation model based on the growth of future discounted cash flows, revenues growth stands as the first and very key factor. The impact of inflation, in the industry segment — not just based on the CPI, must also be taken into consideration.

Understanding and mapping the growth rate is a prerequisite for validating the target or strategic partnership business plan. It is therefore necessary to spend a bit of time gathering a good set of detailed statistics by sector — growth, purchasing power, consumption patterns, flexibility, or rigidity of purchasing behavior — to support the business plan.

Afterwards, it is necessary to check that the marketing data, consolidated by line of products or by product, are consistent with the market structure in terms of asset pricing and volume. These assumptions will be essential for the calculation of future revenues and future free cash flows. In a fast moving economy, a precise measurement and understanding of growth drivers by market segment will often make the difference between a mediocre business plan and a great management tool. The segments' growth must be carefully profiled and simulated, as double-digit growth rates cannot continue forever; it is advisable that a "cool down" option is reflected in the long-term cash flow generation and terminal values.

Although Chinese accounting is clear on the concept of revenues recognition, there are sometimes technical difficulties in defining the consolidated revenues of a Chinese company, especially as intercompany flows can represent a significant undocumented part. This is due to the existence of multiple levels of accounting that do not always reconcile well: group, social, analytical, and tax accounting.

4.1.1.3. *Cost Structure of the Business Plan*

The cost structure of the target must be analyzed by product segment to ensure that all the key elements in the value creation process are included in the calculation of the profit. For example, part of the manufacturing may be carried out by a sister company or a minority subsidiary at favorable conditions, for reasons related to business history and alliances. It is not uncommon that once the company is sold to foreigners, these conditions are revisited with a corresponding negative impact on profitability. When dealing with raw material costs, it is important to look at the final price in China and compare it with international prices. Indeed, one must check that the product costs do not deviate too much from international standard prices. If there are significant differences, this generally means that the quality is not comparable; this can then cause product registration problems, damageable quality issues, order cancellations, or loss of certain customers.

For high-tech applications, it is well known that the quality and the grade (e.g., purity) of materials define the performances. In the case of solar cells, there could be a significant difference if the polycrystalline silicon from which the cells are made of is recycled or not, and the impact on the sourcing of raw material costs is of course very significant. Price variations explained by volume factors are easily identifiable, and one must be careful that quality problems in the core materials are not being masked by possible volume discounts. It is often necessary to start from a zero-based budget (ZBB) to understand the manufacturing costs structure of the target company and check that the presented cost structure makes sense for budgeting and valuation purposes.

4.1.1.4. *Monetary Variables*

The foreign exchange factor is often considered a residual element of valuations. This is an essential factor in managing foreign investment, particularly in emerging markets. Monetary instability can lead to significant drops in investment profitability at a consolidated level. As far as China is concerned, the currency (CNY, RMB) is on a gradual appreciating trend, making the Chinese economy attractive from an investor's point of view. However, the resulting appreciation of manufacturing costs makes low added-value activities less attractive in China than in other low-income countries (e.g., Bangladesh for textiles). In the case of intensive labor and low added-value manufacturing, the decision to settle in China rather than in other country must be carefully assessed. One of the best answers is probably to serve the growing domestic market, to build a high quality workforce, and be able to source raw materials in an appreciating currency, although not yet directly convertible.

The payment of upstream dividends from China to Europe is a problem due to the non-convertibility of the RMB. It is therefore preferable to consider a Chinese presence as a long-term investment in a cash reinvestment perspective. The capitalization of results should, over time, turn out to be a good investment.

China is strengthening its policy on RMB internationalization by promoting a wider use of its currency worldwide. The People's Bank of China signed a number of MoUs with foreign central banks to establish clearing and settlement arrangements, and appointed Yuan clearing banks in Europe and the US.[36] Europe is well positioned to become the largest Yuan offshore market, after Hong Kong, in the future. According to SWIFT,[37] the Yuan is now the world's 7th most used currency for trading goods and services (23rd in 2013).

4.1.1.5. *Net Asset Values*

The historical net asset value has economically little relevance in the context of an M&A transaction or for structuring a partnership, mostly because the tangible assets are not priced at their market value, and because the intangible assets are unlikely to be properly

[36] Jiang Xueqing, "Nation Looks to Boost the International Use of Yuan for Trade," *CHINADAILYUSA*, August 15, 2014; available online at usa.chinadaily.com.cn/epaper/2014-08/15/content_18319861.htm (accessed on October 2, 2014).

[37] SWIFT is a member-owned cooperative, through which the financial world conducts its business operations with speed, certainty, and confidence. It enables its customers to automate and standardize financial transactions. Source: SWIFT website: available online at www.swift.com/index.page?lang=en (accessed on October 2, 2014).

accounted for. In contrast, the revaluated net asset value is frequently used in China for practical reasons like structuring transactions. It roughly corresponds to a simplistic replacement value for a second hand equipment purchase. In the case of partnerships, the most important part will indeed be what the partners have decided to build together in the future.

The proper valuation of each class of tangible assets is not very difficult; but significant cost and time are required to provide a detailed and fairly priced inventory. However, an accurate valuation of liabilities is more delicate and requires an accounting and legal due diligence, but its logic remains the same. The valuation of intangible assets and intellectual property (IP) is always a problem and a topic for heated discussion between the parties. It should be noted that on this issue, Chinese law does not recognize the concept of goodwill, and selling a Picasso for the price of the canvas and painting is unlikely to be a deal appealing to any seller. In this case, an analysis of the market values and business plan to determine a succession of discounted future free cash flows will help in calculating an acceptable valuation based on the industrial assets of the company. A proxy for the goodwill has to be calculated on the basis

Table 4.2. Intangible Assets Ranked by Decreasing Order of Ease to Valuate.

Intangible Assets	Facility to Appraise
Patents	1
Formulas	1
Industrial process	2
Brand names	2
Know how (specific)	3
Licences	3
Distribution channels	5
Business networks	6
*Affectio societatis**	6

Note: *Willingness to partner.

of the future profitability of the company based on future discounted cash flows.

Therefore, it is not uncommon for a Chinese seller to mix the net asset value and the turnover multiple to reach a company value that empirically satisfies him.

4.1.2. *Valuation of the Target*

4.1.2.1. *Impact of Structuring on the Valuation*

The structuring of the deal is one of the key aspects of the transaction in China, as the seller is often concerned about minimizing the tax impact. He will often consider the net cash value of the transaction, meaning the cash on hand after taxes have been paid. In addition, some structures are a mandatory channel for pure regulatory reasons (mandatory joint ventures) or to better manage risks (liabilities of the company). The choice of a structure will impact the value. This can be a difficult point in the negotiations, notably for the valuation of intangible assets.

The valuation of an external growth operation is essentially based on the monetary value of net assets contributed by the partners, as intangible assets are inherently much more difficult to value. However, Chinese sellers will explain at length the value of their branded products on the market in comparison to white labels. In the context of a joint venture creation, it is common for the Chinese partner to provide the land, the buildings, and his business network, while the foreign partner provides the capital and the technology. New forms of joint ventures are emerging, where Chinese companies are providing only the capital and possibly some useful relationships, and the Western partner is supplying the rest.

Although the transfer or buy-back of shares is technically easier, the problem of residual risks related to contingent liabilities and the weakness of liability guarantees are rampant. For this reason, it is not always advisable to buy-back shares. It is only after due diligences that this choice can be made. Some industries where potential liabilities are known to be a recurring problem, e.g., severe environmental liabilities, are very exposed.

4.1.2.2. *Valuation of Intangible Assets*

Assessing the quality of intangible commercial assets, commercial access to the Chinese market, to a portfolio of Chinese clients, and to logistics and distribution is always difficult, much more so than access to technology or industrial assets. In this case, the assessment must be done on the basis of the industrial project, which is to say, on the revenue generated, its future profitability, and the future discounted free cash flow.

Trademarks are sensitive areas for partnerships and China market entry strategies, as China's trademark laws follow a "first-to-file" principle that may reward brand squatters. Some businessmen, called trademark trolls, have made a living on targeting valuable foreign brands and registering them as their own property in China. Firms entering China then have to rebrand their own products, fight in China's courts, or pay to buy-back the trademark.

Tesla Motors, the US electric car, is a recent example of companies facing brand difficulties while doing business in China. A Chinese businessman, who registered rights to the brand before Tesla entered China, wanted Tesla to shut its showroom, service centers, and supercharging facilities in China, stop all sales and marketing activities in the country, and pay him RMB23.9 million in compensation according to a lawsuit filed in Beijing.[38]

The United States-based electric carmaker, Tesla Motors Inc, said it has "completely and amicably" resolved a trademark dispute in China, removing a hurdle that had threatened the company's ambitions to expand rapidly in the world's biggest auto market. "Mr Zhan [a businessman who registered the Tesla brand in 2006, three years after Tesla was founded] has agreed to have the Chinese authorities complete the process of cancelling the Tesla trademarks that he had registered or applied for, at no cost to Tesla," Tesla said in an e-mail statement. Separately, Tesla and Zhan have

[38] Bloomberg, "Tesla Faces Suit over Trademark in China," *CHINADAILYUSA*, July 9, 2014; available online at usa.chinadaily.com.cn/epaper/2014-07/09/content_17689526.htm (accessed on October 2, 2014).

also reached commercial terms for the transfer to Tesla of certain domain names, including tesla.cn and teslamotors.cn, the company said, declining to give financial details.

Tesla's trademark dispute underscores a thorny issue faced by foreign companies doing business in China. Global companies like Apple Inc, Koninklijke Philips NV, Burberry, and Unilever NV have all been embroiled in trademark disputes in the country in the past.[39]

The valuation of intangible productive assets, such as the brand name, the R&D, or the new products pipeline, is essential in some sectors (e.g., luxury, pharmaceutical, chemistry), as the issue at stake is not to simply acquire a production facility that may be built from scratch in the context of a "greenfield" project.

In the case of a joint venture, an important part of the value of the deal is based on the commercial value of the partner and his access to the Chinese market.

4.1.2.3. *Teams are the Key Value of Chinese Companies*

The acquisition (or creation) of companies in China by foreign companies is primarily based on the quality of the local teams running it. They are the ones who best understand the environment and will be better suited to guide the local development. The strategic vision of headquarters must be reinterpreted to take into account Chinese specificities, and to have significance on a long-term basis regarding execution and results.

Some foreign brands have been identified for adopting inconsistent growth strategies in China, based sometimes on a combination of greenfield, small acquisitions, and partnerships. This resulted in a business primer of what should not be done to enter the China market.

---

[39] China Daily, "Tesla Reaches Agreement over Trademark Dispute," *CHINADAILYUSA*, August 7, 2014; available online at usa.chinadaily.com.cn/bussiness/2014-08/07/content_18267296.htm (accessed on October 2, 2014).

Business Case

A Case of Failed Market Entry and Failed Partnership

The senior management of a Western company believed that their existing beauty business and their brand recognition in some part of the Western world should be sufficient to successfully enter the Chinese market and strongly establish their brand on the market. A growth strategy based on the firm's key brand attributes in Europe was quickly designed. Local competition, consumer preference, and retail channels were not given too much attention, as it was assumed that Chinese consumers will follow the track of what made the brand a success in other countries.

A product range to start the business in China was quickly put together by the international marketing team. Unfortunately, the feedback received from the Chinese market showed that the brand needed to adapt to the taste and needs of demanding Chinese consumers, flooded with a comprehensive and well-designed product range from aggressive competitors originating from Europe, Korea, Japan, and the Americas.

A small local team was then hired to deliver quick results, i.e., a payback in less than two years, according to the group's standards. Simultaneously, senior management pushed for constant downsizing of the investment budget to achieve more with less. Enormous pressure was put on the Chinese teams, without offering enough marketing support, training, and good management incentives. As sales were not taking off as planned, the headquarters requested more reporting to better understand the situation, started to micromanage Chinese operations, and became suspicious and awkward with the local team. The lack of trust was exacerbated by the lack of knowledge about the country. Many staff left and had no problem in finding better positions.

(*Continued*)

(Continued)

Starting with a store opening strategy, the group ended up closing all its stores. It later announced a partnership with a large distributor and again the story quickly went sour. The consequences of this ailing partnership were low sales and a low visibility of the brand on the market. In the meantime, the distinctive features of the brand business model were dissected and absorbed by the competition which quickly leveraged this failed entry strategy to strengthen their own brand, using a better suited development plan for China.

Poorly structured attempts to enter the China market have always resulted in the failure of brands which were all well known in the West. It is unfortunate to observe that the initial key ingredients for success were in place. The importance of the quality of local management is nothing new: This is the case for all acquisitions, whatever the country, but it may be neglected, as China is sometimes seen as a country where everything is possible.

Hiring an excellent CEO to run the local operations is probably the first major task of any senior management deciding to move to China. Not only must he be able to decide on the best market entry strategy, but he also needs to be comfortable in a multicultural environment, and build a powerful and effective interface with the foreign headquarters. The China-based CEO's most important task will be to form the best possible team, and secure its commitment to grow the business and their loyalty to the firm. It is necessary to have the best retention and motivation tools, given the high degree of competition to attract the best talents. The worst that can possibly happen after an acquisition is that key talents leave the company due to an inadequate communication and management presentation. One has to expect the competitors and head hunters to pay close attention to change of ownership, and to take advantage of any missteps to attract talents otherwise hard to hire. Clear governance and management rules must be put in place for (i) the strategy to be well understood, (ii) for the expectations to be shared, and (iii) for the decision-making process to be well rounded between the local management and the foreign parent company.

China has a culture of pragmatism, carefully framed by a quite comprehensive legal framework. As a foreign company, it is absolutely necessary to be able to lead by example when it comes to dealing with administrative authorities, and work closely with them when difficulties arise.

4.1.3. *A Few Valuation Specificities of Chinese Targets*

To start with a comforting statement, it must be emphasized that the three main types of valuations are almost the same in all countries, including China: comparable market values, future discounted cash flows, and real options.

However, the structural differences between the structure of emerging and mature markets require certain precautions in order to avoid context mistakes.

4.1.3.1. *Valuation by Local Market Value Is Problematic but Improving*

Market values are objective values on which it is, on principle, always possible to rely upon. The case of emerging markets is however derogatory, as a good correlation between risk and return does not necessarily exist in all market segments. From a practical standpoint, this abnormality may translate into an overvaluation of the assets listed on capital markets or over-the-counter, compared to what one may expect on more mature markets. This is due to markets anticipating growth in emerging economies (higher than those of mature economies), to possible "casino" investment behavior, often less rational in emerging markets (rumor mills, possible manipulation, and importance of speculative buying), and rampant information asymmetry. In this respect, revisiting the basis of behavioral finance may be a useful exercise to explain and increase understanding of the reasoning patterns of Chinese investors, including the emotional processes involved and the degree to which they influence the investors' decision-making process.[40]

Overevaluation may also be a consequence of insufficient supply in the number of products or in the volume of products offered, leading to a scarcity of savings instruments with possible inflated prices — such situations being aggravated when the markets are not fully open internationally.

Recurring problems of investor confidence on the Chinese domestic equities market cause some methodological difficulties for corporate valuation. This is correlated with a very short horizon for individual investors, with a turnover of 44 days[41] on average and about 20% of the holdings on the market. The remaining 80% is held by experienced institutional investors, including funds, who have a much slower turnover of about 143 trading days. In comparison to the West, fewer long-term investors participate in the market. Short-term oriented and relatively inexperienced investors who access a limited supply of competing information, such as high quality equity research, may overreact to rumors and limited accounting information in cutting or increasing their positions. In general, the financial statements of AB-share companies are judged by investors to be of higher quality, due to a dual-GAAP reporting system and a strengthened monitoring role by both domestic and international CPAs.[42]

By early 2011, a series of scandals developed around Chinese companies, from the latest wave of listings on foreign markets and, in particular, in the US. Many involved fraud with features that presented particular problems for investors. Almost all involved misrepresentations in financial reporting that would

[40] Victor Ricciardi and Helen K. Simon (2000), "What Is Behavioral Finance?" *Business, Education & Technology Journal*, 2(2), 1–9.

[41] "CSRC: The Length of Time Buyers Hold Stocks Is Proportional to Their Yield" (证监会:持股时间与收益率成正比), November 20, 2013, *Chinanews* (中国新闻网). Q&A interactive session between CSRC and Weibo users on November 19, 2013.

[42] Charles J. P. Chen *et al.* (2001), "Is Accounting Information Relevant in the Emerging Chinese Stock Market?" *Journal of International Accounting, Auditing and Taxation,* 10(1), 1–22.

have been missed by a standard audit. Many of the scandals involved companies that had listed by reverse merger.[43] As a result, although foreign markets still seem comfortable with the valuation of large Chinese companies, they are not so confident with smaller, less well-known ones. The only exception is probably Hong Kong, where Mainland Chinese companies represent 42% of the exchange's total capitalization. But this points again to the benefits of market knowledge and local expertise: The Hong Kong investment community is close to Mainland China, with a stronger business network and enhanced capacities to early detect leading indicators of problems.

In late 2012, the Chinese government closed the door on initial public offerings, after a spate of new listings performed poorly and some scandals erupted.[44] A series of unfortunate cases dented investor confidence, and finally represented a global threat for the stability of the entire equity market. It made it harder to value corporate equities, as the local benchmarks were possibly unreliable. The situation on the IPO market caused a trauma and a market freeze, which resulted in prolonged valuation gaps between buyers and sellers specific to China.

After many months of preparation, highlighted by the introduction of a fresh approach augmented by a new set of rules, the China Securities Regulatory Commission lifted the year-long moratorium on IPOs, allowing a host of companies to join the rush to raise money from the already beleaguered stock market.

First out of the gate was the drug maker, Jiangsu Aosaikang Pharmaceutical. But it did not get far before the CSRC gave the order to abort, because of glaring irregularities. The Aosaikang IPO debacle has revealed the extent of problems in the Chinese stock market,

---

[43] David Cogman and Gordon Orr (2013), "How They Fell: The Collapse of Chinese Cross-Border Listings," *McKinsey & Company*; available online at www.mckinsey.com/insights/corporate_finance/how_they_fell_the_collapse_of_chinese_cross-border_listings (accessed on October 3, 2014).

[44] As an example, the Guangdong Xindadi Biotechnology IPO was halted in 2012 by CSRC after frauds were uncovered. A string of scandals in 2011and 2012 created a very damageable climate of mistrust on China's stock markets.

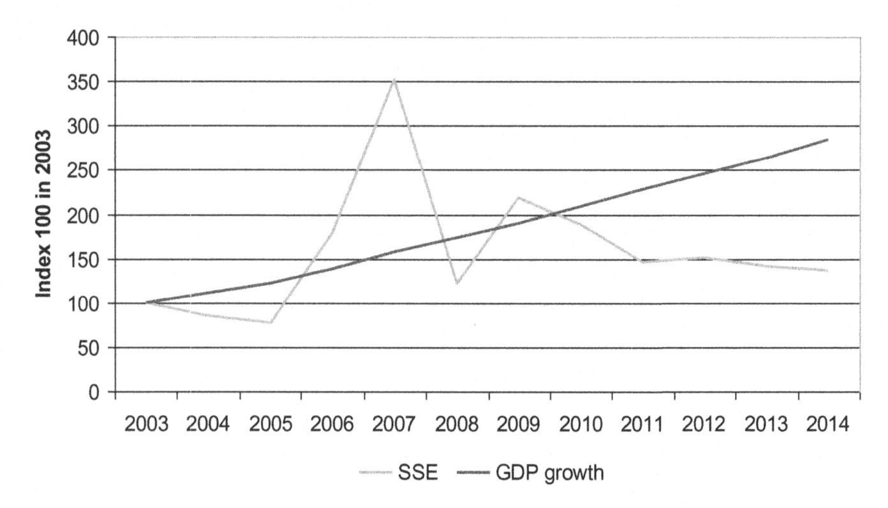

Figure 4.1. Comparative Growth of China's GDP and Shanghai's Stock Market Index (SSE).

which apparently caught CSRC by surprise. Frustrated by the prolonged market slump, Chinese investors have blamed IPOs for draining market liquidity by allowing business owners to cash out.[45]

In recent years, investors have become increasingly disappointed by news that certain listed companies were found to be cheating before listing — with their senior managers rushing to sell their shares as soon as it becomes possible, after listing. As a result, the market has become unattractive to investors. And when it becomes unattractive, it is normal for the indexes to be bearish.[46]

In the immature stock market, fraught with irregularities ranging from insider trading to porous IPO procedures, China's economic booms may not be fully reflected in the stock index changes.[47] The result is a problematic long-term pattern emerging when the market

[45] Hong Liang, "Scandals Show IPOs a Free-For-All," *CHINADAILY.COM.CN*, January 20, 2014; available online at www.chinadaily.com.cn/opinion/2014-01/20/content_17244514.htm (accessed on October 3, 2014).

[46] Xin Zhiming, "Why China's Stock Market Is Bearish," *CHINADAILY.COM.CN*, June 30, 2014; available online at www.chinadaily.com.cn/opinion/2014-06/30/content_17626746.htm (accessed on October 3, 2014).

[47] Xin Zhiming, "Stock Market to Remain Weak," *CHINADAILY.COM.CN*, April 29, 2014; available online at www.chinadaily.com.cn/business/2014-04/29/content_17473489-2.htm (accessed on October 3, 2014).

index (Shanghai Composite Index, SSE)[48] and the GDP growth[49] are compared. Companies are supposed to be valued according to three dynamic criteria, meaning future expectations for: growth, profitability, and risk. As GDP growth does not seem to be a concern, the trust regarding the risk/profitability couple is likely to be what poses a problem to domestic investors since mid-2007 to mid-2009.

4.1.3.2. *Comparable Listed Companies*

Comparables used in China are multiples calculated from the market capitalization of companies listed on the Hong Kong, Shenzhen (mid and small capitalizations, volatile markets), Shanghai (larger firms, more stable market), or even Taiwan stock exchanges.

The different stages of the analysis steps are quite straightforward in theory:

- Identify a relevant sample of listed industry peers with sufficient liquidity at a comparable stage of industrial development and having an industrial profile similar to the target company.
- Establish a well-structured database, in order to identify and download economic and financial data of competitors. This tool can then be shared with business intelligence.
- Calculate market capitalization (share price × number of shares adjusted from different dilution factors) and corporate values (market capitalization + financial debt – cash) to determine their valuations. Market capitalizations are used to calculate valuation ratios for minority investments and the enterprise values are used to calculate ratios for a majority transaction.
- Consistent cross-check between various key performance indicators — revenues, EBITDA, EBIT, net income, net assets — and valuations to determine what the valuation multiples are, company-by-company.

---

[48] Shanghai Composite Index, SSE. Closing every civil year from 2003, closing on June 30 (half year only) for 2014; available online at http://www.google.com/finance?cid=7521596 (accessed on February 4, 2015).

[49] World Bank, World Economic Databank on China; available online at http://data.worldbank.org/country/china (accessed on February 4, 2015).

All these steps help define a table that will be used to calculate an average by industry or the midpoint of the different company values.

These multiples calculated by companies are then consolidated in order to find an average by sector: average corporate values/ EBITDA. The standard deviation must be checked to make sure that the calculation is meaningful. If so, the sample will have to be adjusted and the reasons for this approach documented. Finally, the table consolidating the various indicators will be applied to the target company: ratio of average EBITDA multiple over EBITDA of the target, and so on. It seems so easy that it is hard to believe it takes so many months to learn how do it properly. The resulting valuation set of numbers calculated by indicators and multiples may be scattered. These differences should not be ignored but carefully analyzed and explained. It may seem to be a tedious process, but it will be rewarding at the end to better understand the leading value criteria on the market and finally decide, with a discounted cash flow (DCF), if the contemplated acquisition is worth or possibly overpriced.

A company listed in both Mainland China and Hong Kong will have on each stock exchange a convergent financial capitalization due to the progressive convertibility of the RMB (this has not always been the case), despite the controls and restrictions of entry/exit of capital in Mainland China. This must always be checked and a single stock exchange must be chosen to have homogeneous data in valuation calculation.

The traditionally high savings rate of Chinese households and the growth of financial markets have made certain listed securities a safe haven for investors. Some listed securities have highly speculative profiles resulting in very high volatility and risk. In this case, the market valuation may not be used, as it is not really reliable. One way to spot it is to compare market multiples with peers listed in other stock exchange multiples (emerging markets or not).

The listed comparable companies are "secondhand" shares, as opposed to newly issued shares, which do not include control premiums, except if the company is in play.[50] The control premium

---

[50] See Chapter 6, Case Study Four on the impact on the Huiyuan–Coca-Cola transaction.

is the increase in the average share price to pay in order to acquire the majority control of a company. The necessary adjustments must therefore be made on an ordinary listed share price if the objective

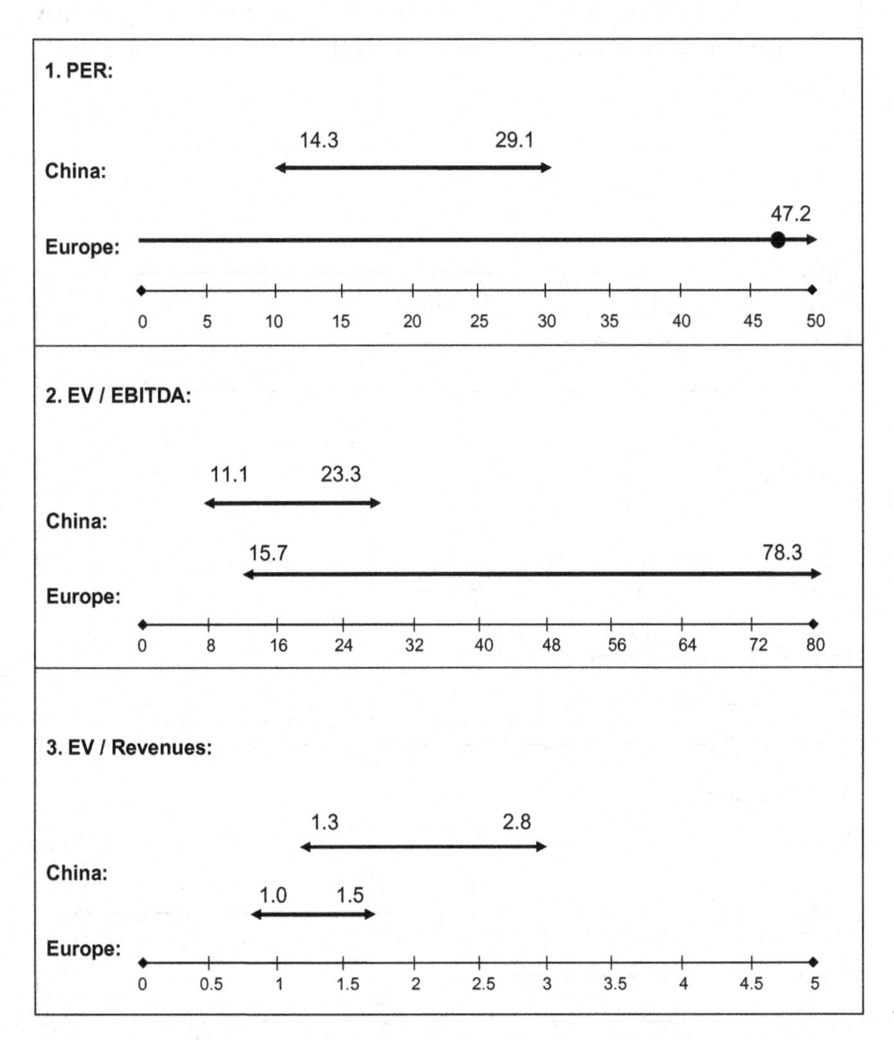

Figure 4.2. Comparative Valuation of Chinese and European Automotive Manufacturers.[51]

Source: March 2011, basis last published accounts in 2009.

[51] See sample in Appendix at the end of the chapter.

is to take control. In some emerging countries, the market is not efficient and stocks do not trade at their fair value on stock exchanges. Therefore, the acquisition of a controlling stake can happen at a discounted price if the share price turns out to be clearly unrealistic and if there is no sufficient liquidity (i.e., supply of shares) at a price level.

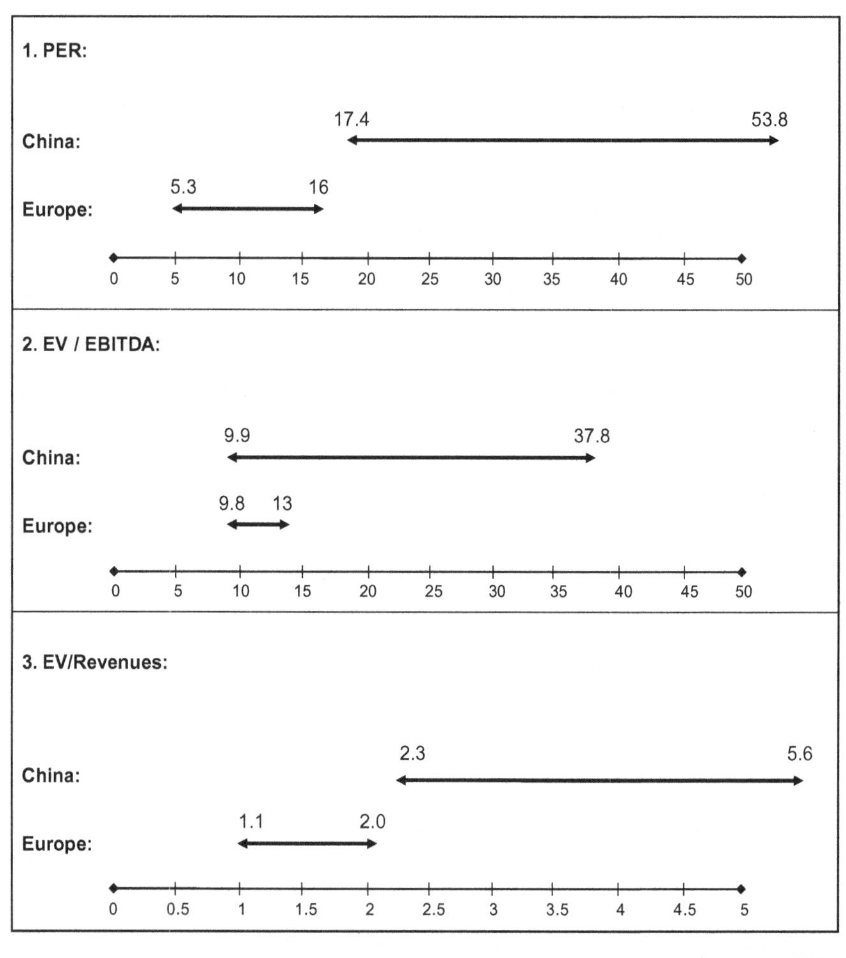

Figure 4.3. Comparative Valuation, Agro-food Firms in China and the West.[52]

Source: Latest published 2010 accounts in March 2011.

[52] See sample in Appendix at the end of the chapter.

An analysis of the compared valuations of Chinese and European car manufacturers in 2011, on the basis of accounts published in 2009, is surprising. The severity of the financial crisis tends to blur the picture, particularly concerning profitability, and the expected misalignment in valuations between Chinese and European companies is not clear.

However, if we compare the differential in value between the agribusiness companies listed in Europe and China on the basis of their 2010 results, Chinese companies, mostly present on the local market, are shining when it comes to investment growth premium in China.

Independently from published or anticipated levels, such high price earning ratio (PER) levels are surprising in China and in other emerging countries. To put it in simple terms and go beyond a simple accounting definition, the PER must also be analyzed as the inverse yield on government bonds (no significant risk), weighted by a sector growth rate and risk variable related to the industry and the sector.

The level of Chinese government bonds in the long run is 4.24%,[53] interpolated over 15 years in March 2010, with sector growths given an average GDP growth of about 7.5%–8% in the last years and risks often well understood by stakeholders in the local market. It therefore results in valuation multiples which cannot compare with those used as a reference in more mature economies. The inverse of a low risk-free rate (e.g., 1/0.04) is a market-neutral PER as high as 25x, which must then be adjusted for growth and risk.

4.1.3.3. *Comparable Transactions*

A first step is to access and collect the transaction data (M&A) of companies with industrial profiles similar to the target. There are a number of databases on the market, but the numbers available are not always reliable. Accessing transaction information with

[53] The China Government Bond 10Y decreased to 4.24% in August from 4.32% in July 2014. China Government Bond 10Y averaged 3.72% from 2005 until 2014, reaching an all time high of 4.85% in November 2013 and a record low of 2.52% in December 2008. Source: www.tradingeconomics.com (accessed on December 2, 2014).

industry characteristics comparable to the chosen target company is always extremely useful, but collecting these data always requires thorough research. It is not uncommon that the seller himself refers to transactions that will serve as a reference to set his own selling price, especially as in China, companies tend to be located together in specialized industrial clusters. When a transaction is made, the information is usually available, and the source is quite reliable; however, buyers should analyse the price in the valuation cycle of the industry. A seller will always push transaction references at the peak to the industry cycle, and in a slowing market, it is usually difficult to explain to the seller that these benchmarks are outdated and require to go deeper in the cycle structure and possibly switch to DCF valuation.

The second step requires to go beyond a simple set of numbers:

- Understand how transaction values are calculated (market capitalization or company value) in a majority or minority operation.
- Take into account market cycles to avoid calculating the top and bottom of the cycle averages that would not be relevant. One will have to notably adjust the multiples of the 2008 crisis to obtain useable indicators.
- Compare these valuations performance indicators with those of the target — revenues, EBITDA, EBIT, net income, net assets — to find out what the valuation multiples by company are. The turnover is a volumetric indicator and therefore of a lesser quality than EBIT or EBITDA, which are both a proxy for real profits (sales volume minus costs volume).

Furthermore, to calculate a good set of ratios, the numerator and denominator must include comparable elements: The enterprise value[54] is always compared to a relevant aggregate such as turnover, EBITDA, or EBIT. Similarly, the market capitalization can be compared to the net income and to dividends, and it is common practice to see it compared with EBIT or EBITDA, even if this is not really appropriate.[55]

[54] Including the value of capital shares + net debt + minority interests.

[55] One must prefer using enterprise value rather than market capitalization in this case.

Table 4.3. Transaction Sample (Last Published Accounts, 2010).

Date	Buyer	Country of Origin	Target Company (Chinese)	Sector	Turnover (€ Millions)	EBITDA (€ Millions)	Total Value (€ Millions)	Shares Bought (%)	Acquisition Price (€ Millions)	Turn-over Multiple	EBITDA Multiple
June 2010	Carlsberg	Denmark	Chongqing Brewery	Alcoholic beverages	254	197	1.994	12.25	244	7.9	10.1
June 2010	Faurecia	France	Xuyang Group	Automotive equipment	150		58	18.75	11	0.4	
June 2010	Carlyle Group	US	China Fishery	Industrial fishing	374	150	969	13.60	132	2.6	6.4
June 2010	QD Asia Pacific	Qatar	Yangziyang Shipbuilding	Shipbuilding	1372	303	2420	2.24	54	1.8	8.0
July 2010	Elica Group S.p.A	Italy	Zhejiang Putian Electric	White goods	14	2	24	55	13	1.7	9.3
July 2010	Charmes Rover Laboratories*	US	Wuxi Pharmatech*	Pharmaceutical development	232	49	1513	100	625	6.5	30.5
September 2010	Vallourec Group	France	Tianda Oil Pipe	Engineering	340	25	357	19.50	70	1.1	14.1
									Highest	7.9	30.5
									Lowest	0.4	6.4

* Acquisition cancelled due to disagreements between shareholders.

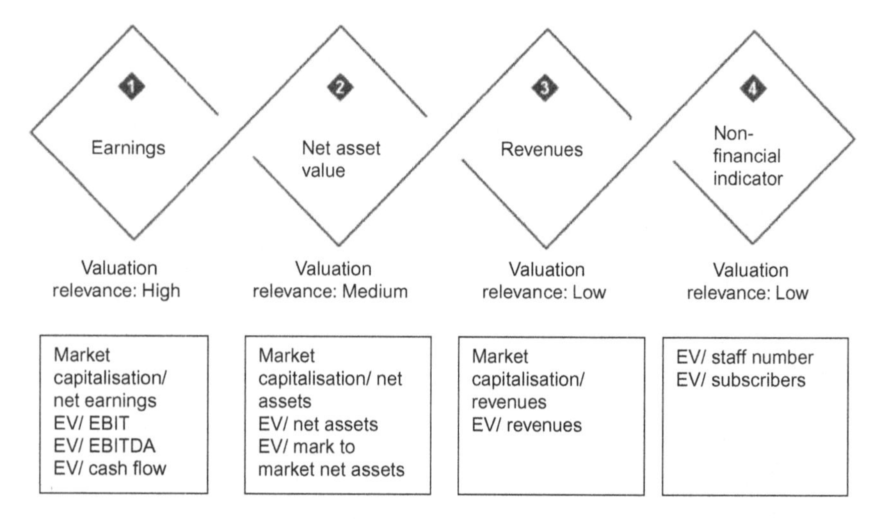

Figure 4.4. Usual Multiples When Using Comparables.

Note: EV Stands for entreprise value = market capitalization + net debt.

Transaction multiples are then consolidated in a table to find a median or an average by sector. The table of indicators is then applied to the target: average EBITDA multiple over the target's adjusted EBITDA, and so on. The calculated values may be scattered, and this must then be explained and cross checked with the market values previously found. Adjusting the target EBITDA is important, as it is likely that the due diligence will uncover some issues to align the accounting practices to national standards.

4.1.3.4. *Net Asset Value Method*

The net asset value method is often used in China due to its simplicity. Valuations by officially certified Chinese appraisal firms for state-owned company valuations systematically used this reference:

- Balance sheet assets are first valued based on replacement values or market values. An additional or corrective valuation can be carried out after the due diligence and a thorough check of property titles.
- It is not uncommon to heavily depreciate receivables, inventories, and tangible assets after due diligences.

- Liabilities must be valued mark-to-market and then added together, or simply removed from the transaction. It should be checked that, even in the case of a transfer of simple assets, unrealized operating liabilities are not associated with them.
- Finally, it may be necessary to establish a cash flow statement based on objective statements for the accrued expenses on certain transferred assets (e.g., electricity bills) to be paid as operation expenses of the industrial building, which the buyer is only partly accountable for.

This type of valuation is necessarily incomplete due to the lack of direct valuation of intangible assets, but may be good enough to buy a simple production unit. Some limited intangible assets can be valued separately and added to the price, e.g., the access to certain key clients. It is necessary that the assets are well-detailed and that market equivalences are found. The main limitation of this method is its static nature, but for a simple transaction this may not be a problem. It tends to undervalue the company, but on the other hand, it gives a value close to the scrap market value which, for companies formerly managed without a real notion of profitability, is not absurd. In the end, this method can be relevant when negotiating on a scrap value basis, but it is not usable as a tool for future business development in China and to calculate precise returns on investment. One must then rely on a detailed budget and DCF.

4.1.3.5. *Valuation by the Discounted Cash Flow (DCF) Method*

4.1.3.5.1. Generalities

Although the DCF method is widely used and has been applied since the '60s, there are still numerous problems when calculating valuations, especially on emerging markets or BRICS,[56] where the world's best finance universities have not reached a consensus. However,

[56]Acronym for the fastest moving economies: Brazil, Russia, India, China, and South Africa.

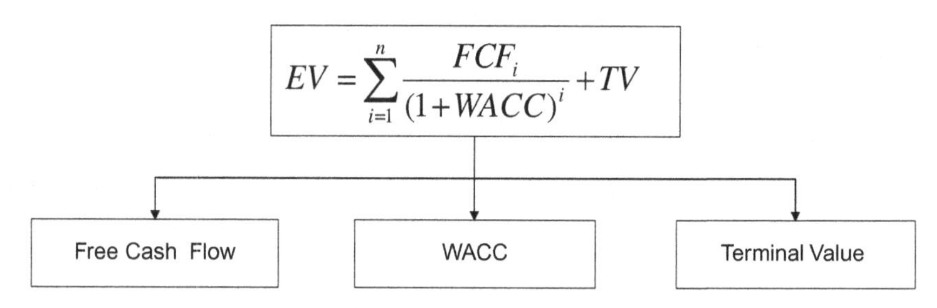

Figure 4.5. Discounted Free Cash Flow Valuation.[57]

using the future discounted cash flow method is probably the most satisfactory method of valuating a target company. It summarizes in a single model all key variables which have to be taken into account for an acquisition. It is more complex to implement in China, but much more useful for both valuation and business development purposes. The optimal use of this method requires an excellent knowledge of the target's positioning and competitive environment, in order to build a business plan and model the free cash flows.

This analytical valuation method is based on the construction of a financial model simulating the expected profitability for the following years. A good business plan will then make the target valuation easier and provide great insights for defining a "walk-away" price. Free cash flows will be driven by the growth rate, the EBITDA margin, the need for investment, and the working capital assumptions. The projection horizon must be reasonable, for example: three years of precise budgeting, and next three years of continuation of trends. The terminal value is the sum of the cash flows infinitely discounted after the last forecasted year.

Traditionally, the free cash flows are discounted using the weighted average cost of capital (WACC), which incorporates the respective cost factors of the debt and equity, as well as the risks

[57]The enterprise value is directly obtained from a future free cash flow model discounted by the weighted average cost of capital (WACC). The equity value is then calculated by deducting the net debt from the enterprise value.

pertaining thereto. This issue will be detailed later. For the record, the free cash flow in year *n* is defined as:

Earnings before interest and taxes (EBIT)
– Corporation tax
+ Depreciation
+ Change in reserves
+/– Change in WCR
+/– Change in investment

Cash flow models used by advisory firms include a large set of adjustable variables and provide a full range of accounting documents, including the income statement, the balance sheet, the cash flow statements, the final valuation summary, and a table of control ratios. After establishing a base case, it is then possible to test various cases and build sensitivity scenarios. Segment revenues are indeed the key variable of any business plan, together with the evolution of the cost structure.

4.1.3.5.2. Main Recommendations When Using Cash Flow Models

1. Have a calibrated future cash flow model. Constructing one's own model may be quite time consuming, especially to ensure that there are no mistakes: It is key to use a reliable and easily configurable model. Many models have limitations and sometimes built-in weaknesses which may lead to making mistakes. Building or selecting a proper one is likely to take a reasonable amount of time. The modelling of the free cash flows is based on the business assumption of what is possibly achievable, in terms of revenues of cost structure in the future. Such cash flows do not include any sort of country risk; they just reflect the capacity of a firm to growth and be profitable through exploiting the opportunities on its market.
2. Work on a timescale consistent with the rapid change of the Chinese market. A scenario based on three + three years is reasonable, and frequently used in order to maintain a certain forecast quality which decreases over time. However, some

capital intensive industries (e.g., cold storage industry, railways) have sufficient visibility and asset resilience to work on long-term forecasts, like real estate, over much longer periods.

3. One must be careful in calculating the terminal value, which is always tricky with the future cash flow method. In China, the obsolescence of business models, the accelerated renewal of fixed assets, and the rapid emergence of local competitors on the most profitable market segments must be taken into account. It is essential that the part of the value based on a visible and easily modelled horizon (three + three years maximum) be more important than the one based on the terminal value; otherwise the company valuation may not make any sense.
4. Calculate the discount rate[58] for future cash flows adapted to the features of emerging markets, even though this is quite difficult. By all means, it may be tempting to increase the risk factor to reflect the lack of knowledge of the Chinese environment. This arbitrary approach leads to incorrect results. The weighted average cost of capital, which has to be used in the calculation, requires to go through the following steps:

   (a) Retrieve the risk-free rate, which must be used for the considered timeline and is published by the Central Bank of China.
   (b) Find the effective interest rate at which the target will access financing — this is a sensitive topic in China. The lack of long-term financing, the use of essentially short-term rates, and the access of companies to indirect financing (e.g., within the context of a stimulus plan, as part of a regional policy), or sometimes, grey market financing, requires some research to calculate an average compounded rate based on the information that the seller is willing to release, which is never easy.
   (c) Calculate the risk premium on equity markets, which can also be difficult. The fact that riskier investments should have higher expected returns than safer investments is central to standard risk and return models in finance. Thus, the

[58] The calculation of the expected return on equity, $i = r_f + \beta_i \times (r_M - r_f)$, is detailed in Section 4.2.4.

expected return on any investment can be written as the risk-free rate plus a risk premium, to compensate for the risk. The disagreement, in both theoretical and practical terms, remains on how to measure this risk, and how to define an acceptable expected return that compensates for such risk. A key number is the premium that investors demand for investing in equities as a class on a certain market, i.e., the equity risk premium.[59] There are three main approaches used to empirically estimate equity risk premiums:

- Survey of investors, expectations about equity returns in the future.
- Historical returns on equities compared to "risk-free" investments.
- Estimated future premium based on the market price of traded assets today.

The financial crisis of 2008 had an unprecedented impact on equity risk premiums. Implied equity risk premiums worldwide rose more during the last quarter of 2008 than in any one of the prior 50 years. In 2009, equity risk premiums gradually returned to pre-crisis levels; however, equity risk premiums have remained more volatile since 2008. The crisis provided a unique opportunity to check how stock markets relate to each other around the planet, and it showed for the first time how the riskier asset classes of the securities markets were closely linked.

(d) Use relevant Betas, as a generally accepted, although imperfect, measure of risk. The Beta of asset *i*, noted β_i is the covariance of asset *i* with the market portfolio/variance of the market portfolio, noted ($\beta_i = \mathrm{Cov}_{i,m}/\sigma^2_m$). Assets with the same market risk as the market portfolio will have a Beta of 1, assets riskier than the market, a

[59] Aswath Damodaran (2013), "Equity Risk Premiums (ERP): Determinants, Estimation and Implications — the 2013 Edition"; available online at SSRN: http://ssrn.com/abstract=2238064 (accessed on October 5, 2014).

Beta > 1, and for those safer than the average, a Beta < 1. The Betas are a measure of the response of a share, bond, or portfolio to a market variation. For example, a stock with a 1.5 Beta has an expected return of 1.5 times that of the market. If the market rates rise 10% above the risk-free rate, the stock must, all things being equal, appreciate by 15%. The Beta is therefore one of the possible ways to measure the risk and correlate it with the expected profitability of the security. The key financial risks related to emerging markets are: expropriation, illiquidity, and information risks.

It may seem strange that emerging market companies consistently have lower Betas, when estimated against global equity indices, than developed market companies, but the Beta is just a relative measure. As far as emerging market stability is concerned, the financial crisis of 2008 has questioned many long-held beliefs about developed economies. It is now possible that international investors, especially those coming from emerging countries, perceive much more volatility in the expected real growth of the Western economies in the future. The problem of emerging markets is that the Betas and the expected rates of return appear to be uncorrelated. The stability of the Beta in emerging countries has also been a controversial issue. As only the historical returns are available to estimate the Beta, it can be questioned if using the historical Beta as an estimate of the future Beta is adequate, especially since empirical evidence shows that Betas on individual stocks are not stable over time.[60]

(e) Define what debt structure deemed "reasonable" should be targeted. It will generally be based on local banking habits and the acquirer financing capacities. In the absence of a precise idea, it can be by default the acquirer's consolidated financial debt structure ratio.

[60] Fama and French (1992, 1996) and Jegadeesh (1992) showed that Betas are not statistically related to returns, and suspected the validity of the Beta in measuring risk.

4.1.3.5.3. The Adjusted Present Value (APV)

Some emerging market investors have developed a taste for the Adjusted Present Value (APV) technique, a variation of the basic DCF methodology, using a three step methodology which is quite simple to understand.

APV = PV(unlevered firm) + PV(tax shield) – PV(bankruptcy costs)

The methodology requires the appraiser to estimate the value of the firm if it was all-equity financed (unlevered firm). The equity-financed base case value is adjusted by the present value of the financing effects from (i) the tax reduction benefits from borrowing money, and (ii) the costs related to the added risk of bankruptcy on emerging markets. The tax shield (fiscal gain) can be determined with a function including the marginal tax rate of the firm, the cost, and level of debt. This methodology works with positive free cash flows only. The evaluation of the bankruptcy cost remains difficult to assess, even if some professionals routinely estimate them to be 15%.[61]

4.1.3.5.4. Valuation Based on Real Options

This valuation method is one of the most advanced, but it remains for advanced types of valuation where the decision to make defining strategic choice is critical, for example, to reorient the business. It also better suits certain types of projects or industrial assets such as mining projects and energy projects. Pricing problems on emerging markets related to the stock market anomalies and the misestimation of the true (historic) volatility from the implied volatility are complicating the use of this type of methodology.

The models used are binomial, or derived from Black–Scholes or Cox Ross Rubinstein. As a reminder, an option is the possibility, but not the obligation, to buy an asset at a given time and price: It is

---

[61] Based on the work of Edward I. Altman (1984), "A Further Empirical Investigation of the Bankruptcy Cost Question," *The Journal of Finance*, XXXIX(4) (September), 1067–1089.

a transaction involving physical and human resources in investment projects characterized by irreversibility and uncertainty. A company can be considered as a portfolio of unlisted options possibly leading to the creation of industrial and financial assets.

Real option models have the following features:

- Create a simulation tool to support decisions involving multiple factors of uncertainty in the investment. They are well suited to China.
- Avoid the "now or never" approach of project assessment, by including probability thresholds for events.

The information on the option market can also be useful to estimate equity risk premiums, as option prices can be used to back out implied volatility in the equity market. This solution is one of the lessons of the last financial crisis, as the link between the equity market volatility and the equity risk premium was clearly established in the last quarter of 2008.

4.2. Risk of an Investment Project in China

A general approach to risk

For a certain investment, the return of a project is calculated through the simulation of a series of future free cash flows discounted by a certain rate — the weighted average cost of capital, which represents the average rate paid to creditors and shareholders for the acquisition of new assets. This rate incorporates a level of risk, including a predefined financing structure.

There are several competing risk and return models in finance, but they share some common assumptions about risk. Risk is defined in terms of variance in actual returns around an expected return, and must be measured from the perspective of a marginal, well-diversified investor putting money in an asset. Therefore, the risk which must be paid for is only an incremental risk to a diversified portfolio. The structure of the risk in any investment is then split into two components: A firm-specific component and a market component that contains risk that affects a large number of assets. It is the latter risk that is not diversifiable and should be rewarded.

The various models will follow different routes to measure and calculate the market risk. The capital asset pricing model measures the market risk by the Beta, which when multiplied by the market equity risk premium on riskless assets, yields the total risk premium for a risky asset. The arbitrage pricing and multi-factor alternative pricing models estimate Betas against the individual market risk factors, and each factor has it own price (risk premium).

In developed countries, it is widely accepted that one of the best discount rates is the weighted average cost of capital (WACC). When the cost of capital is calculated on the basis of the portfolio theory, it is assumed that investors can diversify their portfolio at a negligible cost. Only the portion of non-diversified assets has to be taken into account in the risk calculation. Then, the Beta (β) is accepted as the most common measure of risk. It measures the specific response of a security to a given market change.

In emerging markets, things are a little different, and if one maintains that the Beta is an appropriate measure of risk, many emerging markets would have low investment risks. The portfolio theory supposes that markets are perfectly integrated, meaning that the same securities should have the same profitability, regardless of where they are traded. If the Beta is calculated using returns of a security and returns of a market index formed from security returns from different trading periods, as it happens in almost all the emerging stock exchanges, the Beta are likely to be flawed.

Two problems can affect the quality of the formation of a share price listed on an emerging stock exchange: The stock may be thinly-traded and may display irrational exuberance, sometimes related to pure market gambling, so the share price is used as a proxy for rolling possibly loaded dices. This leads to the problem of non-synchronous trading, where the market prices at the end of a period cannot be accurately matched with the prices of a thinly-traded share. Several methods have been suggested to correct non-synchronous trading[62] in thin markets but so far it does not provide all the solutions to measuring risk in emerging markets.

On emerging markets, Betas and profitability rates are often uncorrelated.[63] The calculated Betas are often too low, and this is a problem for the calculation of a relevant discount rate. Quite often, the risks in emerging markets are perceived as much higher than in mature markets. Therefore, the discount rates are arbitrarily adjusted by the introduction of a "safety cushion" supposedly representing the perceived risk.

Unfortunately, this empirical correction is not consistent with the portfolio theory. It leads to overweighting the risk of misunderstanding a country and increasing safety margins, which consequently leads to incorrect forecasts of real profitability levels of the investment. Indeed, it is generally accepted that investments in developing countries are substantially more risky, and create less added value for investors and shareholders than more mature economic environments. However, the main error is to perceive risk as an entirely negative factor creating underperformance. The less risky countries are not necessarily the most attractive and, using the same logic, those who have a higher risk are not necessarily the less attractive countries. Risks have to be mitigated by information and verified local macroeconomic and competitive data, such as growth rates or the company's competitive advantages compared to competitors.

Risk structure on emerging markets

Emerging economies are characterized by a less structured and more volatile economy than developed countries. They certainly present a wider range of risks. Those risks can be related to: The volatility of the local currency or its convertibility, the weakness of the legal framework, the failures of the education system, social instability, or the fragility of institutions in general. Foreign investors who are not

[62] Blume (1971), Vasicek (1973), Klemkosky and Martin (1975), Scholes and Williams (1977), and Dimson (1979).

[63] The major focus of the CAPM tests has been to check whether returns are statistically positively related to Betas.

familiar with these risks are likely to make costly mistakes during the early years of their business activity. This unfamiliar environment will take them longer than local players to understand the global picture and be able to reach an acceptable internal rate of return.

To address this higher degree of risk and given their lack of knowledge of the market in emerging countries in general, many investors frequently and arbitrarily perform some adjustments to the risk premium to load the model. Typically on the market, as aversion for risk increases, equity premiums will become fatter to compensate for perceived risk. Using a larger equity risk premium unilaterally will increase the expected returns for all risky investments, and by extension, reduce their value. It can be often observed that:

- A risk premium is added to or subtracted from the discount rate. The premium as such, is quite subjective and depends on the country in which one is located.
- The relative volatility of the local stock market index is added to the equation.
- An additional adjustment is made to take into account the level of risk of the country and depends on the expected (or, worse, past) average rate of return of foreign investments.

For most discount rates calculated for developing markets, an adjustment is simply added in the form of a so-called "sovereign risk premium" to the equivalent discount rate in developed countries. However, adding such a premium to the discount rates goes against the principles of the portfolio theory for the following reasons:

- The different projects and/or businesses are not exposed to the same level of risks in each considered country.
- If a "country risk premium" is added, this implies that the risk of this country is present in a systematic way.
- The economic risk of a country is neither stable nor constant in the duration of a long-term investment.
- Generally, this risk premium is simplistically added to reflect the default risk of developing countries.

In real life, it is very difficult to simultaneously evaluate the degree to which the risks of a country are diversifiable or not, i.e., from how many base points the discount rate should be impacted and how to adapt the portfolio theory without altering it. If the country risk really changes the DCF discount rate, the WACC must be adjusted. Most of the time, adding a risk premium is based on perceived risks. In that case, these adjustments do not reflect, in any way, objective information concerning the real risks of such an environment. More substantially, this does not encourage managers to reduce these real perceived risks by digging deeper on how they can manage it. On the contrary, many companies tend to overestimate risk in the discount rate, in order to keep sufficient safety margins in case some unknown risks come to the surface. This is a bit like calculating a route when skipping a boat and adding multiple corrections factors based on judgment, but not on objective parameters, such as wind speed or current. This is not likely to lead to any good result.

Such a so-called "safe approach" only distracts the management from an in-depth analysis of risk factors that must be handled. It is thus dangerous because it destroys any analytical effort. And yet, in many cases, the decision to invest cannot be separated from the investor's risk management policy. The various stakeholders of the project each give more or less value to different risk factors (depending on their expertise), and will reduce or increase their acceptance of these risks. Any investor must classify the risks according to whether or not he can possibly tame or manage them, and not by an external perception of the risk severity on just a theoretical scale. It should clearly answer the ability or inability of the company to manage a risk typology.

As a last resort, the equity risk premium can be generically defined on the basis of historical empirical studies backed up by a study of large equity markets over the 20th century, which concluded that the historical risk premium is close to 4% and possibly a bit more.[64] Generic target risk premiums can be considered for

[64] Elroy Dimson, Paul Marsha, and Mike Staunton (2002), *Triumph of the Optimists: 101 Years of Global Investment Returns*. New Jersey, US: Princeton University Press. A much lower risk premium than the 6% cited by Mehra and Prescott (1985).

emerging markets as the historical data is often irrelevant, or inexistant, due to the immaturity of the stock markets.

4.2.1. *Risks Should Be Analyzed, Understood, and Classified*

Initially, it is a good practice to define an analysis matrix[65] of the perceived risks of the planned investment in China by type of investment (majority, minority, business partnership), in order to understand the risk differences compared to an investment in a more mature economy:

- Country related risk — although capturing it in the Beta is potentially tricky.
- Macroeconomic risks — they are often singled out but must be embedded in the country risk analysis using aggregated indicators,[66] or specific indicators such as bond default spreads or credit default spreads, used as proxies for country risk and directly added to the cost of equity and debt.
- Industry risks — a very specific set of risks compared to the global economy, e.g., the food industry compared to the Chinese economy.
- Operational risks — supply, demand, local environment, international markets.

Admittedly, the scale of these risks is very different, depending on whether one is located in China, Ukraine, or Algeria. The quality of the development of China shows that the country is striving to achieve, and in some case even exceed, the investors' expectations, notably regarding the development of quality infrastructures:

- Country related risk, e.g.: Payment difficulties is not a relevant factor as the banking system in China is reliable.

---

[65] Donald R. Lessard (1996), "Incorporating Country Risk in the Valuation of Offshore Projects," *Journal of Applied Corporate Finance*, 9(3), 52–63.

[66] The Economist and the Political Risk Services (PRS) group produces country risk rankings from 0 to 100 including political, financial, and economic risk indicators.

- Macroeconomic risks, e.g.: Currency fluctuations — the Chinese Yuan appreciated with the development of the economy.
- Operational risks, e.g.: gap in education — China has a solid education system and excellent universities, even if all regions have not reached the same level of development. It is quite possible to recruit talents during the business development, even in some regions more "remote" than the large coastal cities.

Completing the analysis grid allows for a much clearer, structured, and rational framework of what the perceived risks of an investment really are.

Following this analysis, it is likely that the rationally measured risk, initially perceived compared to the risk, will have substantially diminished, which shows that risk is not a static factor. This is due to the decrease of the risk of not being familiar with a given environment, which is a diversifiable and manageable risk, unlike the sovereign risk which, save in specific cases, is an exogenous constraint — for example, in countries where there is no rule of law.

The dynamics of risk tend to be different from those prevailing in a familiar environment. For example, the investment risk in an emerging country can differ depending on the accessibility and support of administrative requirements to foreign companies compared to local companies. In China, unlike in India in the past, the government has put very significant efforts to attract foreign companies and ensure that they would feel comfortable in the long run. They were encouraged to inject capital and train their talents to support the country's development. From this risk typology, it is possible to create a detailed matrix, which allows to empirically calculate a global Beta by assessing the magnitude of the risks, by analogy between the risks mapped for a developed country and those mapped for an emerging country.

The comparative advantages related to the ability to cover the encountered risks may be caused by the following facts:

- Information is not shared under perfect market conditions.
- Investors are likely to have different levels of control on the probability that certain risks will materialize. This may be related to

their professional experiences and the quality of the relationships built with the country in the past.

- Investors may differ in their ability to diversify risks (as a consequence of the two reasons above).

To illustrate the three advantages seen above, the example of a Korean company investing in an independent Chinese car manufacturer can be reviewed. The advantage of this investor lies in his past experience and his long lasting practice of successful acquisitions and investments. The Korean company thus has a good understanding of the economic development of China, which is a neighboring country, and is able to make reasonably good forecasts for the years

Table 4.4. Risks Matrix in Emerging Countries.

Risk Typology	Foreign Strategic Investors/ Operators	Local Strategic Investors/ Partners	International Investors	Local Investors	International Fund Providers (e.g., World Bank)
		Investor Profile			
1. Supply chain					
• construction	+	+/++			
• operations	++	+?			
2. Demand					
• GDP growth	+?	+	+	+?	+
• distribution channel		+			
3. Local environment	+?	+	+	+	+
• regulations	+	+		+?	+
• economy		+		+	
• stability					
4. International markets					
• oil price			+		+
• steel price			+		+
• interest rate			+	+	+

Note: ? = applicable to the case

to come. This understanding and familiarity with China enables it to work better on the key factors of success, and simultaneously reduce potential risks. There are several methods in order to carry out a risk analysis, but the most effective is to build a risk matrix and refine it by successive iterations.

This risk matrix is based on four types of risks: (a) supply chain, (b) demand, (c) local environment, and (d) international markets. Usually, risks related to international markets are considered exogenous, unless the company is a significant player and its products are traded on the local or international market. In case the company is a coffee producer (beans), one can anticipate that adverse climate changes will have a negative impact on harvests, reducing supply and then resulting in higher coffee bean prices, down to the end user.

(a) Supply chain: Through its technical expertise and its local experience, our Korean company is likely to have a significant advantage in the management of supply risks. This competitive advantage makes his company more prone to accepting being exposed to great operational risks, compared to a European one without any significant business knowledge of China. In the case of a minority joint venture, the Korean company could even attempt to negotiate an additional share of profit — more than the one owned from its equity investment, as a reward of an exceptional performance measured by a set of operational benchmarks.
(b) Demand: Comparative advantages regarding the ability to cover risks heavily depends on institutional stability and the quality of the economy of the country. Our Korean company may nevertheless have a problem on systematic risks diversification if this project is only part of a large industrial project portfolio targeting China.
(c) Local environment: This risk is related to the probability that the local rules may change. Contrary to what may be initially assumed, emerging countries are not inherently less stable than developed countries. The frequent changes in tax policy or regulations in Europe or the United States have clearly proved this.

The key questions are rather the following: Is the asset protection of foreigner owners guaranteed? Will the gross domestic product and the gross national income per capita increase? How can the risks related to local price fluctuations be hedged on international markets?

(d) International Markets: The exposure of the project to international prices fluctuations is linked to a precise understanding of the world commodity market, the company's ability to diversify and cover its risks, and its ability to pass the raw material price increase to the end customer. For example, the launch by Nestlé of a new take-away cold coffee drink in China is sensitive to the price of some key materials — the price of coffee, milk, quality water, plastic for the container, and electricity to refrigerate the bottle — all of the risks related to these raw materials being sorted and prioritized in the price of the end product. The risk of raw materials does not only apply to one company but also all its other competitors. In some cases, the volatility of one key component of a product may be cushioned by some new regulations promulgated by the Chinese authorities (e.g., electricity supply at a preferential rate), but these practices are more restricted since the entry of China into the WTO.

4.2.2. *Free Cash Flows Must Be Risk-Adjusted with the Discount Rate*

In an emerging country, one must take into account a broad spectrum of risks and isolate the "symmetrical" risks from the "asymmetrical" risks. Both ends of the spectrum will impact the valuations calculated by the free cash flows method.

"Symmetrical" risks are related to the sensitivity of the target to price fluctuations on international markets. They will have an impact on the risk level and not on cash flows. They reduce the value of an investment insofar as they contribute to the increase of the volatility of an asset portfolio, and consequently increase the profitability requirement of this portfolio. The impact of such additional investment on the portfolio of an investor is measured by its Beta (or its variation) compared to the Beta of the market. These risks will have a limited impact on cash flows but will be taken into account in the discount rate.

"Asymmetric" risks are related to the sensitivity of the target to its external environment and in particular, expropriation, riot, war risks, and not being familiar with the country and its culture. These risks have a higher probability to negatively impact cash flows rather than positively impact them. They will decrease cash flow forecasts by impacting total revenues and the present value of the investment, whatever its contribution to the portfolio volatility or the IRR of the investment. These risks usually have limited impact in terms of portfolio volatility, but lead to lower cash flow expectations.

As an example, the risks that most contribute to the volatility of a European portfolio are those related to economic factors specific to Europe or to international markets, such as the quality of the EU member sovereign debt. In contrast, the risk related to social unrest, riots, or social cash in small countries, for local reasons, will have little impact on the volatility of a diversified European portfolio. However, an investment in an emerging market, whose value is derived from the state of the world economy rather than local factors, will result in a higher risks premium, e.g., the return of investment in a tar sand or oil shale extraction project is related to the international oil price. In such a case, the discount rate used should be higher than the average discount rate of the market. As a result, free future cash flows of projects exposed to well-identifiable downside risks will be lower than those which would be forecasted, all things being equal, in an economically stable environment. The decrease of future cash flow is *de facto* comparable to the increase of the discount rate, but the impact on cash flows, by comparison to the increase of the discount rate, will be more specific and limited in time. This is illustrated by the experience curve which can be modelled as a financial penalty decreasing with time, correlated to the lack of knowledge of a defined economic environment.

It will always take some time to build a good economic model of the project, integrating the key financial data and the asymmetric risks in the calculation of free cash flows. Then, a simulation based on a Monte Carlo model can be used to establish the probability law for the company or the project's values.

The results must then be crossed with those from scenarios using different discount rates, in order to obtain a correct multiple entry table for facilitating the decision-making process.

4.2.3. *Adjusting the Calculation of the Cost of Capital to Emerging Countries*

The fundamental technique to assess investments in emerging countries is the calculation of an IRR using the discounted future cash flows method. The standard approach to this calculation by discounted free cash flows (DCF) is based on the correct calculation of the free cash flows, the real cost of debt, and equity.

The weighted average cost of capital (WACC) discussed previously is the cost of real money that a company should pay back to its creditors (cost of debt) and to its shareholders (cost of equity) to finance the acquisition of additional assets in the company. The weighted average cost of capital is then the minimum yield that a company must generate to satisfy its creditors, shareholders, and other backers. The weighted average cost of capital is defined by the cost of equity (Ke) calculated with the capital asset pricing model:

$$\text{Ke} = r_f + \beta(u_m - r_f).$$

The first part of the sum (r_f) is the long-term risk-free rate, usually calculated by using the rate of a first category government bond.

The second part is the additional risk premium required to remunerate this type of investment on the stock markets.

The formula $\beta(u_m - r_f)$ is the result of the Beta of the investment, measuring the volatility of a stock, more precisely, the variation factor of a stock with regards to market fluctuations, multiplied by the market risk premium (the premium paid to investors to invest in a stock market rather than in a risk-free government bond rated AAA). As it was previously discussed, the issue of emerging markets, and therefore China, is that risk measured by Betas and yields measured by dividends seem uncorrelated. This situation makes it difficult to calculate a discount rate accurately representing the risks taken by investors.

In the CAPM model, the relevant risk is the market risk that measures the returns sensitivity of a particular risky security or a portfolio of risky securities, to the returns of market portfolio. The CAPM is based on the availability of two fundamentals — a true market portfolio and the market risk — and it is probably one of the most tested models in the financial literature. The French-American mathematician, Benoit Mandelbrot, father of the fractal theory, calls into question the validity of the Markowitz theory and its corollary, the CAPM, developed by Sharpe.

In his numerous studies, including his historical study of the exchange rate of cotton for over more than a century,[67] Mandelbrot considers the Chicago School theories to be disconnected from financial market realities, in particular, in the case of crisis or irrational exuberance leading to the extreme behaviors of actors. The classic theories have been repeatedly challenged since, in particular, during the various stock market crashes that they were unable to predict. They have led to risk management errors and wrong decisions in most financial institutions.

The WACC is based on a normal distribution assumption (Gauss law), which strongly underestimates the "unlikely" events such as economic crisis or crashes, when they are ultimately much less rare than this probability law predicts. Furthermore, the assumptions on which these theories are based seem too simplistic (investor rationality, continuity and independence of price changes, etc.).

After having gauged the limits of the available tools, it is necessary to adjust the calculation of the Beta specifically to emerging countries in order to calculate the cost of equity, or radically change methodology. In the latter case, however, one must be wary of the market consensus; unconventional methods, as accurate as they are, will cause pedagogy problems if they are used during negotiations.

---

[67] Benoit Mandelbrot (1963), "The Variation of Certain Speculative Prices," *The Journal of Business*, 36(4), 394–419.

Calculating the Beta of a project in emerging countries, in relation to a benchmark portfolio, can usually be "synthesized" using two empirical methods:

- Directly, by regressing the profitability of a relevant sample of local stocks in relation to a local stocks portfolio, which will be adjusted for the most obvious anomalies and differences in financial structures. This requires to pay special attention to the choice of the portfolio components, especially in China where risk can be uncorrelated to profitability.
- Indirectly, by estimating the Beta of the project in relation to a portfolio of local assets prioritized according to an analysis based on a multifactor risk matrix, whose result will be multiplied by a country-related risk coefficient, China's Beta, compared to the country of the investor's Beta portfolio (probably close to 1 for a European player).

4.2.4. *Using Advanced Composite Discount Rate*

A pioneering work was done by Donald R. Lessard in MIT (1996), who tried to solve the problem of unreliable local information by combining emerging market information with mature economy data, and designed the first of the so-called hybrid models. He calculates the cost of equity by determining the risk premium investors would require for a comparable project, if it were based in the US. This premium, which is calculated on the basis of US equity market data and a comparable project's Beta, is then multiplied with the country Beta of the investment's geographical location. However, he stresses that the risk is declining over time and that it could be reduced by additional work to better understand the country.

Godfrey and Espinosa (1996) later argue that the application of the country Beta as computed by Lessard often leads to confusing results, if the valuation takes place in the context of emerging markets. Countries like Venezuela or Sri Lanka have a negative country Beta in relation to developed markets, leading to negative risk premiums for investments in these countries, due to the absence of correlation between the market returns in emerging markets with those on the global level.

Another model developed for Goldman Sachs by Mariscal and Hargis (1999) is elegantly derived from the above ideas, but introduces more company-specific components:

$$R_E = R_{f,US} + (R_S + R_C) + \left(\frac{\sigma_L}{\sigma_{US}}\right) \times \beta_{S,L} \times MRP_{US} \times (1 - corr(S, B))$$

The concept of an individual company-specific risk is an elegant and new factor, R_S, which can be positive or negative, and depends on the company and industry characteristics with the country risk premium, R_C, just added on top.

Mariscal and Hargis prefer using the relative volatility risk, σ_L/σ_{US}, instead of the covariance used by Lessard, when determining a specific country's risk. The model also accounts for the target company's Beta to the local economy with the factor, $\beta_{S,L}$. Finally, the last term adjusts for the double counting of risks that occurs by using the sovereign spread as country risk premium.

The Goldman-Sachs model is designed to provide clarity in the analysis, and splits the various risk drivers that constitute and influence the discount rate. Firstly, the US risk-free long-term interest rate and the stock market equity premium determine the global investor expectations. Then, the country risk premium and the relative volatility risk are the domestic macroeconomic indicators measuring the risk of the target company's economic environment. In addition, the company-specific risk premium and Beta take the individual risk characteristics of the object into account.

However, there are no guidelines on how to calculate the sensitive company-specific risk premium, R_S. In addition, combining the Beta of the target company with the local market data calls for only even more questioning on mixing together so many unreliable long-term data in emerging markets. Finally, adjusting the Beta by the relative volatility factor has been heavily criticized as meaningless.[68]

---

[68] Harvey (2001).

4.2.5. *Pricing on Downside Risk*

Risk can be revisited on how poorly an investment can perform if things go really wrong; there is now increasing evidence showing that downside risk is priced by investors. A pricing model based on downside risk aims at replacing the Beta and the CAPM with the downside Beta and the D-CAPM when estimating the cost of capital in emerging markets. The correlation between returns and the downside Beta was found to be much stronger than between returns and the Beta. The downside Beta outperforms the Beta not only in terms of statistical significance but also of economic significance.

The measure of downside risk was developed at about the same time that Markowitz developed the mean-variance theory. Roy (1952) was the first to formally model downside risk. In his model, an investor would prefer safety of principal first, and the resulting technique is termed "safety-first" technique. Estrada (2002) later argues against the use of the traditional CAPM, as its founding assumptions are violated in emerging markets. In addition, Estrada argues against the Beta, as the variance of returns is a dubious measure of risk, applicable only to symmetric and normally distributed values. And, as the CAPM basic foundations are already heavily debatable in developed countries, they are even more debatable in developing countries where the markets are imperfect and access to information difficult.

As a measure of the downside risk, the semi-deviation of returns captures the very risk that investors want to avoid, rather than performance. The idea is to turn risk upside down and focus on what the likely economic impact of a counter performance is if one only considers the left-hand downside tail of the returns distribution in the calculation. Calculating downside risk is simple, and practitioners can apply it just as easily as the conventional CAPM to calculate a D-CAPM.

For an asset noted A_i, its required rate of return R is:

$$R_i = R_f + M_i * \text{MRP}. \quad (1)$$

The required rate of return R_i splits into two parts: a risk-free rate (R_f) and a risk premium. MRP is the world market's risk premium, and M_i the risk of the asset i, that is to say, its Beta in the portfolio theory.

The first part is the time value of money of a risk-free asset; the second part is the additional risk premium required to remunerate an investment on the stock market.

Under the downside risk approach, the downside risk of A_i is set as the downside volatility of the asset relative to the downside volatility of the market portfolio. The downside volatility is then measured as the semi-deviation on asset returns. The semi-deviation on the returns of A_i is the standard deviation of the asset's downside returns.

Denote semi-deviation with respect to any equity benchmark B, as $\sum B$, which can be applied to A_i, and we have:

$$\sum_B = \sqrt{\left(\frac{1}{T}\right) * \sum_{t=1}^{T} [\min(R_t - B),\ 0]^2}. \qquad (2)$$

When B is the mean return, semi-deviation measures the spread of outcomes under the mean. Semi-deviation can be measured to any benchmark returns, thus making it a very flexible and effective tool in risk analysis. This measure of downside risk is widely used by capital investment professionals to evaluate fund performance.

As can be seen from the formula, only returns below a certain threshold would be considered in semi-deviation. Thus, the focus is on the downside of asset returns. This is consistent with investors' perception of risk.

The downside risk measure for an asset i can be calculated as the ratio of the semi-deviation of the returns of asset i to the semi-deviation of the returns of the world market portfolio, in the form:

$$M_i = \frac{\text{semi} - s_i}{\text{semi} - s_M}. \qquad (3)$$

It is then easy to derive the cost of capital for investing in asset *i* as:

$$R_i = R_F + \frac{\text{semi} - \text{s}_i}{\text{semi} - \text{s}_M} * \text{MRP}. \tag{4}$$

The return must be calculated on the basis of log returns, which are more accurate than simple returns. The advantage of pricing downside risk is that it is a statistical observation and not a qualitative assessment, and has the following advantages:

- In emerging markets, the stock yields are usually correlated with a systematic risk (and specific risk) measured by the Beta.
- Yields on equity markets are correlated to the total of the risks measured by the standard deviation.
- The stock returns are correlated with the downside risks measured by the semi-variance of yields, in accordance with the average or downside Beta.
- Calculating the cost of capital based on the semi-variance seems more rigorous than a calculation based on the systematic risk or the total risk (systematic + specific).

This approach seems fairly robust in theory and is easily usable by practitioners. Moreover, it can be used at a macroeconomic and microeconomic level. This approach is based on a pure statistical measure and a necessarily subjective judgment (as opposed to risk premiums calculated from score cards). It can be used at the market level and at the company level, and can be adjusted to any desired benchmark return to capture the downside risk that investors want to avoid.

The differences in results between this method and the synthetic Betas are too important to overlook, as it was found that that around two-thirds of the time standard Beta would underestimate the downside risk.[69] Estrada has conducted extensive research which

[69] James Chong, Yanbo Jin, and G. Michael Phillips (2013), "The Entrepreneur's Cost of Capital: Incorporating Downside Risk in the Buildup Method," MacroRisk Analytics Working Paper Series; available online at www.macrorisk.com/wp-content/uploads/2013/04/MRA-WP-2013-e.pdf (accessed on October 7, 2014).

provides evidence that the D-CAPM is better able to explain the cross-section of returns in emerging markets than the traditional method. The downside Beta is on average 50% higher than the standard Beta for emerging markets, whereas the difference is much smaller for developed countries. This result shows that emerging market risks are better captured by the downside volatility than by traditional CAPM. On average, the D-CAPM leads to an increase of the required cost of equity by 250 basis points.

4.3. Getting Ready for Negotiations in China

4.3.1. *Choosing the Right Chief Negotiator*

The first important decision is to choose the chief negotiator as he/she needs to be well-accepted by the corresponding Chinese negotiating delegation; soft power is important to conquer the China market. A large part of the success of the negotiation will be on his/her shoulders. Choosing the right person is not a light decision to make, as it will be a defining decision for the success of the contemplated transaction. One must be prepared to allocate a substantial amount of time to the case and make sure that all the details of the negotiation are properly monitored.

Chinese people are very sensitive to power, honor, and hierarchy in general. Therefore, this individual, male or female, must have a title, a good academic background, and a professional track record capable of empowering him to naturally lead the discussions without any doubt. However, it is understood that he/she may not be the only decision-maker in the process, but soon the Chinese negotiators would like to know who the decision-makers are *in fine* and who is responsible for what.

Maturity is equally important and Asian tradition automatically gives a higher status to seniority and grey hairs. The negotiator is expected to know China and to have kept regular contact with this country. This knowledge of Asia is likely to help him understand that patience is important and to keep control of his temper even in the worst of situations. Those in a position of authority cannot afford to admit lack of knowledge or mistakes which will likely cause them to "lose face".

It is important that he can stand as a seasoned professional with a flexible but determined personality capable of adjusting to the style of negotiations as needed, and keep a clear mind on the objectives without compromising the global economics of the transaction.

This may sound a bit of a surreal description of the needed profile, but this is actually what is needed for the job. And people capable of fulfilling this task are not that many.

4.3.2. *Greeting Your Future Partner Properly as First Impressions Tend to Last*

About everyone knows now that it is not very auspicious to forget or neglect to bring one's business cards for an important meeting in China. A substantial amount must be brought, and they should be bilingual in order to be able to introduce oneself properly. The exchange of business cards is one of the first steps in getting to know one's partner and it is part of the Chinese etiquette. However, officials will tend to be reluctant to give their business cards, but will happily accept yours.

In the West, getting to know one's partner socially is deemed less essential, and it may even be the opposite: It is after doing some business that people try to get to know one another. An objective negotiation based on hard facts often takes precedence over personal relationships even in a simple business transaction in China. In the West, it is almost the same: For complex and possibly long negotiations it is certainly necessary that the future partners develop a form of empathy to better trust and understand each other, and in due course, learn to moderate their respective corporate egos. Both cultures are thus not so different. A deeper level of knowledge may be necessary, in some industries, and specifically if the relationship with the seller takes the form of a partnership. A specific part of the due diligence is dedicated to this aspect.[70]

It is easy to pick up on the most visible part of the Chinese culture, but it is more difficult to understand more subtle signals or real

---

[70] See Section 3.1 on third party due diligence.

concerns. Therefore, some prudence is required in professional relationships and one must beware of the feeling of being too comfortable. The progressive access to these deeper elements of Chinese culture allows a better understanding of the other party. However, this takes time and good guidance in order to properly address this dimension. Nothing replaces experience and immersion in the Chinese world. One must pay attention to Chinese and Western values which are often symmetrical to one another. This applies to, in particular, respect for seniority in business, the style used to solve problems (direct or indirect), hierarchy, and consensus.

It is therefore essential to quickly find the best partners on two levels: industrial (to develop the core business) and friendly sponsors (to build a strong base and a brand image). This approach will help level many difficulties later and help expand one's network. This should be treated as an initial investment and considered as part of the entry ticket to China. The cultural wealth and diversity of the overseas Chinese diaspora can help bridge this knowledge gap with China. This option should be carefully reviewed though, without forgetting that Chinese counterparts in the West may not necessarily make the best local partners back in China to understand local issues.

It will never be possible to understand everything and control every step while conducting business in China. It is therefore necessary for the partnerships to operate smoothly, and to be able to test whether the parties are capable of having a quality relationship and balanced ego trips to work properly together. Part of the business has to be delegated after explaining what is expected, repeatedly if necessary, and controlled with a smooth, but firm, manner that ensures the results are in line with the objectives previously set.

"Face" is a term both essential in business behavior and in the status of a person. It is the sense of personal honor and the dignity of an individual facing his peers. Foreigners should pay close attention to this, and avoid offending their Chinese counterparts, often clumsily, which limit their chances for a possible collaboration. A few careless comments or bad jokes can do much harm.

One has to experience it to really measure its impact, understand how to manage business, and move forward while taking into account these peculiarities. A mutual understanding will deepen the relationship, develop a friendly and trusting relationship, and mitigate the risk of embarrassing the other party by an inappropriate comment.

4.3.3. *Developing Your Network*

Business relationships often first come from a friendly face-to-face personal relationship ("Guanxi"). This term is quite untranslatable for the Chinese; it expresses network, proximity, contact, personal knowledge, relationship, and trust. It is an essential ingredient to grease the wheels of a rather complex economic and politic machinery at both the national and local levels. However, when this concept is expanded to the business environment at large, it quickly collides with the increasingly precise set of laws and internal corporate regulations collected under the compliance umbrella, including the US Foreign Corrupt Practices Act (FCPA), the United Kingdom Bribery Act (UKBA), and the Chinese Anti-Corruption laws. Each of these laws aim at levelling the playing field by, in one way or another, forbidding the bribing of those responsible for deciding on commercial contracts.[71]

It must however be remembered that the Chinese regulatory-legal system is not based on Guanxi and exemptions, especially when there are foreigners involved in a deal. There are specific laws applicable to M&A and partnerships which constitute a comprehensive framework that every businessman should know and respect. The involvement of any political connections in a case should not lead one to think that the law can be broken without consequences: One must, on the contrary, be especially vigilant and meticulous in respecting the law, and quickly search remedies if, due to problems

[71] Ken Kedl (2013), "RISK MANAGEMENT: Reading Backwards to Assess Risk," in *Orientation China Guidebook: Opportunities and Challenges for U.S. Small and Medium Enterprises in China's Growing Consumer Market*, p. 30. Shanghai, China: Amcham.

of interpretation, the line is passed. Chinese traditions and the increasingly precise anti-corruption set of laws are creating a complex and riskier environment for doing business in China, especially if commercial practices are not carefully regulated by the company's code of conduct and strictly enforced at the highest level.

The Party's clear statement that it will go after both "tigers" and "flies" in corruption cases could result in a new, far-healthier relationship between politics and business. Wu Hui, an Associate Professor of governance at the CPC Central Committee Party School, said that although publicly funded extravagance fuelled the consumer sector in the days before the crackdown, the prosperity it created was "illusory" and had to be stopped. "When businessmen invited officials to dinner or gave them gifts, they expected something in return. The 'return result' was intangible, but represented a huge loss of national wealth."[72]

As any other relationship, Guanxi is bilateral. This is quite normal and understandable and it has to be developed in this direction in order to bring one's credibility and empathy in China to fruition. The reciprocity associated with it, which the Chinese call "hui bao", is a crucial element of the relationship that is otherwise not considered as moral. One must, by way of reciprocity, capitalize on Guanxi, which is the vector of trust in China. A lack of reciprocity will result in bringing the relationship to an end, or even in developing a bad relationship in the future.

It goes without saying that a relationship by e-mail or telephone does not have the same impact. These personal relationships will be later transformed into trade relationships and may become an essential part of the long-term growth of any company in China. They will then often come in addition to a contractual relationship through which everything cannot be predicted. In the changing environment of Chinese law and its national, regional, and local enforcement, this relationship is essential in order to avoid being

---

[72] Zheng Yanpeng, "Austerity Campaign Takes Corruption off the Menu," CHINADAILY.COM.CN, March 7, 2014; available online at www.chinadaily.com.cn/2014-03/07/content_17328984.htm (accessed on October 8, 2014).

involved in litigations that would likely result in a loss of precious time and credibility. In parallel, a well-structured politic of public relations is vital to better understand the complexities of the Chinese world and develop relationships based on a mutual understanding, allowing to explain the mission and objective of the company. A regular attendance with a good involvement in events serving public interests will enable the company to strengthen its relationship with the community by sending out a more profound and genuine image of the social responsibility of the company.

4.3.4. *Enticing Good Luck*

Luck is a central concept of business in China and related matters must be watched out for; other countries like India are also very sensitive to auspicious or unauspicious times to do business. Chinese businesses will tend to be sensitive too, especially as the size of their business increases, and they will chose important business meetings according to times and locations prone to entice luck. The latter is also a matter of harmony and intimacy with the elements: water, wood, fire, earth, and metal. Each of the elements represents a different state of energy in interaction with each other; they are closely related to Chinese geomancy and astrology.

Some numbers are important for Chinese people and, very often, this belief resides very deep in their mindset. Numbers like 6, 8, or 9 are considered lucky and auspicious. The number 8 ("Ba") is good, as it is referring to the 8 diagrams, the 8 immortals, the 8 treasures, the Buddhist eightfold path to enlightenment. Others, especially the number 4 are not considered lucky; 4 ("Si") is a doomed number as its pronunciation in Chinese is close to the word "death".

Chinese businessmen are generally very careful about this. It is recognized that the environment is based on an invisible life energy (the "qi" — the vital breath), which, accumulated, provides harmony, prosperity, wealth, and honor. Conversely, when poorly channelled, the "qi" brings plagues and misfortunes. Meaningful budgets are spent by Chinese businessmen to study and dispose of their business according to the "feng shui" (wind-water) principles. Feng shui stems from the Taoist movement based on the complementary yin and yang. The feng shui masters are consulted, almost systematically in Southern China, to answer these questions and determine the layout and the orientation of the openings of offices and homes to better channel the "qi" and good luck.

4.3.5. *Understanding the Chinese Cultural Context*

Chinese people are always very proud of their ten thousand years of continuous history, making China one of the world's oldest civilizations. Therefore, summarizing the history of Chinese culture is a challenge much beyond the scope of this book. In a nutshell, Confucianism, Daoism (Taoism), and Buddhism are generally considered the three pillars of Chinese philosophy.

The first written evidence of Chinese culture can be found as early as the Shang dynasty (c. 1700–1046 BC), although ancient texts such as the *Records of the Grand Historian* (ca. 100 BC) and *Bamboo Annals* suggest the existence of a Xia dynasty before the Shang dynasty.

The constituents of the Chinese culture are plural. In the course of history, acrimonious debates have opposed the various schools of spirituality, philosophy, and wisdom that together constitute China's cultural fabric. Confucianism, Daoism, and Buddhism were never unified, but divided among a variety of schools under the stewardship of numerous masters. Furthermore, while several of these schools have been dealing with the practicalities of state and family government, their aim and scope were loftier and larger. Chinese thought cannot be summarized into a set of "ready-to-made" advices and rules of conduct: Its favorite channel of expression was storytelling and conversations, and stories are susceptible to receiving a variety of interpretations in space and time that keep their ultimate meaning open.[73]

---

[73] Benoit Vermander (2013), *Corporate Social Responsibility in China*. Singapore: World Scientific Publishing, p. 48.

(i) A (very) brief overview of Chinese classic philosophers

Chinese philosophers like to illustrate, in vivid and lively short stories, situations where the wise man can find a way to assert his capacity to step back and master a complex situation.

Many of them derive their teachings from the ancient culture of China, inherited from the thinking of classical masters, including Lao Tze (6th century BC), Confucius (551–479 BC), Zhuangzi (4th century BC), and Mencius (4th century BC). Daoism stands alongside Confucianism as one of the two great religious/philosophical systems of China.

Lao Tze sees nature as the founder in a world in perpetual movement, lacking stability, but not without harmony. He highlights the existence of a path (harmony), the importance of non-doing, and the existence of two superior forces: the "Yin" and "Yang". Yin: Earth and moon, the feminine side of nature, shows flexibility, rest, and unresponsiveness. Yang: Sky and sun, the masculine side of nature, marks rigidity, movement, and activeness. The world is thus blurred: the good/evil, the feminine/masculine. Civilization is vain and contradiction is a condition of the world. Taoism is a philosophy and a Chinese religion.

Confucius forges a network of values whose goal is the harmonious relationship of human beings. He seeks to establish a positive moral, structured by "rites" and invigorated by "sincerity", emphasizing studies and rectitude. His teachings, although mainly directed towards the training of future men of power, was open to all. The basis of culture is made by society, of which family and clan are the pivots and prevail over individuals. The man of virtue, the gentleman ("junzi"), is opposed to the little man, ignorant and vulgar ("xiaoren"). He attaches great importance to the ethics of kindness, a virtue of humanity in order to keep at bay sources of misfortune or suffering for others. He stresses the importance of human virtues such as filial piety, loyalty, justice, fidelity, wisdom, and courage.

Zhuangzi does care about human beings — the only being trying to break away from the "Dao" by imposing its action and speech. The attempts to talk about reality, aiming to acquire the basis of the founding knowledge of actions, are futile because speech only divides this reality. He advocates a philosophy of skepticism, realizing himself in non-action, and raises the question of reality: "Confucius and you are both dreaming! And when I say you are dreaming, I am dreaming, too."

Mencius is probably best known for the view that "human nature is good"; a view of human nature on the basis of which he defended the Confucian ideal and developed an account of the self-cultivation process. He elaborated on the Confucian ideal by highlighting four ethical attributes — *ren* (benevolence, humaneness), *li* (observance of rites), *yi* (propriety), and *zhi* (wisdom). Mencius regarded the transformative power of a cultivated person as the ideal basis for government. In addition, he spelled out more explicitly the idea that order in society depends on proper attitudes within the family, which in turn depends on cultivating oneself.[74]

(ii) Military strategy as a guide for business acumen

Military strategy has a well-defined space in the mindset of Chinese people, as the art of winning a battle closely interacts with philosophy, recreation, and aesthetics. Chinese chess (Xiangqi) is a very popular game in China, and references to the game date back to the Warring States period. The traditional Xiangqi board is a grid of ten horizontal lines and nine vertical lines. The object of Xiangqi is to either checkmate or stalemate your opponent's General. Your opponent is checkmated when you have attacked his General (placed him in check) and he cannot eliminate the check with any move.

The Xiangqi tactics, together with the "Art of War" by Sun Tzu (544–496 BC), are probably the most popular pieces of strategy in the Chinese psyche. They are present, a bit like watermarks, in the mindset of Chinese businessmen. Tactics are considered a must, especially if the objective is noble, and making money is a perfectly noble one. This sometimes results in this strange impression that Chinese negotiators are concealing some of the "truth" (as defined

---

[74] Bryan Van Norden and Kwong Loi Shun, "Mencius," in Edward N. Zalta (ed.), *The Stanford Encyclopedia of Philosophy* (Summer 2014 Edition); available online at http://plato.stanford.edu/archives/sum2014/entries/mencius/ (accessed on October 8, 2014).

in the West), as they are trying to find a way to focus on more important things to reach their objective.

Sun Tzu, a military strategist and General who served the State of Wu near the end of the Spring and Autumn period (770–476 BC), is considered the author of *The Art of War*, but the piece is likely to have been written early in the Warring States period (475–221 BC), at a time when China was divided into six or seven belligerent states at war with each other in their struggle for supremacy.

The Art of War is a systematic guide to strategy and tactics for rulers and battle commanders. It analyzes various manoeuvres and the effect of terrain on the outcome of battles. Ruse is considered a cardinal virtue worthy of appearing at a higher level of the Chinese culture. *The Art of War* emphasizes:

- The importance of accurate information about the enemy forces, dispositions and deployments, and movements. This is summarized in the axiom — "Know the enemy and know yourself, and you can fight a hundred battles with no danger of defeat."[75]
- The unpredictability of battle and the use of flexible strategies and tactics.

The book's insistence on the close relationship between political considerations and military policy greatly influenced some modern military strategists. The Chinese communists took from *The Art of War* many of the tactics they utilized in fighting the Japanese invaders and, later, the Guomindang, a political party that governed all or part of Mainland China from 1928 to 1949.

Finally, it may be useful to reflect upon some of the classic "stratagem" maxims (*Thirty-Six Stratagems*) as it may help inspire one's own grid of reading and negotiation.

- Lure the tiger out of the mountain.
- Toss out a brick to attract a piece of jade.
- Conceal a dagger with a smile.

[75] Sunzi Sun Tzu (1994), *The Art of War*. New York: Basic Books, Chapter 3.

- Lure the enemy onto the roof, then take away the ladder.
- Muddle the water to catch the fish.

(iii) Religions

Since 1949, China has been governed by the Communist Party of China (CPC), founded in July 1921 in Shanghai by Chen Duxiu and Li Dazhao. The Party suffered heavy losses fighting with the Kuomintang (KMT) in 1926–1927, and a new party was built by Mao Zedong and Zhou Enlai. The new CCP consolidated its leadership and cadre during the Long March, 1934–1937; was able to drive out the KMT after the defeat of the Japanese; and in 1949, declared the founding of the People's Republic of China (PRC).[76] In the Sino–Soviet split of the '50s, Mao distanced himself from Marxism–Leninism and developed a Chinese interpretation of Communism. After Mao's death in 1976, Deng Xiaoping shifted the ideal of China towards "market socialism". The CPC founded mainly on ideology and politics is the ruling party of Mainland China (PRC). The CPC, an atheist organization with 86.7 million members, regulates the practice of religion in Mainland China. It formally and institutionally recognises five religions in China: Buddhism, Taoism, Islam, Protestantism, and Catholicism.

Buddhism provides China with another set of cultural resources that are deeply ingrained in Chinese culture. Present in China for the two last millennia, the Buddha's teachings have been an inspiration for the philanthropic efforts deployed by generations of Chinese officials and entrepreneurs. At the same time, Buddhism in its Chinese garb has been often criticized for putting an excessive emphasis on the acquisition of "merits" (*gongde*) through donations to temples or charities, without leading powerful or wealthy individuals to look at the roots of their decisions and behaviors.[77]

---

[76] "Chinese Communism: Who's Who"; available online at www.marxists.org/subject/china/whos-who.htm (accessed on December 19, 2014).

[77] Benoit Vermander (2013), *Corporate Social Responsibility in China.* Singapore: World Scientific Publishing, p. 53.

Daoism (Taoism) designates both a philosophical tradition and a religion organized back to the second century CE, which in modern China, are identified separately as *daojia* and *daojiao*, respectively. Daoism includes: the ideas and attitudes peculiar to the Laozi, the Zhuangzi, the Liezi, and related writings.[78] The Dao is a divine reality, and Laozi is seen as the personification of the Dao. Daoists focus on understanding the nature of reality, increasing their longevity, ordering life morally, practicing rulership, and regulating consciousness and diet.[79]

Monotheism: Catholicism and Protestantism, Muslims, and Jews have been present in China for centuries. The Catholic Church made great efforts to build a cultural bridge between China and Europe, especially through Jesuit missionaries. S. J. Matteo Ricci arrived in Macau in 1583, and later compiled the first Portuguese–Chinese dictionary. According to Chinese Muslims' traditional legendary accounts, Islam was first introduced in China in 616–618 AD by companions of Prophet Muhammad. The first major Muslim settlements in China consisted of Arab and Persian merchants. Jewish settlers have been identified as early as the 7th or 8th century. Some Chinese Jews, the Kaifeng Jews, are members of a small China Jewish community in Kaifeng (Henan) who have assimilated into Chinese society while preserving some Jewish traditions and customs, and seem to have existed since the Northern Song dynasty. Their existence was unknown to the West until one of them visited Matteo Ricci.

(iv) A complex cultural fabric is the result of this rich heritage

In the 21st century, deep and far-reaching constituents of these philosophies remain rooted, at various degrees, deep into the very fabric of Chinese contemporary culture. Ethnologists are still working to uncover the rich and diversified cultural heritages of ethnic groups

---

[78] Anna K. Seidel, "Daoism," *Encyclopaedia Britannica on Daoism.* Last updated on November 4, 2014; available online at global.britannica.com/EBchecked/topic/582972/Daoism (accessed on December 19, 2014).

[79] Ronnie Littlejohn, "Daoist Philosophy," *Internet Encyclopaedia of Philosophy*; available online at www.iep.utm.edu/daoism (accessed on October 8, 2014).

from various parts of China. In the Yunnan province, an ancient rite for offering sacrifices to the sacred tiger, Tiger Dancing, is a living remnant of primitive totemism among the Yi people. From the perspective of "memory", Tiger Dancing is a unique means for presenting and expressing historical memories among the Yi ethnic group. While the Lolo people dance through time, their memories are being carried on through a process of constant composition and reconstruction.[80] This process is typical of the continuous reinterpretation and transmission of the Chinese culture across space and centuries.

A wealth of diversified traditional, intangible cultural heritages are still very much alive in various parts of China. Indeed, it may take some efforts in large cities to discern the survival of such ancient traditions after the impact of the Cultural Revolution and the wave of consumerism, literally at least.

The history of the People's Republic of China in the last 60 years has not always been peaceful. The Cultural Revolution and the war are still reminded with pride, but as a painful and difficult time for Chinese, and some issues are still very much unresolved. The opening of the country has changed mentalities, but for a long time, conditions were such that the two primary objectives were to ensure one's own survival and that of one's family. Mentalities are still pervaded by these times, even if the success of China economic development has deeply changed perceptions, especially for the young generation. Too often, only the end justifies the means, but there are many exceptions, and foreigners should pay specific attention to find trusted local allies, sharing common values, to build their business over the long-term on solid foundations.

A good negotiation starts with a good positioning of the M&A discussions on the national-local axis and on the public-private axis, with both axes intersecting. The four cardinal directions operate as a compass to navigate during the negotiations. A good understanding of each party's expectations is thus a necessary prerequisite for a good start.

---

[80] Gu Yuejuan and Wang Yixiang (2009), "Tiger Dancing of Yi Ethnic Group in Shuangbai County," in He, Ming Kunming (ed.), *Fieldwork Image of Intangible Cultural Heritage Series*, 6–8. China: Yunnan People's Publishing House.

Chinese businessmen are sometimes perceived by Western negotiators as slow, inefficient, and sometimes irrational. Western negotiators are sometimes perceived by the Chinese as impulsive, impersonal, and aggressive. These differences in perceptions actually reveal very deep cultural differences. They must be well-understood and integrated for discussions to be more fruitful.

"Yes" is often the first word of a negotiation in China, but rarely the last, as saying a straight "no" can be seen as an offense. For a foreigner, a successful negotiation in China is a multidimensional work that has to be managed with patience, great professionalism, and in a climate of trusted cooperation with its local Chinese partners, to possibly grease the wheels when needed. One of the worst situations one can possibly encounter is to lose a promising lead due to poor preparatory work. Thus, a sloppy company presentation or inadequate legal documentation, which would greatly fail to impress the Chinese parties, can weaken the perceived standing of the candidate and, consequently, his negotiating position. Such errors are likely to make an external growth operation or partnership go wrong. It must be remembered that the competition will stay strong through negotiations, especially if the opportunity is attractive.

4.4. Negotiating Well in China

4.4.1. *Negotiation Framework*

Understanding and speaking Chinese (Mandarin, which is the official language) brings a significant advantage to any party willing to be more involved in China's business community, but one must remember that China uses at least seven languages and more than four hundred dialects. Even with a good command of Mandarin, a translator is useful to be comfortable during technical negotiations and avoid making mistakes or lead the other party to unintentionally lose face. However, speaking Chinese is indeed useful in building the friendship and the trust, as one Chinese counterpart will always be appreciative of the effort made to learn their language.

Before starting negotiations and disclosing key information, it is essential that one knows its bottom line, otherwise, the discussions are not likely to go anywhere. Then, it is also common practice that the parties ensure their discretion and their mutual good faith. General principles will be agreed upon and even though this part seems a bit tedious, one must remember that this will become part of a framework very likely to be included in the letters of intent and various problem resolution procedures after the contract is signed. Trust must be established so that all the information needed for the decision-making process can be exchanged as smoothly as possible. A confidentiality agreement, and later a Memorandum of Understanding (MoU) including a privacy clause, should be signed.

The Chinese have a reputation to start meetings on time; however, the date of the meeting may be postponed if they have unresolved issues or more important matters to deal with. They are known for being tough and sharp negotiators. One must be well-prepared for discussions and pay particular attention to the following subjects and pitfalls:

- Mutual understanding of the parties prior to the negotiations, which involves a good knowledge of the negotiators' and deciders' biographies. The importance of individual relationships between the parties should not be overlooked — check that an agreement on main principles can be reached and that the parties can do business together.
- Duration of negotiations. It is difficult to negotiate quickly in China, as issues are likely to be addressed sequentially.
- Negotiating teams. The Chinese often negotiate in large numbers; therefore, a corresponding team in number should also be prepared.
- Protocol and hierarchical management of negotiations (importance of title and social status).
- Translation difficulties. An excellent translator is a key asset for a negotiation to avoid misunderstandings; this point cannot be prepared at the last minute. It is worth mentioning in the contract, which will generally be bilingual, that both versions are identical but that the negotiations were conducted in English or Chinese, as appropriate. Chinese (Mandarin) will prevail on Mainland China contracts.

4.4.1.1. *Use the Right Levers at the Right Level*

The art of negotiation in the West is often based on an analytical priority-based approach, while it is based much more on a global picture in China. The key success factors of the negotiation may be seen in a more superficial way, but gradually every point will get tightened. The concept of synthesis in China is essential to achieve harmony and consensus among the various parties involved at the right hierarchical level of representation ("shehui dengji").

Contemporary Chinese society is very hierarchical, and it is essential that negotiations can take place in an orderly way at the right hierarchical level. Chinese behavior is rooted in the acceptance of paradoxes, resulting from the merger of a very ancient, predominantly agrarian culture with the communist–socialist ideal that has been an essential vector of transformation towards a more urban society. Understanding these historical, geographical, and economic paradoxes is necessary to deal with the tensions that may surface when discussing different options. One must therefore keep an open mind, be patient in order to cultivate contacts, and persevere in a flexible style, but determined way, to achieve one's goal.

The different values influencing the perception of the parties involved can be analyzed as follows:

Table 4.5. Comparison of Corporate Values between the West and China.

West	China
Individual	Clan/nation
Consensus	Hierarchical
Analysis, details	Helicopter view
Sequential logic	Möbius curve
Balance	Best deal
Objectives	Resources
Long-term results	Short-term results

4.4.1.2. *Codes and the Respective Priorities in Negotiations*

The differences influencing the partnership or acquisition negotiations can be analyzed in Table 4.6.

Negotiations in China always begin quite formally around a table, so that delegations from both sides of the table can get to know each other. Chinese teams can sometimes be constituted of several tens of people. This can create a sense of being overwhelmed, which may not be very comfortable. The proper way to deal with the situation is to focus on the speakers, as the rest of the audience is

Table 4.6. Comparison of Key Negotiating Values between the West and China.

West	China
Initial contact	
Work meetings	Mutual contact
Informal	Protocol
Direct	Intermediaries
Efficiency	Harmony
Methodology	
Sharing relevant information	Gradual knowledge
Negotiator	Negotiator + decision-maker
Rational price	Acceptable price
Definition of deal	Possible options
Contract	Mutual understanding
Closing process	Impact of closing
Decision	
Rational logic	Multifactor logic
Schedule	Patience
Sequence, decision tree	Hierarchy
Balance	Possible options
Transaction structure	Partner knowledge
Quick conclusion	Conclusion in due course
Quality of transaction	Impact of transaction

likely to remain very quiet. Negotiations can, in some cases, be preceded by official speeches, a strategic presentation, and a quick "technical" lunch, after which Chinese officials will leave without talking much about the deal. Dinner is likely to take place at a more advanced stage of the discussions, when things move in the right direction. It is essential on this occasion that the foreign party's representatives match the Chinese party with people of the same hierarchical level. This preamble allows the parties to gauge one another. Statements of cooperation and sincerity in the process are of particular importance.

Negotiations continue in an atmosphere gradually more informal to build trust; some relaxing topics can be discussed to break the ice, hobbies and family being on top of them. A first round of negotiations around the table is likely to be followed by a meeting of a smaller committee, including higher-level decision makers, in another reception room furnished with chairs typically arranged in an open rectangle. This room often has a symmetrical arrangement, each side presenting a pair of chairs and sofas. The central position will be occupied by the highest-level people; then, the other negotiating parties will sit around according to hierarchy and protocol.

If the negotiation is strategic, it is necessary to ensure that the CEO is available in order to meet, several times if necessary, its Chinese counterpart. One should always remember that the three trips to Beijing by John F. Smith, who was then CEO of General Motors, to meet with his counterparts in Shanghai Automotive Industry Corporation (SAIC) in 1995, had certainly something to do with the extraordinary success of the Buick brand (owned by General Motors [GM]) in China. Other automakers' CEOs have not been so motivated about showing their commitment at the right time and their firms ended up being almost nowhere on the China market afterwards.

4.4.1.3. *Usefulness of Good Intermediaries*

The local intermediary ("zongjian ren") has a key role as a facilitator in China to introduce a negotiation, help on with the agenda, and summarize the topics to be discussed. He is also there to reduce differences and facilitate the decision process. As it is inconvenient to say directly "no" in a negotiation and question too directly the other party, well-rounded and unbiased intermediaries can help smooth the sharp angles.

Intermediaries can also act as an interpreter for the parties. Negotiations can come to an end if the Chinese party fears losing face, especially as ego trips can become a problem. Negotiations can then be turned around by intermediaries who will find clever ways to overcome the differences and put the discussions back on track. An intermediary will have an essential role in defining social, extraprofessional activities necessary to the creation of a good working environment during the deal: dining at a restaurant (around 18:00), touring a local scenic spot, or visiting a place of interest, such as a country club, or more informal activities, such as golfing or wine tasting. Purely professional discussions will usually be set aside during these meetings.

The chief negotiators must be carefully chosen and replaced, as necessary, if they do not fit or if the parties are not comfortable. This point must be especially monitored during the early moments of the negotiations and backup solutions must be prepared. The beginning of any new negotiations, especially with a foreigner, will often be greeted by an equivalent part of enthusiasm and suspicion, which can be overcome by a good understanding and a mutual appreciation of the leaders.

The decoding of visual signals, and especially the body language of our Chinese friends, is particularly difficult for Westerners: modulations, mood, facial expressions, and body positions. It is useful to have one or more local intermediaries who can provide valuable information on the psychology of one's interlocutor. A good intermediary should also translate not only the language, but also the emotions, for both parties.

To avoid misunderstandings, it is nevertheless important to use intermediaries carefully and avoid crossing the red lines, especially when it comes to corruption. This is now a very sensitive topic, as China wishes to get rid of bad habits of the past.

To better assess the complexity and the weight of tradition, one can possibly recall a story from the Western Zhou Dynasty[81] (1046–771 BC), carved on a bronze vessel which stands as a judgment recording, and possibly the very first case of a civilian accusing government officials and a judge of taking a bribe.

The story written on the bronze vessel recalls the following: "One day, a man named Mu Niu sued me, his administrator. Chief Judge Boyangfu sentenced him for making a false accusation and attempting to accuse me, his administrator named Zhen. Mu Niu was indeed very heavily sentenced to give five slaves to Zhen, get caning a 1,000 times, get tattoos on his face, and have black silk cover his face in the rest of his life as a punishment. In order to get a commutation to this very harsh sentence, Mu Niu offered 3,000 Ai (equivalent to 2,000 Chinese Tael in the Han Dynasty) to Chief Judge Boyangfu. Then, Boyangfu changed the court verdict to only 500 times caning, and no tattoo-on-face punishment. Boyangfu took the 2,000 Tael and he had Mu Niu swear not to accuse Zhen any more. If Mu Niu ever accused Zhen again, the court verdict will be reversed to the original verdict before Boyangfu took the bribe."

One must have a clear idea of what is unethical and illegal, and keep away from it, even if extrajudicial settlements are officially possible in different legal systems in the world.[82] It must be added that the benefits of corruption are usually short term and

---

[81] This bronze artifact ("Zhen Ye") is a basin to wash one's face, dated from the mid-Western Zhou Dynasty (1046–771 BC), with an animal shape and four legs. There are 157 letters carved on it. The vessel is 20.5 cm high, 17.5 cm wide, 12 cm deep, and weighs 3.85 kg. It is kept in the Qi Shan County Museum and a copy was displayed in August 2014 at the Kunming Green Lake Park (金殿公园) Western Zhou dynasty exhibition.

[82] For example, in the US, the SEC charged several institutions with engaging in illegal cross trading during the financial crisis, which agreed to settle the charges by paying a financial penalty and returning money to harmed investors; quoted in "SEC Enforcement Actions," *U.S. Securities and Exchange Commission*, August 21, 2014; available online at http://www.sec.gov/spotlight/enf-actions-fc.shtml (accessed on October 8, 2014).

create unhealthy dependence relationships that may, years later, cause the loss of the benefits of a long-term effort. It is best to progress, sometimes, a little more slowly but on a sound and solid basis.

4.4.2. *The Negotiation Ritual Unfolds Like a Game*

4.4.2.1. *The Negotiation Ritual*

In China, negotiations are more like a strategy game with twists and turns, rather than a classic legal and economic Western-type negotiation with multiple rounds. The information is often multi-faceted, incomplete, and of uncertain quality, and plays a key role in the quickly evolving environment of an emerging market. The game is played in several dimensions through official and informal channels.

The smart use of these two lines of dialogue enables one to better finalize negotiations and to influence peripheral parameters in a transaction to ensure the success of key issues. The game unfolds as a series of exchanges — requests and responses, then more detailed explanations — until the right formulation is found. Concessions must be carefully prepared on a reciprocal basis and carefully gauged. Being always professional and patient ("chiku nailo") will serve one as a great asset in China. One must not hesitate to go back several times on an issue if it is not sufficiently clear or understood. Until the contract is signed, things can change, and they are likely to continue to change after the contract has been signed. There is, therefore, no room for complacency before the actual closing of the negotiations.

The setting of the interviews, the best time for negotiation, and the use of multiple information channels are part of a process which Chinese businessmen master.

4.4.2.2. *Opening Negotiations*

The Chinese will frequently use similar patterns to open the negotiations. They will never negotiate alone and the team involved could be quite numerous, with each member focusing on a specific area of expertise in the discussions. They will always make group decisions and usually do not like to be singled out.

The Chinese like to control every aspect of the meeting as this gives them a sense of comfort: arrival by car, seating, greetings, and agenda. When entering the meeting room, the highest ranking person in the team will lead the delegation. They like to have the foreign party do the same so that they will know the hierarchy.

The oldest member of the team is likely to start with the greetings, and you will be quickly asked to present your company and introduce your plans. They are likely to let you go first, as this is will always be an important learning opportunity for your Chinese counterpart, and first impressions tend to last. For any foreign company, a good presentation translated in Chinese will always be a strong asset and will impress your audience. A messy documentation will make the exact opposite impression, and it will be difficult to change it afterwards.

The Chinese counterparts' leader will continue the meeting and lead the negotiation process for the rest of its team; other team members are unlikely to jump spontaneously in the discussion, except if they are invited to do so by their leader. At the early stage of the discussions, especially with an SoE, the leader may not be the highest ranking person depending on the opposing team, intentions, and level of maturity of the discussions. Finally, except for family-owned businesses, the lead negotiator usually does not have the power to make the final decision and the case must be decided at upper levels. Any significant concession or change in the negotiation must be discussed with peers and formerly approved. A straight "Yes" should never be taken as an agreement with you but rather interpreted as: "I am hearing you, and I will see what I can do about this."

One of the Chinese businessmen's favourite tricks is to track inconsistencies in your presentations to later leverage it as an advantage; you can expect the tough questions to surface many times if the answer is not satisfactory. No wonder the Chinese team will carefully take notes and carefully review the minutes of past meetings before starting a new one. In addition, the whole session is even likely to be recorded or even video recorded without you being asked whether you feel comfortable or not, which may be disrupting if the Western party is unprepared for it. In addition, you must be prepared to hand over part or all of your slide shows (this point must be prepared in advance), but in any case you should not be surprised to see your counterparts taking pictures of the presentation with their smartphones. Depending on the level of the negotiation, you may have someone from your team enquire for the details of the organization and ask for no recording of the session, but it may be very difficult to control this point.

4.4.2.3. *Negotiation Habits in China*

Trust will be built slowly and keeping harmony is important to adjust the relationship to the desired level. Your Chinese counterparts will be studying your psychology and sincerity. And if they decide they do not like you, they will not be doing business with you.

Their actions will be based on a pragmatic assessment of objectives rather than principles. Telling the other party what it wants to hear can be considered an acceptable attitude to build harmony, even if this does not fully represent the reality.

Impressions of disrespect must be avoided, like showing anger, holding the gaze of someone during the meeting, or too openly showing disagreement with the other party. This kind of confrontation is considered provocative, rude, and inappropriate during a negotiation. It will be usually difficult to get one's direct opinion, as the Chinese do not believe that doing so will provide them with any advantage in the negotiation. This information must be gathered as peripheral information.

The Chinese will need to have a sense of what their counterpart can quickly communicate, especially the preliminary details of possible transactions, all being subject to future negotiation. They will need to understand the key expectations and motivations of the other party. One of the frequent mistakes is to let the other party know that you have some obligation or deadline, as this will greatly help them build a significant competitive advantage in the course of the negotiation.

A famous example of negotiations getting sour is related to an international fine chemical producer, A, formerly in a joint venture with a Chinese company, B (in the process of being acquired by company D), negotiating another partnership with a Chinese Party, C:

- Party A could not help telling Party C that he needed to quickly resolve a problem of production licence.
- This was after Party A's former partner, Party B, was acquired by another foreign company, D, and that Party D threatened Party A to stop producing its products in China.
- Party C was well aware of the B/D deal but unaware of Party D's threat.
- Party C immediately started to raise the level of the requested concessions from Party A, including technology transfer, higher prices, and minority position in the partnership.

4.4.2.4. *Business Banquet*

Business banquets have a particular importance in starting the friendship, unlocking sensitive issues, and later, in fine-tuning the details to close the transaction. After having a meal with your future partner, one usually starts to exist as an individual and not just as a rather anonymous negotiating or presenting entity. One must remember that strangers are usually not treated with more than indifference, so getting beyond that point is critical. Many parties usually attend and are likely to be involved in creating a sense of welcoming the future partner into the group. The appreciation for Chinese cuisine will be noted as a positive contribution to building a constructive environment of understanding and friendship.

Chinese negotiators may go to great lengths to know about their guests' preference, in order to create a sense of comfort and possibly leverage it later for concessions. It is then not uncommon to drink excessively and sing, although this has become less prevalent in the larger cities, where moderation is now seen as a virtue. However, it is important to participate. This more relaxed atmosphere will allow the Chinese to express what they really want outside the formalism of the negotiation table.

Your Chinese counterpart may show interest in various topics considered a bit private in the West like your age, your family, your salary, whether you own a property, the brand of your car, and even sometimes your religion. No topic, except maybe internal politics, is unlikely to be discussed and one must be prepared for it. They may in return, share some of their passions, from Chinese contemporary painting to golf or Bordeaux wine millésimes.

4.4.3. *Common Negotiation Tactics in China*

The cornerstone of any Chinese negotiation tactic is to understand what you want and understand in detail what you are prepared to give them for this. The end game for them will be to obtain more and give you possibly less. The idea of a "fair" or "balanced" deal is not a concept which has the same definition in China, and this is a bit of a Western chimera. The Western idea of "win–win" is not something they like — in a negotiation, there is always a winner and a loser, and the stalemate is not an acceptable result for them, especially if a foreign party is involved.

Western style negotiations tend to put on the table fair proposals where details can be adjusted between the parties; on the opposite side, Japanese or Korean style negotiations tend to offer unbalanced proposals, to leave ample room for the other party to discuss and negotiate concessions. Being too straightforward from the start is likely to be a problem later in order to get what one wants to end up with. Negotiation leaders need to be capable in showing that they can move the lines.

For this reason, Chinese negotiators will spare no efforts to keep you off-balance to create and build a durable negotiation advantage. Multiple letters of intent may be signed with various competitors to increase the pressure on you. The golden rule is to never give up anything without a corresponding concession and know your bottom line, or the whole outcome of the negotiation is likely to be a disaster on your side.

However, it would be too simplistic to consider that Chinese businessmen will just try to extract as much as possible from you. Like any others, they can be very generous when you have gained their trust and touched their heart or their interest, and this is the ultimate challenge when you develop real business friendships in China. But this will take time and effort.

4.4.3.1. *Negotiations Preliminaries*

The Chinese often like to negotiate with an excellent knowledge of balance of power to get, in a friendly climate, the most concessions possible. They are often particularly well-prepared and avoid any sentiment in doing business. It is, therefore, recommended to do the same and devote the necessary time to prepare for meetings. It is not uncommon for negotiations to go in multiple directions after a series of endless questions. This style ("zhengti guannian") is more "old school" and tends to fade away.

The new generation of businessmen often raised as a single — and sometimes spoiled — child will come faster to the point. Preliminary discussions will be shorter, and they may even be very blunt and outspoken, especially at the highest levels. They will carefully study your company to build their advantage, a bit like poker or chess players, with the advantage of knowing China better than you. Keeping too defensive a position will only help them push their advantage, especially if they feel that one needs them more than they need him: An agenda of short and well-articulated meetings, a clear analysis of the payout for the partner, and credible backup options must be prepared to keep the opening very unemotional.

It is recommended to prepare carefully the negotiation and slice it into key modules, including options such as: the price corresponds to the type of offer, and also to consider a table of possible concessions, in exchange for other concessions from the other party. These elements must be kept confidential and attention must be paid to keep the more sensitive documentation secured. Careful planning by the Chinese party on the negotiation schedule and the key events, such as the attendance of CEOs to the main milestones meetings, the requests for clarification of specific aspects of the contract, or the discussion of extras to be annexed to the transaction (e.g., technical assistance or training abroad) should be interpreted as positive signs in the course of the discussions.

4.4.3.2. *Negotiation Patterns in China*

A number of negotiation patterns can be identified over time and there could be numerous variations on these classic schemes:

(a) Multiple level negotiations: Once "finished", negotiations often have to be subject to upper-level approval. It is then common that negotiations resume with another party which may ask for a substantial change of the conditions. One should, in this case, remain open and flexible while firmly holding to the baseline conditions of the negotiation.
(b) Round-robin negotiations: They are both a part of the protocol and of getting to know the parties in the context of the Chinese environment. It is useful to be flexible about touring the city for a few days if necessary and about discussing many things other than the contract. Showing interest in what surrounds the negotiations is considered courteous and allows getting closer before they start.
(c) Indirect negotiations: They allow, through the use of influential intermediaries, to prepare each party to the requests of the other by explaining the constraints of each side. The goal is to make quick progress without incidents in order for both parties to make concessions.
(d) Negotiations in parallel with competitors: They allow the use of competitors to bargain and get the best deal without initially having to present the negotiation as open to other competitors. It is to be expected as it is almost systematic in China, and this should not be interpreted as a sign of duplicity or distrust. Bargaining is deeply rooted in China's culture.
(e) Silent negotiations: During price negotiations, the Chinese can use silence and patience. They always believe that it is better to talk too little than too much. This can destabilize the other party

who does not know what to do to restart the negotiation. This tactic is particularly effective when facing talkative interlocutors in a rush to close. Rather than getting impatient, it is more constructive to resume the negotiation by asking a few questions about the structure of the competing offer in order to find loopholes and get a better deal.

(f) Postponed negotiations: Their goal is to modify the course of the negotiation and the agenda. The negotiating efforts of the Chinese focus on only the key elements with real value for the buyer. This can cause these parts to be overvalued and force the buyer to make substantial concessions on accessory elements which will, when the time comes, will be of great importance to the Chinese (for example, buying a business because it has a manufacturing license difficult to obtain in return for keeping most of the employees).

(g) Loose-end negotiations: Their goal is to see how far you will go in the negotiation, especially if in the course of your due diligences the Chinese party's focus is on another matter than selling their company. Therefore, they may not be ready to allow you to sign a partnership or invest any more, unless one can put substantial, better terms on the table. Last-minute amendments to the contract may show up at the signing to try to force more "final" concessions.

4.4.4. *Some Misconceptions about Negotiating in China*

There is always a price lower than the one at which a deal is negotiated. In spite of the absurdity of this idea, it happens to be a market reality, but this is not without risk. For each level of price there is a level of quality, and risk increases, especially when the Chinese party cannot generate a sufficient margin. This can later lead to very bad surprises for those who are not careful enough.

Regardless of the contract, what matters is one's word and the friendly atmosphere of the discussions. All contracts in China are deemed to evolve over time as the relationship and the constraints of the business also evolve. What has been written contractually at the end of negotiations will be the basis for further negotiations.

The contract is, in fact, a negotiating tool in China which represents the position of the parties at a certain time. The contract must provide mechanisms for risk management and conflict resolution, which ultimately gives the advantage to the party who has best negotiated. The contract is primarily for the use of the parties involved and not really for third parties. This means that in case of a disagreement, the parties will have to make their best efforts to find a solution without the use of third parties. Several European groups have witnessed that the law enforcement did not necessarily lead to the expected results and had to restart negotiations.

Relationships ("Guanxi") take precedence over the rest. Supposedly "what you know about China is not as important of whom you know". However, this can also be a simplistic shortcut that can generate bad surprises. The "Guanxi" is a concept fruitful over the long term and not in the moment; the "Guanxi" should be cultivated as a precious plant that should always be cared for. Guanxi is based on small committee discussions, exchange of little tokens of recognitions, and mutual services to grease the wheels in a system which is sometimes a bit complicated or opaque. Guanxi is not to be confused with corruption.

Guanxi is dealing with reciprocity and of course mutual appreciation, but the emotional part of the relationship is not so important. A similar concept exists in Korea or in Japan — it is no surprise that both these countries master it when dealing with a Chinese counterpart. The only possible exception is the existence of very old historical ties, such as family and clan. These are issues often out of the scope of foreign investors.

The closing of negotiations is not necessarily indicated by the date set for the signature of the contract. Chinese businessmen like to negotiate until the last minute, especially if they feel that the other party is in a hurry to close the deal. Pushing it through the end with persistence is also part of the agrarian and ancient Chinese culture, much like carefully transplanting rice in this small rectangular place that is a rice field. Yield requires care and the edges are no less important than the center of the field.

Chapter 5

Closing the Transaction

The negotiation of contractual documentation is important to formally end the acquisition process. It must comply with a specific process of signing by the contracting parties and authorization of information by the supervisory authorities. The importance of contracts has sometimes been minimized in the success of acquisitions in China, but this idea about business in China is usually erroneous. However, it is true that Chinese businessmen tend to prefer framework contracts with lesser details than in the West, as they feel all issues are likely to be renegotiated at a later stage, especially if they keep a significant equity stake in the business. In such a case, one should think of it as a partnership rather than a straight majority acquisition. The acquiring party can be certain that the remaining shareholders will later open another round of negotiations that will be time consuming.

This is also why, typically in the last version of the contract, Chinese businessmen sometime like to include some provisions which will allow the parties to renegotiate as needed. One must be specifically careful when it comes to signing the final draft.

The Western vision of the contracts is close-ended; the Chinese vision is usually open-ended, as contracts are considered the beginning of a series of possible adjustments in the developing relationship.

The use of expensive and time consuming contracts, which may be difficult to enforce in a Chinese court can be questioned and one can legitimately wonder if this is not a waste of time in China.

As China joins the WTO, contracts cannot be ignored any more and are particularly important as they will always serve as a reference, especially as people and times change. They are also useful to discuss face-to-face the details of extreme situations and see how the other party reacts. However, if the conditions of the cooperation are not based on shared values and trust, it may be a better idea to look for another business partner closer to one's corporate values.

5.1. Getting Approval from the Chinese Authorities

5.1.1. *The Approval Process for Foreign Investment*

All foreign investments in China, including M&A, are subject to the review and approval of the Chinese authorities: at a national level, usually the Ministry of Commerce, MOFCOM and the State Administration of Industry and Trade (SAIC); at a local level the Commission of Foreign Trade and Economy Cooperation (COFTEC) and the Administration for Industry and Commerce (AIC). Since August 1, 2008, the date of the entry into force of the Anti-Monopoly Law, the anti-monopoly control authorities, Anti-Monopoly Enforcement Administrations (AMEA), are also in charge of the control of concentrations in mergers' operations.

The time needed for the approval of foreign investments by the Chinese authorities depends on the nature and amount of the investment, the required level of approval (local and/or provincial and/or national), and the complexity of the operation. On average, for a simple acquisition of a Chinese company by a foreign investor, it takes between three to five months after the filing of the case has been done.

The main levels of approval are generally (see Table 5.1):

Table 5.1. Main Levels of Administrative Approval.

Encouraged investments	If the total project investment is: ■ Less than USD100 million — local COFTEC. ■ More than or equal to USD100 million but less than USD500 million — MOFCOM. ■ More than or equal to USD500 million — MOFCOM, with submission to the State Council for audit.

(*Continued*)

Table 5.1. (*Continued*)

Authorized investments	If the total project investment is: ▪ Less than USD100 million — COFTEC. ▪ More than or equal to USD100 million but less than USD500 million — MOFCOM. ▪ More than or equal to USD500 million — MOFCOM, with submission to the State Council for audit.
Controlled investments	If the total project investment is: ▪ Less than USD50 million — provincial COFTEC. ▪ More than or equal to USD50 million but less than USD100 million — MOFCOM. ▪ More than or equal to USD100 million — MOFCOM, with submission to the State Council for audit.

Source: Ministry of Commerce of the People's Republic of China, www.mofcom.gov.cn/article/b/c/201409/20140900723361.shtml; The Central People's Government of the People's Republic of China, www.gov.cn/zwgk/2013-12/13/content_2547379.htm.

The approval process could be reduced to a registration process for investments in the field of encouraged and authorized investments by FIEs which have already been approved during their initial establishment. In addition, asset deals made by FIEs with a business track record within the limit of their corporate purpose are, in principle, not subject to any approval or registration process provided that they are not subject to a capital contribution. However, asset deals made by foreign investors before the creation of an *ad hoc* FIE into which the assets are brought are subject to these processes.

Share deals involving listed companies are subject to a specific approval process. Foreign companies wishing to acquire a stake in a company listed on the Chinese market can only, in principle, acquire class B shares. However, the measures from December 31, 2005 for the administration of strategic investments by foreign investors in listed companies provide foreign companies which want to make a mid- to long-term investment, including in terms of managerial know-how and technologies, with the opportunity to acquire, under certain conditions, part of the class A shares of a Chinese listed company. In particular, the foreign investor must be in good financial health, internally apply the good governance principles, have a capital of at least USD100 million, or in the case of holding companies, control stakes of companies whose total combined share capital is greater than or equal to USD500 million and never have been convicted by a supervisory authority in its home country or in China during the three previous years.

The acquisition can be structured in several stages, but the first one implies acquiring at least a 10% stake in the company. The acquisition of Class A shares can be done by signing a share transfer agreement by subscription to a capital increase or any other type of acquisition allowed by the law. The acquisition must respect the constraints related to the acquisition of an interest by foreign investors (catalogue, prohibited sectors, etc.). In particular, if the company is a wholly- or partly-owned state enterprise it must also respect the laws related to the acquisition of SoEs. In the case of an acquisition by a foreign subsidiary of the acquirer, this subsidiary must provide a guarantee of the parent company and accept the liabilities originating from its Chinese subsidiary. The principle and details of the acquisition must be approved by the Ministry of Commerce and the China Securities Regulation Commission (CSRC) when a foreign investor takes over a listed company.

This approval will be valid for a period of 180 days after which the transaction will have to be completed or will be invalidated. It is, however, possible to obtain an extension of the deadline at the discretion of the approval authorities. When a foreign investor has carried out an acquisition under the strategic investments regime, any additional investment in the same listed company will have to be carried out under the same regime.

The shares thus acquired will be subject to a lock-up period of three years, during which they cannot be sold. The acquisition of a stake by a foreign strategic investor will automatically change the status of the target company into a foreign investment enterprise (FIE), the latter having to apply for an approval certification within the 10 days following the closing of the transaction.

As soon as the new operating license is issued by the Chinese authorities registering the operation, all other registration certificates of the structure in China should be updated (fiscal, customs, bill of exchange, statistics, etc.).

5.1.2. *"Fake" Foreign Investments: Acquisitions by Chinese Companies Owned Abroad*

To avoid "fake" foreign investment, i.e., investments actually carried out by Chinese nationals who have set up companies abroad to serve the purpose of an acquisition, the 2009 set of regulations prescribe an obligation to inform the authorities on the origin of the investor and an approval process. After examination of the case, the Chinese authorities can then deny the acquirer the status of foreign investor or, in some case, completely reject the transaction. Moreover, the 2009 regulations set up a strict control process for the acquisition of stakes in Chinese companies through an SPV located offshore, controlled directly or indirectly by a Chinese company or citizen in order to be listed abroad. The regulations provide an especially complex approval process required by the Ministry of Commerce which also involves the intervention of the CSRC.

5.1.3. *Merger Control and Anti-Monopoly Law*

Regulations for the acquisition of domestic firms by foreign investors had provided, in its 2006 version, for some rules on merger control, which were then removed from the 2009 version to become part of the Anti-Monopoly Law published on August 30, 2007 and its various implementing regulations.

The Anti-Monopoly Law mainly aims at preventing and controlling monopolistic behaviors and anti-competitive business practices, as well as protecting a healthy market resulting from the normal competition between operators.

According to the law, the Chinese authorities have to approve the mergers of companies that eliminate or weaken competition in China and even outside the Chinese territory. The following are subject to the requirement of mandatory preliminary applications: specifically "mergers & acquisitions" and, more generally, situations where an operator takes control of other operators or is able to have a decisive influence contractually or by any other means, which includes *de facto* strategic partnerships.

On August 4, 2008, the State Council published a text enforcing the anti-concentration law which aims at clarifying the details about merger regulations and, in particular, the notion of take-over and the provisions for the filing of thresholds. According to the State Council ruling, an operator takes control of one or several other operators if he:

- Acquires 50% or more of their shares or assets.
- Becomes a majority shareholder or owns the majority of the assets.
- Acquires the voting rights, giving the power to control decisions or to appoint half or more of the board members.
- Has a decisive influence on the decision-making process related to operations and daily management.

But such criteria can be interpreted in various ways and, for example, in the case of many small shareholders, 5% of the shares may be enough to become a majority shareholder.

The planned merger must be subject to a preliminary application if one of the following thresholds is reached:

- The previous year's consolidated worldwide turnover of all entities involved exceeds RMB9 billion and the turnover in China of two of the entities each exceeds RMB300 million.
- The previous year's turnover in China of the entities involved exceeds RMB1.7 billion, and the turnover in China of two of the entities each exceeds RMB300 million.
- The merger will consequently concentrate 25% of the worldwide market share in China.

Large companies could thus be quasi-systematically subject to the approval of Chinese authorities, including for small transactions in China.

5.1.4. *Control of State Security*

This matter was already mentioned in the 2006 and 2009 revised regulations regarding the acquisition of domestic companies by foreign investors. Since February 3, 2011, the control of state security issues by the Office of the State Council does apply to the acquisitions of domestic companies. Henceforth, the procedure of control of state security is required when the target of a planned acquisition by foreign investors is both:

(i) In a designated sensitive industry, such as defence, agricultural products critical to the state security, energy, infrastructure, important transport, strategic technologies, and key equipment manufacturing.
(ii) This target may be taken over and controlled by foreign investors.

According to this text, the actual control of the company will be deemed to be held by foreign investors in one of the following cases:

- A foreign investor and its majority stake parent company, and one or more of its subsidiaries where the investor has a majority control, will hold after the acquisition more than 50% of the target.
- More than 50% of the capital of the target will be owned, after the acquisition, by its foreign investors.
- The percentage of the total shares held by investors in the share capital of the target does not reach the 50% threshold, but the voting rights held by these foreign investors, due to their stakeholding, will have an important impact on the shareholders' decisions and on the board of directors of the target.
- Other factors that will ensure that the effective control of the target in terms of operating decisions, finances, human resources, and technology will belong to a foreign investor.

Based on this set of rules, it is clear that that the Chinese authorities now have discretionary power in deciding whether or not an acquisition project by a foreign investor may be approved.

5.1.5. *The Future of Employees*

Managing human resources is critical to ensure the success of M&A, especially for materializing synergies and functionally integrating the activities of the target company. The rules relative to the transfer of employees in such projects differ, depending upon the type of deal conducted and the nature of the target company.

The acquisition of all, or part, of the shares of a domestic company has, in theory, no effect on the status or the employment of employees, for the employer (the target company) does not change.

The labor contract law, effective on January 1, 2008, also stipulates that changes in the corporate name, in legal representatives, in key members or investors in the company, do not change the terms of the labor contracts. It should be noted that in the case of an acquisition of a Sino-foreign joint venture, the employees of the Chinese partner will be able to keep their the seniority in terms of the severance package and will receive an amount calculated from their employment in the joint venture. They can also take advantage of the transformation of their temporary contract into a permanent contract after 10 years of service, calculated based on the date of their entry into the joint venture.

In the case of a merger or spin-off of a company, the law provides that the surviving entity is required to take over existing contracts and substitute the original employer in their execution. However, it is common for this type of deal to be followed by a labor contract readjustment during the integration of the target. If negotiations with employees regarding their contract adjustment fail, it is now possible under the labor law to carry out, under certain circumstances, a collective layoff plan, that it is to say, involving the departure of at least 20 employees or when the proportion of employees affected exceeds 10% of the total number of employees. The covered situations are those where the company changes its products, makes substantial improvements to its technological processes, or adjusts the way it manages its activities and in these cases, it is still necessary to layoff employees despite a first amendment to the employment contract.

Finally, the cases where the objective economic circumstances in which the contracts were signed have considerably changed and where the employer cannot fulfil his obligations pursuant to the contract are also covered by the law. In these circumstances, the employer must inform and explain the situation to the labor union or to the overall employees 30 days in advance. After having solicited the union or the employees' opinion, the employer can layoff the necessary number of staff, provided he reports the details and reasons of this downsizing to the Labor Bureau. The text also provides that certain categories of employees, especially those in long temporary contracts and permanent contracts, or employees supporting minors or seniors have to be protected, and that in the case the employer hires additional personnel in the following six months, he must notify the authorities and give priority to the dismissed employees. The employer cannot, however, layoff employees in exceptional situations, for example, employees disabled for occupational diseases, receiving medical treatment post-disease, pregnant women, or employees close to retirement, etc.

The purchase of assets of a domestic company does not entail, subject to exceptions, an automatic transfer of employment contracts.

Special rules regarding projects involving the disposal of core assets or shares resulting in a change of control of state-owned companies exist. In particular, an employee reassignment plan must be set up and approved by the employees and the employee council, and then be submitted to the approval authority and included in the transfer contract.

Apart from considerations concerning the adjustment of the number of employees, an investor considering a merger or an acquisition must also consider the employment conditions of its employees, the content of the various existing agreements and/or contractual commitments between the employer and employees (especially related to non-compete and confidentiality issues), and the payment by the target company of the various social contributions. All these elements will have to be carefully studied during the legal and tax due diligences.

5.1.6. *Contract Signature*

There are two aspects to consider in a restructuring and M&A project: First, the contracts that will allow concluding and ensuring the transaction and, second, the contracts which will be transferred during the transfer of shares or assets, or the merging of entities.

5.1.6.1. *Contracts Accompanying the Implementation of Restructuring and M&A Operations*

- Signing the LOI (Letter of Intent) or MoU (Memorandum of Understanding) and confidentiality agreement.
- Assignment contract of shares or assets.
- Shareholders' agreement.
- Joint venture agreement, if necessary.
- Investment agreement.
- Guarantees (escrow agreement, asset or liability guarantee agreement, etc.).

The signing of a LOI, an MoU, or a confidentiality agreement is not mandatory in China for the closing of an M&A operation, but it is a very common practice that allows the parties, before the signing of the final contracts concluding the deal, to demonstrate their good faith and their intention to close the deal. These pre-contracts reassure the parties; the seller, when a buyer has clearly shown his interest in buying assets or shares, will be more inclined to communicate/expose information during the subsequent stages of due diligences.

Similarly, from a legal perspective, the investment agreement to be concluded between a foreign investor and the local authorities from where the investment project is to be concluded is not mandatory for the creation of a company and the development of projects in China. But it is also a very common practice which aims at allowing on the one hand, the local authorities to attract investors with the promise of a number of advantages for their investment project and, on the other hand, aims at enticing investors to obtain guarantees on such promises. Therefore, such an agreement, which is a contract, must accurately describe the obligations of each party. The question as to the possibility of obtaining the enforcement of the execution of this type of agreement or damages has been raised for a long time, notably when it is signed by a political authority which does not necessarily have an independent legal existence and which is a non-official government-related organization. But as most authorities have a commercial entity with which legal contracts and agreements can be signed, this difficulty can in practice be largely circumvented.

5.1.6.2. *What Happens to Contracts in Case of Restructuring or M&A?*

In China, the principle of extending existing commercial contracts prevails in the case of a share acquisition. However, in the case of an asset acquisition, contracts are not automatically transferred but can be subject to new negotiations. It should be noted that some contracts, in particular, those related to know-how and intellectual property, can include termination clauses in case of a change in control or ownership. The legal due diligence helps highlight such possible clauses and involve the relevant external parties in the negotiation, on a case-by-case basis.

5.2. Financing of the Deal and Fund Transfer

While China's set of regulations appear to allow many forms of payment for M&A, the payment in cash is by far the most frequent practice and the one favored by the Chinese authorities.

5.2.1. *Debt Financing*

5.2.1.1. *Borrowing Gap Issue*

The debt financing of M&A for foreign investors is not prohibited by the Chinese laws and regulations, but it is in practice severely limited by the requirement to respect the ratio of capital/total investment, or borrowing gap. As a result, leveraged debt financing, including leveraged buyout (LBO) are very limited in China.

They may exist in the case of offshore structuring and the acquisition of a Chinese entity by a holding located offshore, the payment of dividends from the Chinese entity being used to repay the debt. In fact, assuming that a foreign investor creates a holding company in China to conduct its acquisitions and restructuring, lending money to one's subsidiaries is permitted to a certain extent, which can help manage the cash flow, but the debt of the holding company itself will have to meet the legal requirements of the capital/total investment ratio, a fundamental concept in the Chinese regulatory system regarding the supervision of foreign investment.

Established when China started to open to foreign investment, this concept defines the ratio between the volume of share capital of a Foreign Invested Enterprise (FIE) and the total investment of this company, which combines the amount of share capital and working capital. It was reiterated by the regulation on the acquisition of domestic companies by any foreign investor. When the share capital of an FIE resulting from an M&A operation initiated by a foreign investor is:

- Less than USD2.1 million, the total investment of the FIE cannot exceed 1.43 times the amount of share capital.
- More than USD2.1 million and equal to USD5 million, the total investment cannot exceed twice the share capital.
- Greater than USD5 million and equal to USD12 million, the total investment cannot exceed 2.5 times the share capital.
- USD12 million, the total investment cannot exceed three times the share capital.

5.2.1.2. *Business Partners' Current Accounts*

In order to inject the minimum amount of capital, an FIE can be partly financed through business partners' current accounts located outside of China. As previously mentioned, the amount lent by the business partners will need to comply with the regulatory ratios of capital regarding total investment. In addition, the loans denominated in foreign currencies can be only converted into RMB at the following conditions:

- Amounts in excess of USD50,000 can only be used to pay for salaries, increase the statutory reserve, or pay third parties, in this case, immediately after the loan has been granted.
- The loan cannot be used to refund another loan denominated in RMB.

It must be noted that these monies can be put on a long-term interest bearing account or used to hedge foreign currency exposure. The financial proceeds derived from an interest bearing account will be subject to a withholding tax.

5.2.1.3. *Domestic Loans Denominated in RMB*

Loans in local currency (RMB) to finance the acquisition of assets in China can be negotiated with local Chinese banks, with the branches of the international banks based in China or with the branches of the Chinese banks based outside of China. These RMB acquired through the international branches of Chinese banks can now be used to invest or make acquisitions in China.

The interest rate of reference is the People's Bank of China's (PBC) base rate, as the Chinese banks are not authorized to lend money at a rate below 90% of the base rate. The PBC administers two different benchmark interest rates: one year lending and one year deposit rate. If the loan is approved, the final interest rate is expected to include a significant spread on top of the reference rate. In July 2014, the benchmark interest rate in China stood at 6%. Interest rate in the PRC averaged 6.41% from 1996 to 2014, reaching an all-time high of 10.98% in June 1996 and a record low of 5.31% in February 2002.

5.2.1.4. *Entrusted Loans*

The mechanism of entrusted loans is based on loan agreements between a bank and companies from the same group. One cash positive entity of the group will entrust the bank to lend this money to another company of the group in need of cash. The interest rate of an entrusted loan must be aligned with the corporate rates used on international markets.

5.2.2. *Cash Payment*

This is the preferred means of payment for the Chinese authorities and the most frequently used in daily business life, together with some specific contribution in kind — most frequently in the form of land or industrial properties. The corporate law stipulates that the contribution in cash to the share capital cannot be lower than 30% of the registered share capital. Foreigners will contribute in foreign currency to the capital of the acquired companies. The share capital can be used to pay for the operating expenses of the company in RMB, after conversion or directly in foreign currency from the share capital account.

China uses different types of banking accounts according to the type and final destination of the payment. As an illustration, there is a specific account denominated in foreign currency for the share capital, and there are current accounts in RMB or foreign currencies for the operating expenses. In case there is a loan granted from a parent company to its subsidiary, a special account must be opened and authorized by SAFE, so that the loan can be refunded or converted into equity.

In August 2008, SAFE defined the rules regarding the payment and contribution to the capital of FIEs, with the objective of enhancing the administration process of such companies and facilitating controls regarding such payment and contribution to capital. SAFE further added that FIEs, including holdings, must use the injected capital in foreign currency or it must be converted into RMB, within the limits of the approved social object. As a general rule, the capital in RMB cannot be used to make other domestic equity investments. This restriction aims, in particular, at those doing capital investment operations under the cover of WFOEs, as they cannot set investment funds in RMB without a Chinese partner. Similarly, with the exception of companies whose purpose is to make real estate investments, FIEs are not authorized to acquire real estate assets which are not dedicated to their own business. However, in theory, FIEs can use their capital to invest in financial products without any limitation in terms of percentage of capital invested.

5.2.3. *Contribution in Kind*

The laws and regulations on companies and joint ventures authorize the contributions in kind to the share capital, in the form of tangible assets (real estate, equipment and machinery) and, more importantly, intangible assets (brand licences, patents, know-how) up to 70% of the registered capital. However, it is unlikely that any administrative authorization will be granted for registration if the contribution in kind is in excess of 50% of the registered capital. In addition, the valuation of the contributed assets must be appraised by a registered Chinese professional, which creates uncertainty of the result of the final value contributed.

5.2.4. *Financing of an Acquisition by Exchange of Shares*

Financing by exchange of shares is now authorized in China. It is possible to offer to a Chinese party equity from a foreign company in exchange for all or a fraction of the shares of a Chinese company. However, the foreign company must be listed, and the complexity and limited experience in this type of transaction in China makes it possibly lengthy and likely difficult to manage.

The exchange is made possible in China if a number of conditions are met, in particular, if the share price is stable enough during the year just before the transaction, and after the satisfactory review of these conditions by M&A experts accredited by the Chinese authorities, which creates uncertainty of the result of the appraisal.

5.2.5. *Fund Raising on the Chinese Market*

Raising funds on the Chinese market for an acquisition in China is not an available option for the moment. This implies the future listing of Chinese subsidiaries of international groups on the China market to serve this purpose. This may become another financing solution one day but this is still very much "work in progress" for the moment. In the meantime, private equity solutions do exist on a limited scale but they should not be neglected, especially for mid-sized transactions.

5.2.6. *Payment of the Full Acquisition Price*

Until early June 2014, the full acquisition price was supposed to be paid no later than three months after receiving the new business licence of the acquired company. By the approval of the transaction approval authorities, the payment period could be extended to one year, provided (i) that the supporting documentation explaining the reason for a delay was accepted, and (ii) that 60% of the acquisition price was paid no later than six months after receiving the new business licence.

Such restrictions on acquisition price payment timing has been abolished by a circular of MOFCOM, dated June 17, 2014. From now on, the buyer and the seller are free to define the timing of acquisition price payment.

5.3. Leveraging and Integrating Acquisitions in China

As the number and the path of acquisitions and partnerships have increased in China, one should wonder if one factor rather than another is more decisive for the success of an M&A operation in China. The key success factors are:

- The quality of the relationships established with the owner during the transaction (proportional to time invested).
- The quality of one's business network and the knowledge of Chinese politics.
- The technical expertise and knowledge of China's business life.
- The capacity to execute a flawless deal and well-managed transaction smoothly with a good team of professional advisors.

What matters most is how to organize and prioritize factors related to strategy, finance, master the legal environment, combine knowledge with the usual Chinese negotiation techniques, perform useful due diligences, and leverage China's "cultural" codes of conduct.

5.3.1. *Managing a Harmonious and Effective Acquisition Process*

The work done with many Chinese and international clients show that they are very sensitive to the following:

- Strong M&A expertise (in particular, references and track record).
- Strategic understanding of the envisaged M&A operation and associated risks.
- Sectorial knowledge and industrial "empathy".
- Understanding of Chinese specificities.
- Business sense and personal well-rounded presentation.
- Capacity to grow a quality relationship with the owner(s).

Transaction expertise, knowledge of China's industries, and business sense seem to be real prerequisites to manage harmoniously a multifaceted team of professionals, navigate smoothly in a network of requested administrative approvals, and finally close the transaction.

This is not too surprising — that partnerships and acquisition methodology intrinsically compares well with other complex industrial processes. Thinking a bit "out-of-the-box" using some non-business related skills can shed even more light on what could be the key success factors for a transaction in China. Can fine arts, and more specifically, collaborative fine arts like music or drama teach us something about dealing effectively with partnerships and acquisitions in China?

The analogy with the creation of an art piece as the opening of a new world may draw an interesting parallel.[83]

---

[83] As defined by Karlheinz Stockhausen, a German music composer, widely acknowledged by critics as one of the most important but also controversial composers of the 20th and early 21st centuries.

5.3.2. *Musical Direction as an Analogy for Transaction Leadership in China*

In Western countries, external growth management can be compared to the structure of a Chamber music orchestra. The work is modelled on a quartet structure between strategy experts, corporate finance advisors, lawyers, and auditors. The musicians are closely connected to each other and the deal leadership flows like music being softly relayed between the players at each step of the mission. There is usually a leading musician in the group who plays the role of an informal leader; it may change according to certain criteria such as: composer, style, difficulty, and so forth, but it is usually the investment banker's role to lead. The treaties of musicology remind us that when music was started to be played by orchestras, there was no director. Gradually, as music became more complex, and as the number of musicians increased, especially in the 19th century, the presence of a director became a condition for a good performance.

As a first step, an orchestra director must be able to reconstruct the work internally before expressing it through his direction (guiding the orchestra). He can give a new life to the piece, being careful of its dynamics, its balance, tempo, and colors contributed by each musician or group of instruments. He will also pay much attention to the style and, in particular, the respiration, silence, and musical inflexions which will all give a specific style to his interpretation of the musical piece.

In China, the large number of professionals participating in the success of a transaction suggests that managing an acquisition or structuring a partnership is closer to conducting a small symphonic orchestra, than playing quartet or quintet chamber music. Unlike quartet chamber music, the leadership cannot be informal, and the deal "conductor" must be not only a leader but also a seasoned transaction professional with a strong knowledge of Chinese culture.

Key transaction management skills in China may be compared to conducting a symphonic orchestra. Therefore, perfect music will be unlikely to flow at the first rehearsal and a precise preparation of all the musicians, as a team, is of the essence. Musical direction requires finesse, clarity, and empathy to achieve excellent teamwork.

But "it is quite sure that this music will lead you to a musical space that will manage to be a surprise for you".[84]

As Leonard Slatkin put it, "[c]onducting is not about learning how to keep time or how to read a score. It is about what a major, professional orchestra needs from a conductor and how a conductor must relate to the whole ensemble." The mission of a conductor requires a broad skill set and a deep artistic know-how. It requires a demanding training, specifically in musicology, composition, analysis, instruments, and a broad musical culture, possibly ranging from confessional music in Counter-Reformation France to the effect of motor neurons on musical empathy. Studying for music direction encompasses understanding the work of all repertories for all musical formations — from duet or trio to lyrical and symphony orchestras.[85]

The mission of the conductor is to lead a great performance with his brains and with his heart, and respect the work of the composer beyond the sum of the individual interactions of the musicians. The objective is to deliver together a superior level of pleasure and performance. It is not a coincidence that the Juilliard School curriculum, one of the best musical education curriculums in the world, associates the highest level of education in the arts together with collaboration between such music, dance, and drama, to break down traditional barriers across disciplines and people. A parallel can be drawn with China for business management and, in particular, successful partnerships and acquisitions.

Leading such a large project in China requires making sure that every member of the "orchestra" develops a unique relationship with the "conductor" in order to play its part in time with passion and dedication to the team. Some musicians may need more time to

---

[84]Karlheinz Stockhausen, during a conversation with Julia Spinolla (September 11, 2001) in the Musikhaus for the FAZ. "We in Music Are Like Physicists," September 11, 2009; available online at kaganof.com/kagablog/2009/09/11/we-in-music-are-like-physicists (accessed on January 27, 2015).

[85]Conservatoire National Supérieur de Musique et de Danse de Paris, Department of Composition and Orchestra Direction; available online at www.conservatoiredeparis.fr/disciplines/les-disciplines/les-disciplines-detail/discipline/direction-dorchestre-ler-et-2e-cycles-superieurs/ (accessed on January 27, 2015).

adjust than others but this will not necessarily affect their ultimate performance, and possibly enhance it.

Although diversity is essential in making the music flow, the relative importance of one skill compared to another is irrelevant in the symphonic orchestra framework. An excellent violin solo cannot make up for the mediocre performance of the rest of the orchestra. The performance is altogether a success or not. The success of the whole performance depends on the excellence and timely participation of each of the "instruments".

The conductor is ultimately responsible for driving the process transforming instrumental diversity into global musical harmony. Its artistic inspiration, the precision of his advice, and the quality of his relationship with the musicians will finally be decisive in delivering a mediocre, passable, or a seminal performance. Without leadership, the performance would be flawed, irrespective of the talent of each member of the orchestra. Each of the musicians (team members) is part of a wider vision requiring music knowledge, personal skills, and commitment to the group. In this respect, the conductor must ensure that each musician is supportive of the other in order to achieve a superior collective performance.

Coming back to partnerships and acquisitions, this tells us that the advisor team must be assembled with care and reflect a reasonable degree of professional diversity and complementarity. Selecting the right team members is a prerequisite for all the communities involved in the process (strategy and finance experts, lawyers, auditors, administration) to find common grounds and quickly interact with each other.

The structure of a successful transaction includes:

- A rigorous identification of possible targets/partners and their rightful selection according to the acquirer's strategy.
- The definition of a reasonable framework for the transaction, including price and general terms and conditions.
- The selection of an appropriate transaction structure.
- The management of the legal environment.
- The identification of the key points for discussion after conducting appropriate due diligences and before closing the deal.

5.3.3. *Do Not Fear Heuristic M&A in China*

Despite the legal and administrative constraints, doing business in China means keeping a rigorous but flexible open mind to opportunities and innovations as a strategy for success.

Pierre Boulez, conductor, teacher, composer, and winner of 26 Grammys, shared his views as an outspoken defender of the music of the 20th century, saying that one could not live without curiosity. "[I think that] a work [for me] has to have a kind of specific sound, and even with combinations of instruments which are really very unusual, you can find combinations which are quite unusual...I find also that performers have a lack of curiosity," Boulez continues, "They are happy in their own surroundings and don't pay attention enough to what is going on elsewhere."[86]

Growing one's business presence in China through acquisitions or partnerships, just like contemporary music, means pushing forward on new territories, using new structures, and exploring new possibilities to do even better business. Sometimes this will mean taking a route that may substantially differ from a Western transaction. For this very reason, "inspiration" cannot be dissociated from an in-depth preparation on the understanding of the business environment and a very serious preparation of the leadership teams. First impressions will always be lasting and of key importance for the success of the deal.

5.3.4. *Identifying Quickly Pay-offs and Pitfalls*

It has been noticed in the past that some acquisitions or partnerships are driven by the tendency to imitate success stories, to fulfil personal ambitions, and satisfy senior management and shareholders. These ego-minded transactions explain why, in the past, so many transactions missed their target. But as the consequence of such ailing motivation has been analyzed, this is now changing. One

[88] Evan Fein, "Boulez Visits Juilliard on a Mission for New Music," *The Juilliard Journal*; available online at www.juilliard.edu/journal/boulez-visits-juilliard-mission-new-music?destination=node/14363 (accessed on December 19, 2014).

must be certain that past examples of partnerships or acquisitions will be carefully reviewed and analyzed by the seller or the future Chinese partner.

Successful transactions are driven by compelling economic logic rooted in globalization, acquisitions of competitive advantage, and independence.

5.3.4.1. *Globalization or Semi-Globalization*

The positioning on mega regional market positioning, such as Greater China, ASEAN, the European Union, and the US comes with the deregulation of world markets, creating more competition in terms of price, costs, innovation, and marketing. Rapid impacts on overseas markets or demand restructuring can more easily be done through acquisitions and partnerships. The business history of SoEs in China shows that the best ones managed to transition quickly to the market economy under the stewardship of excellent management. Privatizations coupled with foreign partnerships, mostly to consolidate a market segment, have unleashed the best players' creativity and their capacity to focus on and grow their best assets.

MNCs, both Chinese or non-Chinese, must be in a position to generate economies of scale, economies of scope, and optimize the way they address their markets on a global scale. Lenovo, ICBC, Haier, or CIMC are some successful examples. Chinese MNCs have also well understood this concept, as illustrated by the May 2013 successful acquisition by Shuanghui of Smithfield Foods (US), the world's largest hog farmer and processor founded in 1936, for USD4.7 billion at a total value including debt of USD7.1 billion. This is a 31% premium on the May 28, 2013 Smithfield share closing price.

5.3.4.2. *Competitive Advantage Such as Access to New Technologies*

New technology — energy (e.g., hybrid vehicles), pharmaceuticals (e.g., new chronic disease therapies) — redefine markets, reshape

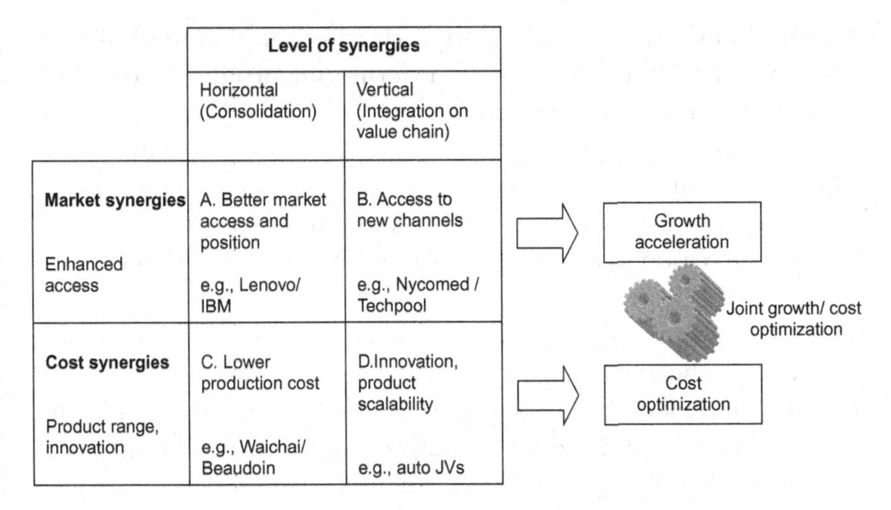

Figure 5.1. Synergy Levels.

business models, growth strategies, and critical sizes; internal growth and domestic markets are just not sufficient to recoup rising R&D expenses and mitigate the risks of a new product launch. Nor are they sufficient to cover the rising market entry cost of new products with possibly shorter life cycles.

5.3.4.3. *Independence and Financial Power*

Global financial investors are ever more merciless in demanding competitive focus, sound business practices, and shareholder value creation. Corporates willing to keep their independence and to continue raising cash for growth need to show consistent above-market performance.

The business rationale underlying external growth strategy is that the value created by the market capitalization of merged corporations must be higher than the sum of the pre-merged ones, despite some possible transitional adverse impact. Value creation remains the main economic engine behind acquisition and partnership decisions, but the social conscience of corporations (through Corporate Social Responsibility) is gradually strongly awakening and certainly a factor to be accounted for in future decisions.

Responsibility, sustainability, and social impact (creating shared value) will hopefully mitigate short-term and profit-only oriented motivations to shape a better economy.

Managing the corporate portfolio of somewhat different businesses requires a clear assessment of each segment's performance and a different pool of talents. Pruning the less promising segments is always a legitimate reason to divest a business and strengthen the others:

- For cash burning businesses, the reasons for keeping them in the corporate business portfolio must be regularly assessed.
- For cash making businesses, the profit should be invested in the consolidation of the existing business and the preparation of a possibly disrupting future.

Increased size and speed in order to gain world leadership is often seen as a critical reason for engaging with external growth operations. Size matters, for example, to establish a stronger brand name and a larger market footprint, and to negotiate with suppliers, retailers, and customers. Size does contribute to the creation of real synergies in a disciplined and cost-conscious company. However, size to flatter one's corporate ego usually provides short-sighted payback, although a good board governance should provide sufficient protection against that. Economies of scale must be felt on revenues but also at multiple cost levels, including the reduction of unit cost through better mass production processes or lower cost to access the distribution channels.

A stronger image, powerful brand, and better market position on the one hand, and increased profit margins and better returns on invested capital on the other hand, are the final post-acquisition goals for operations.

This objective can be achieved through a well-designed integration scheme. It requires a specific and well-designed training of the federating entity to make sure that size results in additional corporate muscle, not in fatness. Size should not give a better advantage to more agile, performing, and versatile competitors, which will become tomorrow's leaders.

5.3.5. *Avoiding Frequent Mistakes*

The experience gathered about partnerships and acquisitions in the last 15 years shows that 60% of the transactions missed their objective to create the targeted corporate value or just failed completely. However, as the actors are ramping up the knowledge curve, there are good reasons to be optimistic and confident that past performance is not indicative of future results. Lessons from the past are drawn and these already have an impact on the way inbound and outbound transactions are designed. Companies with sound governance, and good financial and management information are likely to be chased and acquired with a premium, compared to those incapable of providing the same quality of information. The latter are likely to be acquired with a discount, and sometimes based on asset transaction, to limit risks.

The 2008 crisis helped reset valuation benchmarks; this is likely to have a long-term downward impact on overinflated companies and acquisition premiums. One must remember that in China, in the '90s, acquisition premiums were north of 50% before the crisis caused the premium to decrease to 27%. The Chinese stock market became a bit of a disappointing investment due to past excessive valuations, lack of transparency, and the various scandals which have resulted in lack of investor trust.

Industry leaders tend to refine their acquisition strategies according to their key market objectives. Acquisitions and partnerships in China are usually carefully planned based on a rigorous mapping of the competitive landscape. Revenue size, per say, has never been the only sufficient and valid reason to justify an acquisition — leveraging the target together with sustainable and sound profitable growth appears to be much more important.

Operational risks related to external growth must be carefully analyzed and understood to ensure that the post-merger integration process is under control, effective, and possibly smooth. In order to extract the maximum value from both partnerships and acquisitions, two contributing factors must be highlighted: speed of integration and rigor in the post-transaction execution. Therefore, the appropriate team must be prepared to come into action very quickly after the decision to do the deal is made.

In the West, managers of acquiring firms report that only about 56% of their acquisitions can be considered successful against the original objectives set for them.[87] A number of visible examples in the history of M&A transactions have shown that these are not only textbook cases — Daimler had to separate from Chrysler acquired 10 years before (automotive); the unsuccessful merger of Adidas and Salomon (sports gear); or the sale of NCR by AT&T (IT) for USD3 billion after acquiring it for USD7 billion four years earlier — show how risky the integration process can be, especially for large scale acquisitions[88] and prominent companies where the recruitment of talents should not be a problem to ensure the success of the external growth strategy.

Four classical mistakes, taken alone or combined together, can lead to an M&A disaster:

- A weak industrial strategy underlying the acquisition or the partnership.
- Inadequate leadership and senior management team to quickly put the new venture on track to success. In the case of China, this includes finding a real decision-maker — a leader capable of mastering the Western and Asian environments, and capable of recruiting a top regional business development team.
- Incompatible cultures between the target and the acquirer, in particular, business ethics, corporate responsibility, personal ambitions, work style, and possible disrespect for each other.
- Sloppy post-acquisition integration process; benefits from the merger and synergies are difficult to extract; the two companies see each other as a burden.

---

[87] R. Schoenberg (2006), "Measuring the Performance of the Corporate Acquisitions: An Empirical Comparison of Alternative Metrics," *British Journal of Management*, 17(4), 361–370.

[88] Yaakov Weber, Christina Oberg, and Shlomo Tarba (2013), *A Comprehensive Guide to Mergers & Acquisitions: Managing the Critical Success Factors Across Every Stage of the M&A Process*. New Jersey, US: FT Press.

5.3.6. *Seven Conditions Precedent to a Successful M&A Transaction in China*

The guideline of a successful integration process is long-term and sustainable value creation, not only for the shareholders but also for the other stakeholders. Therefore, a clear process must be defined according to the following principles:

(1) Integrate the target quickly
Expected synergies, especially when it comes to mutualising resources, need to be achieved as quickly as possible and without stressing key people in the whole organization. This is one of the ways to amortize the majority premium paid for the acquisition, typically the difference paid between the price of any listed company before the acquisition and the real amount paid at the moment of the acquisition, which is usually higher.

In addition, the staff must be quickly informed of the new strategic direction of the company and expectations of the senior management. This must be communicated in such a way that people feel clear and comfortable with the direction set. Nothing is more detrimental than a long period of uncertainty and the feeling that senior management is unable to communicate what needs to be done due to internal disputes or lack of consensus.

(2) Communicate effectively, mix cultures
The staff needs to understand what is expected from a quantitative and qualitative standpoint and have a clear understanding about their new environment. People need to know what changes are implemented, how they mix with the new partner, what resources are made available to them, and how this is going to change their life. A smart communication of the senior management objectives is critical for the staff buy-in and focus. Workshops with newly acquired entities are usually a good way to break the ice and start sharing efforts towards achieving a common goal.

(3) Appoint the new management and define the organization
This point must be addressed very quickly, ideally in the first month following the acquisition. Key people must be already identified, and

time must be spent to motivate the staff and take them on board the new corporate project. The staff must trust the integration process and recognize that the appointment of the new management or the continuation of the existing one is based a rational analysis of professional value. Securing the key people's loyalty is a critical topic for both partnerships and acquisitions, especially in China, where the employee turnover tends to be higher than in the West.

(4) Appoint a dedicated team to facilitate and focus on the integration process

In China, the integration organization process must deal with three layers as follows:

- Heavy duty functions such as IT, shared industrial resources, and headquarter (HQ) services.
- Operational divisions such as the organization of the production process.
- Division responsibilities such as marketing, price policy, or sourcing.

The staff of the two companies partnering with each other must be closely associated in the integration process. It is important that each one brings its own ideas, contributes with a positive spirit, and has the feeling that the integration process is well-rooted at various corporate levels, typically from the factory floor to the executive management. It cannot be a just add water, "ready-to-mix" formula prepared on the sole recommendations of external consultants. The opportunity to exchange ideas is necessary for the staff of the two companies to start working together, know each other, and forge their own solutions to find best solutions for the integration. Shared success always makes a long-lasting impression in a company, and creates positive business stories that people remember and pass to each other, to lay the ground of their common culture.

(5) Leverage the integration as a new business start

An acquisition or a significant partnership is always an opportunity for a new start. This should be leveraged to possibly redesign a more effective and better corporate organization, strengthen best areas, simplify others, and even possibly outsource some sub-functions as needed. The "non-invented-here" syndrome is always lurking around, and a lot of attention must be paid to those who will systematically ban much-needed ideas to entrench their position and play internal political games to their sole advantage.

(6) Solve the technical problems related to integration
It is expected that the senior management leads the integration process, and this must be felt and known in every location and at every level in the company. The impression that key decisions are floating must be avoided except when tactically needed. Adjustments and arbitrage in the organization must be decided, and in order to do that, three competence centers must be set:

- A center of integration decisions (arbitrage and priorities).
- A dedicated HR center.[89]
- A dedicated communication center under the responsibility of both corporate communications and the senior management.

The senior management must communicate its vision, ensure that the integration process is on track, and make fast and just decisions when problems or conflicts surface. The management of the process is by nature slightly uncomfortable but such a transition shall not become a perpetual undefined state, where people have the impression that no decisions are taken. The art of the senior management will be to simultaneously run parallel processes and go smoothly through integration milestones without shaking the grounds of the whole organization. When a corporate focuses on the rules, synergies are usually extracted on time and people find themselves at the right place in the new organization. Therefore, one can be reasonably confident about the probability of success of the merger.

---

[89] See Section 3.3. Human Resources Risk Management.

(7) Quickly identify and deal with both synergies and liabilities post-acquisition

The financial and industrial due diligences must help in identifying as early as possible lower hanging fruits, i.e., easily actionable benefits from the transaction. It will always be beneficial to plan early for staff redundancies, identify key people, and negotiate with the previous owner or partner a productivity and retention plan. In addition, it will be necessary to obtain guarantees that the best staff do not resign after the deal is signed to follow the previous owner in a similar or different venture.

The operating conditions in the newly invested company (FIE) in China are likely to be quite different from the past. The upgrading of the management, the quality of the internal controls, the definition and the follow-up of industry benchmarks, and the integration of the target IT system have to create synergies and contribute to the investment payback. But one must also be prepared for additional costs related to the system upgrade. As an example, the accounting practices, usually traditional paper bookkeeping, must be aligned with the group's best practices, probably fully computerized, in order to be smoothly consolidated later in the group's reports. This workshop is usually time consuming and requires a specific team to run the process.

In most cases, the new management of the company will impact many critical areas including corporate culture, quality control, commercial policy, client relationships, and sourcing. If the due diligences have revealed some weak areas such as fiscal and environmental concerns, or corrupt practices, it is obvious that they will need to be taken care of early. These action plans must be staffed and budgeted. In a matter of months, the company process will need to be gradually aligned with the rest of the organization, with close monitoring and the objective that the work done becomes a reference for further acquisitions. The implementation of best practices and compliance programs, including extensive staff training and follow-up on the factory floor, will be useful to steadily ramp up quality and motivate the staff.

It is expected that the swift implementation of this integration strategy will lead to a transformation of the newly acquired or

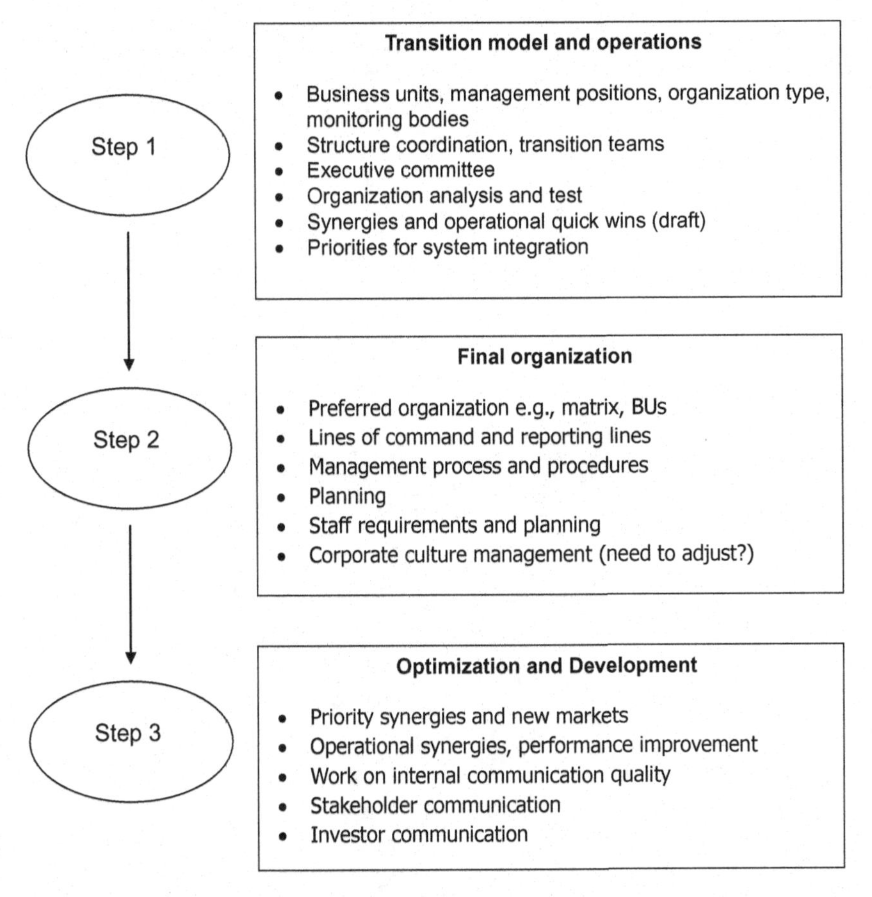

Figure 5.2. Design a Transparent and Practical Organization.

formed entity (in the case of a partnership) in the best interest of both parties. In case these recommendations cannot be applied following the closing of the transaction, this is a clear indicator that something has gone very wrong in the relationship with the Chinese counterpart, especially when it comes to his assessment of the payoff related to the common venture. In this unlikely event, some well-prepared working session together should help avoid coming back to the negotiation table to find a mutually acceptable solution to ramp up the company business plan before the partnership hits the headlines of the local press and hurts the foreign firm development strategy if it ends up in court.

Seven Case Studies of Mergers & Acquisitions and Partnerships in China

Case Study One

Partnership with and Acquisition of Hsu Fu Chi by Nestlé

Nestlé set its commitment to not only accelerate its footprint on an emerging market but also to be a truly local player in China. In Nestlé CEO Paul Bulcke's development plan, emerging markets would account for 45% of Nestlé's total revenues by 2020, with a current share of 33%. Despite mediocre revenues in most developing markets in 2011 (sluggish or declining sales), Nestlé enjoyed a double-digit increase of 11.9% in emerging markets in 2011; the growth in Greater China Region was even stronger, of 15.5%.

The founders of Hsu Fu Chi were always seeking ways to sustain the group's business and vision of making the "Hsu Fu Chi" brand a hundred-year brand. In the course of exploring possible joint venture options with global confectioners for over the past few years, they identified Nestlé S.A. ("Nestlé") as a suitable strategic partner.

Confectionery constituted only 10.9% of Nestlé's 2011 turnover. In the confectionery market in China, Nestlé fell behind its main competitors. According to Euromonitor, Nestlé accounted for only 1.8% of China's confectionery market in 2010, ranking fifth and lagging behind Mars (13%, market leader), Kraft, and Unilever. Hsu Fu Chi (HFCI:SP), listed on the Singapore Exchange Securities Trading Limited (SGX), ranked third in China with a 3.9% market share. Nestlé estimated that its market share would climb to the second position behind Mars after the acquisition and it would be instrumental in creating a deeper presence in China. Following months of discussion, the possible acquisition of a 60% stake in Hsu Fu Chi got approved in December 2011. This was Nestlé's second major transaction in an Asian country, after it agreed in April 2011 to buy 60% of Yinlu Foods Group, Nestlé's partner for ready-to-drink coffee. Yinlu is also a well-established household brand in China, and a significant marketer for ready-to-drink peanut milk and ready-to-eat canned rice porridge.

CS1.1. Nestlé Plans to Strengthen Its Position on the Chinese Confectionery Market

Hsu Fu Chi has been leading the Chinese confectionery market for years and outperformed its Chinese competitors. According to the National Bureau of Statistics, Hsu Fu Chi's confectionery products topped the sales for this category for 13 consecutive years ever since 1998.[90] The firm was founded in China in 1992 by Taiwan-born Hsu Chen and his brothers. Hsu Fu Chi's portfolio includes sugar confectionery, cereal-based snacks, jelly, pudding, and packaged cakes including the traditional Chinese snack *sachima*. The firm is China's second largest confectionery company after Mars Inc. The Company enjoyed a CAGR of 17% over the last five years and reached RMB5.2 billion in 2011.

In 1997, a private equity firm from Singapore, Transpac Industrial, invested in and introduced new ideas to the Company. In 2006, Hsu Fu Chi was successfully listed on the main board of the Singapore Stock Exchange. In 2009, a subsidiary of Baring Private Equity Asia, Star Candy, took over Transpac's share and took an active position on the board. After the listing, the Hsu Family held 56.5%; the two largest independent shareholders: Arisaig Partners and Star Candy held 9.0% and 16.5% respectively, and the public, 17.5%.

---

[90] National Bureau of Statistics of China's annual survey in 2011. Hsu Fu Chi International Limited, Annual Report 2011, p. 3; available online at http://quote.morningstar.com/stock-filing/Annual-Report/2011/6/30/t.aspx?t:AS5&ft=&d=43cf3ce5a7485bd3d33lc201426f8f8e (accessed February 4, 2015).

CS1.2. MOFCOM Approved the HFC Transaction

In the light of a vision to make Hsu Fu Chi a hundred-year brand, the group had in July 2011 announced the proposed establishment of a joint venture between Nestlé S.A. ("Nestlé") and the current majority shareholders of the company, namely Mr Hsu Chen, Mr Hsu Keng, Mr Hsu Hang, and Mr Hsu Pu.[91] As at September 20, 2011, approximately 17.5% of the Company's shares were held in the hands of the public.

MOFCOM announced its approval of Nestlé's USD1.7 billion acquisition of a 60% stake in Hsu Fu Chi International in December 2011. It took about seven months for the Chinese authorities to clear the transaction. The brand "Hsu Fu Chi" would not disappear, and its CEO and board chairman, Xu Cheng, would remain chief executive. The Hsu family still owns 40% of the company and ranked 16th on the Taiwan Rich Forbes List in 2013 (estimated wealth of USD1.8 billion). The company will apply to be delisted from the official list of the Singapore Exchange Securities Trading Limited.

According to the scheme, Nestlé offers a cash price of SGD4.35 for each share of Hsu Fu Chi, which represents a premium of 24.7%

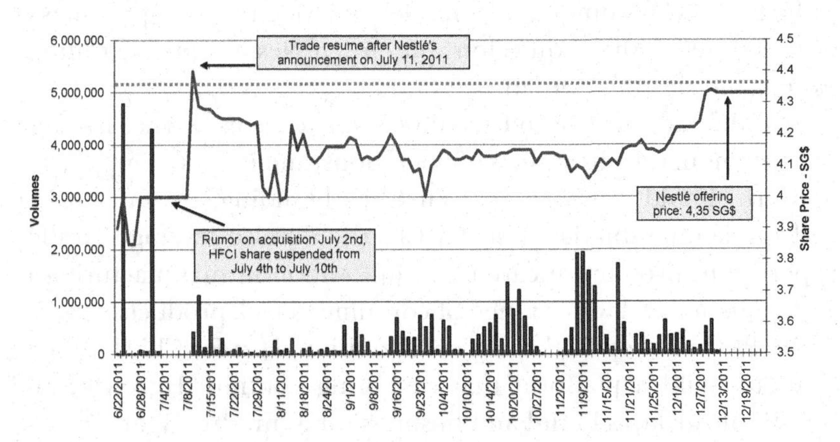

Figure CS1.1. Evolution of the HFC Share Price before the Transaction.

[91] *Ibid.*

over the volume-weighted average share price over the last 180 days. Nestlé acquired the 43.5% stakes held by independent shareholders and the 16.5% from Xu family's current 56.5% holding. The total price paid is approximately SGD2.1 million (USD1.7 million). Considering Hsu Fu Chi's 2011 EPS of 0.16, the Price-Earnings Ratio (P/E) for the deal is 27.

CS1.3. Nestlé Will Benefit from Hsu Fu Chi's Strong Distribution Channel

The most obvious acquisition synergy for Nestlé is to access the strong distribution channel of Hsu Fu Chi all over China, as 99.5% of the products are sold in China. As of the financial year ended June 30, 2011, Hsu Fu Chi owned 128 sales branches, approximately 9,000 sales and logistic personnel, more than 20,118 direct retail points, and around 3,500 specialty counters in supermarkets nationwide.

Furthermore, with two production bases in Guangdong and Henan, Hsu Fu Chi has a deep presence in Tier 2 and Tier 3 cities in China. Hsu Fu Chi operates a total industrial floor plant of 500,000 m^2 split into 47 large scale manufacturing plants, with over 220 production lines and 736 units of high speed packaging equipment. Also, with Hsu Fu Chi's unique sales model and wide range of products of over 500 items, the acquisition will enrich Nestlé's product line in China, and possibly abroad.

Nestlé's advanced food technologies, team expertise, managerial systems in various aspects of operations, and its global supporting network should enhance Hsu Fu Chi's branding, manufacturing, and marketing abilities. Hsu Fu Chi should also leverage Nestlé's expertise in product research and innovation in manufacturing to build a better and wider range of consumer snack products targeted at the PRC market. With such collaboration, Hsu Fu Chi should be able "to build a platform that can bring continued growth, and sustain the group's brand and business for a hundred years"[92].

---

[92] Hsu Fu Chi Corporate Presentation 2001; available online at wenku.baidu.com/view/87817621915f804d2b16c149.html (accessed on December 19, 2014).

Case Study Two

Caterpillar's Purchase of ERA Mining Machinery Ltd.

Caterpillar, the world's leader of tractors and excavators, was considering strengthening its position in one of the key mining/energy sectors in China, as it was convinced that China's government would require more safety and efficiency improvements by mechanizing more mines. China produces almost half of the world's coal and is forecasted to continue growing coal over the next decades, especially since 80% of China's mines are underground.

Caterpillar had already a long history in China and, during the past three decades, Caterpillar has grown from a single sales office in Beijing to a cross-country footprint — including 16 manufacturing sites, four R&D facilities, three logistics and parts centers, and other offices. In addition, Caterpillar had made significant investments in China and announced a wide range of new facilities. At the time, more than 20,000 people worked in China to support Caterpillar customers.

The opportunity to acquire ERA, a holding company incorporated in the Cayman Island, materialized during the year 2011. ERA was a leading non-state-owned hydraulic roof support manufacturer in the People's Republic of China through its wholly-owned subsidiary, Zhengzhou Siwei Mechanical & Electrical Equipment Manufacturing Co., Ltd.[93] Siwei, a former state-owned enterprise,

[93]Caterpillar SEC filings 2012; see "Caterpillar Form 8-K"; available online at http://phx.corporate-ir.net/phoenix.zhtml?c=92466&p=irol-SECText&TEXT=aHR0cDovL2FwaS50ZW5rd216YXJkLmNvbS9maWxpbmcueG1sP21wYWdlPTg2NjQ2NTEmRFNFUT0wJlNFUT0wJlNRREVTQz1TRUNUSU9OX0VO

was taken over by two entrepreneurs through ERA Mining in 2007, and ERA was then reverse listed in Hong Kong.[94]

Siwei, a stand-alone company known for its deep expertise, possessed a strong manufacturing base of 600,000 m^2 in Zhengzhou, Henan province, and primarily designed, manufactured, and sold roof support equipment to underground mining customers in China — spatula-like hydraulic arms that keep underground coal mines from collapsing. It has established a clientele of coal mining producers, primarily located in 13 of China's provinces and autonomous regions. Since its inception in 2003, Siwei has been the fastest-growing companies in China in this area. In 2009, Siwei posted revenues of USD181 million and a profit of USD18 million. How trustable this numbers were, and what happened to the subsequent income, are still a matter for debate.

However, Caterpillar was also happy to find there a strong management, and retain the firm key executives and its base of employees. Following the completion of the offer, current Chairman and CEO, Wang Fu, would continue to lead the operations of the business.

CS2.1. A Great USD677 Million Acquisition and an Award Winning Transaction

Adding to the strategic fit with Caterpillar, Siwei also had three high-profile investors with American ties. This was another reason that Caterpillar may have felt even more comfortable with the acquisition.

VElSRSZzdWJzaWQ9NTc%3d (accessed on December 22, 2014); see also "Caterpillar Form 10-K"; available online at http://phx.corporate-ir.net/phoenix.zhtml?c=92466&p=irol-SECText&TEXT=aHR0cDovL2FwaS50ZW5rd2l6YXJkLmNvbS9maWxpbmcueG1sP2lwYWdlPTg3MzY4NTgmRFNFUT0wJlNFUT0wJlNRREVTQz1TRUNUSU9OX0VOVElSRSZzdWJzaWQ9NTc%3d (accessed on December 22, 2014).

[94] Simon Montlake, "Cat Scammed: How a U.S. Company Blew Half a Billion Dollars in China," *Forbes*, January 21, 2013; available online at http://www.forbes.com/sites/simonmontlake/2013/02/13/cat-scammed-how-a-u-s-corporation-blew-half-a-billion-in-china/ (accessed on December 22, 2014).

The M&A project was presented to the Caterpillar (CAT) board on October 2011. In November 2011, the CAT board was informed that Siwei needed an urgent USD50 million cash injection due to aging receivables. However, the acquisition and the loan for working capital were authorized.

In November 11, 2011, Caterpillar and ERA jointly announced a pre-conditional voluntary offer by Caterpillar, through a wholly-owned subsidiary, for all of the issued shares of ERA, which at that time was a publicly traded company on the Hong Kong Stock Exchange.[95] If successful, the transaction would be the largest foreign machinery acquisition in Greater China since the country opened up for business in 1978.

As outlined in a joint announcement submitted to the Stock Exchange of Hong Kong, the offer consisted of two options:

(i) An all-cash alternative to acquire the shares in consideration for HKD0.88 per share; and/or

(ii) A loan note alternative, which will entitle the loan note holder to receive a minimum of HKD0.75 and up to HKD1.15 per loan note upon redemption. ERA shareholders will be able to elect to receive the all-cash alternative in relation to some of their shares and the loan note alternative in relation to the remainder of their shares, or to elect to receive either the all-cash alternative or the loan note alternative in relation to all of their shares.

Dependent upon ERA's performance and the number of shareholders who elect the cash alternative or the number who prefer the loan note alternative, the Caterpillar offer valued ERA between HKD4.5 billion and HKD6.0 billion.

In the tender offer, Caterpillar received acceptances in respect of 98.89% of ERA common stock and approximately 98.26% of all

[95]Elisabeth Behrmann and Masumi Suga, "Caterpillar Offers $885 Million to Buy ERA," *Bloomberg*, November 11, 2011; available online at www.bloomberg.com/news/2011-11-10/caterpillar-to-buy-era-machinery-for-up-to-885-million-to-add-china-sales.html (accessed on December 22, 2014).

outstanding options to purchase ERA common stock. Based on the distribution between ERA shares tendered for the all-cash alternative and the number of shares tendered for the loan note alternative, the final purchase price was estimated between HKD5.0–5.7 billion, depending on ERA's performance.

Caterpillar announced its intentions to exercise its right to acquire the remaining shares of ERA's common stock that it had not purchased to date under applicable provisions of the Cayman Island Companies Law, under which ERA is incorporated.

In June 2012, Caterpillar announced the completion of its tender offer for ERA[96] after the deal received a go-ahead from MOFCOM.

CS2.2. The Post Merger Integration Excavated an Accounting Mismanagement

On November 2012, the Caterpillar advisors were toasting the top deals of the year in Hong Kong and picking up an award for their cross-border deal of the year. That very day, three Caterpillar lawyers were wrapping up an eight-hour grilling of Siwei's Chairman Wang Fu. Major accounting problems had been excavated at the Siwei headquarters. On January 18, 2013, Caterpillar announced that an internal investigation had uncovered deliberate, multi-year, coordinated accounting misconduct at Siwei. This included improper cost allocation that resulted in overstated profit, inventory problems, and also improper revenue recognition practices. As a result, Caterpillar had removed the faulty senior managers and a new leadership team had been put in place.

Following the announcement, the situation triggered legal action against Caterpillar. New Jersey investor, Michael D. Wolin,

[96]Caterpillar Press Release, May 16, 2013 — "Caterpillar and Mining Machinery Limited Announce Settlement Agreement Related to Siwei Acquisition," Corporate Press Releases, May 16, 2013; available online at www.caterpillar.com/en/news/corporate-press-releases/h/caterpillar-and-mining-machinery-limited-announce-settlement-agreement-related-to-siwei-acquisition.html (accessed on December 22, 2014).

sued its Chairman Douglas R. Oberhelman and 13 directors for failing to heed "red flags" that should have alerted them as they were overpaying for the Chinese mine-equipment maker.

In 2012, Caterpillar announced the resolution of its outstanding issues with Siwei regarding Caterpillar's acquisition of ERA. This closed for Caterpillar an embarrassing chapter, which had so far overshadowed the company's benefits from the acquisition. Cleaning the mess had incurred a goodwill impairment charge, of approximately USD580 million for Caterpillar in its fourth quarter of 2012 results, wiping out around half of its expected income. Caterpillar alleged that its target's value had been inflated by accounting irregularities from unnamed parties.

The previous Siwei management acknowledged weaknesses in Siwei's accounting procedures and an inexperienced finance team, but continues to deny that any fraud had been committed. The former Siwei chairman has since established a new company intending to compete with Caterpillar.

Caterpillar still owed USD164.5 million for the acquisition of ERA. As part of the agreement between Caterpillar and former directors of ERA and two other interested parties, Caterpillar's total obligations have been slashed by USD135 million to USD29.5 million. In exchange, Caterpillar has agreed to end any litigation targeting ERA's former directors or auditors related to the alleged accounting misconduct.

The noise around these post-acquisition problems apparently impacted business and new orders for hydraulic roof supports were rumored to be quite weak. On November 2013, it was decided that the Siwei brand needed to be phased out and it was announced that the company name had been changed to Caterpillar (Zhengzhou) Ltd.

Case Study Three

Acquisition of 51% of Jonway Automobile by ZAP

ZAP (Zero Air Pollution), founded in 1994, is one of the oldest electric automobile manufacturers still alive in California. ZAP has a rich history of producing all sorts of electrical vehicles, from electric bicycles to electric SUVs. Since its creation, it has sold more than 117,000 vehicles in 75 different countries. Given the size of the automotive industry, it is a dwarf, but compared to the electric vehicle fleet, it is one of the visible players. The company started international operations with small but significant deals, such as the sale in 1995 of 500 electric propulsion modules for electric bicycles to China Forever Bicycles. This deal was a remarkable one on the Chinese market at this time and it shows the visionary plan of this company. About 15 years later, more than 100 million electric scooters and bicycles were riding on the roads of China.

Given the possibility of an energy peak and due to the interest of the market for electric propulsion, ZAP decided to become one of the world leaders of light electric transportation systems. The company showed its innovative capacities with a car, the Alias, the first electric vehicle capable to run on a highway. This new three wheeled vehicle was also one of the fastest electric cars at the time, with a maximum speed of 135 km/h, produced at an affordable price (around USD11,000).

CS3.1. ZAP is an Innovative Company Struggling to Find Its Market

At the end of 2009, the firm did not have more than 35 staff in the US and was struggling to design the right product to find a stable market, deliver a meaningful number of vehicles, and price them accordingly. This was probably the result of huge investments in R&D and weak production capacities. In fact, ZAP had become some kind of invention think tank for electric vehicles.

After reviewing the firm's competitive environment, ZAP's CEO, Steve Schneider, pointed out that the market for individual electric vehicles was not mature enough — "Currently there is no practical infrastructure, and the consumer, it doesn't matter where in the world, will have the same issues, which is known as range anxiety. The average consumer may drive 25 miles a day in their average driving practice, but every so often they might want to drive 100 or 200 miles. In that case, they cannot make today's electric vehicle their primary vehicle."[97]

ZAP therefore decided to focus on the development of professional vehicles for large corporation fleets or federal administrations. The company is producing vans, pick-ups, and SUVs for private and commercial use on private estates where the number of daily kilometers driven can be easily forecasted. "We are the only manufacturer producing a full size electric pick up, a full size electric SUV, which is what Jonway manufactures, and a full size electric van. We have several other utility vehicles as well. No one else is doing those three core vehicles at the moment. Although they are a smaller part of the market, it's the market that is more mature for the technology available today."

After the 2008 financial crisis and the subsequent economic slowdown, ZAP core customers did not have the means to acquire electric vehicles, more expensive on average than classic vehicles. In addition, the American government chose to help, as a priority, the most important American automotive manufacturers close to bankruptcy, to save jobs and protect the economy. No assistance was provided to ZAP.

The ZAP share price[98] fell to USD0.26 in early January 2009, a level 15 times lower than its historical peak of USD4.09 at the end of

[97] Available online at dario-zap-beijing.blogspot.fr (accessed on December 22, 2014).
[98] The ZAP share has been listed on the US OTCBB stock market since 1996 — "ZAP (ZAAP.PK), *Reuters*; available online at www.reuters.com/finance/stocks/companyProfile?rpc=66&symbol=ZAAP.PK (accessed on December 22, 2014).

2004. These adverse economic conditions pushed ZAP to distance itself from its original US market and broaden its horizon. 2004 was also the very year when automobile production in China overcame the US. As it became aware of China's ambitions in new green energy technologies and of the needed consolidation of its fragmented automotive industry, ZAP's senior management realized that China may again become an interesting opportunity.

Zhejiang Jonway Automobile (Jonway), a subsidiary of the Jonway Group, a privately funded Chinese company, specialized in the manufacturing of short series petrol SUVs (6,500 vehicles sold in 2010). The Jonway assembly line seemed to complement ZAP's, with a good automotive know-how, and sufficient capacities to develop new vehicles and increase production.

CS3.2. The Chinese Government Was Pragmatic

ZAP and Jonway announced on July 2, 2010, that they had reached a final agreement: ZAP will acquire 51% of the capital of Jonway for USD30 million. When ZAP got the approval of the governmental authorities for the transaction, it became the first American company to be authorized to buy the majority of the capital of a (small) Chinese automotive manufacturer.

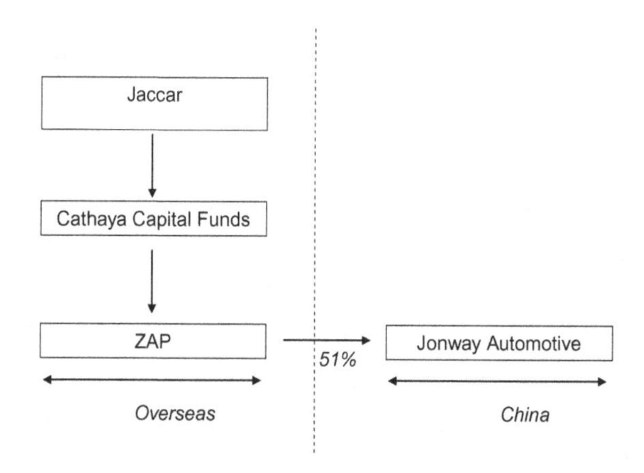

Figure CS3.1. ZAP Jonway: Transaction Financial Structuring.

The take-over of an automotive company by a foreign firm was previously considered impossible by the experts. But after six months of discussions and the desire of the Chinese authorities to encourage green gas energy vehicles and, in particular, carbon dioxide reduction (–40% by 2020), this decision was not such a surprise. Some flexibility on a traditionally strict rule was serving a broader vision to build a better environment, and it was not the first time that China's automotive industry was successfully cooperating with foreign manufacturers.

ZAP's CEO explained that much to his surprise, at the 2010 Beijing Auto Show, 600 electric cars were presented, much of them from Chinese manufacturers. After discussions with the Chinese International Chamber of Commerce, the Chinese Automotive Forum, and many officials, he realized that only a fraction of these electric vehicles would likely hit the Chinese roads and contribute to the 2020 carbon dioxide reduction target.

Another important clause of this transaction is the possibility for Jaccar to acquire 49% of the remaining capital of Jonway at the date of the transaction (March 30, 2011) or at another valuation, as needed.

ZAP and Jonway have communicated their intention to make this transaction a first step to later combine their respective industrial expertise. With the combination of the electric vehicle expertise of ZAP, together with the automotive production skills of Jonway (ISO 9000), the new entity will be in a position to produce a large number of new electric vehicles.

The key reasons behind this merger are quite clear:

- The merger gives to ZAP an industrial tool to produce a range of electric vehicles well-adapted for emerging markets.
- The manufacturing facilities of Jonway can be filled with the ZAP light commercial vehicle range (taxis, light bus, delivery vans).

Jonway always had a good stream of revenues and no financial debts but its future was uncertain due to the government decision to consolidate a fragmented automotive sector.

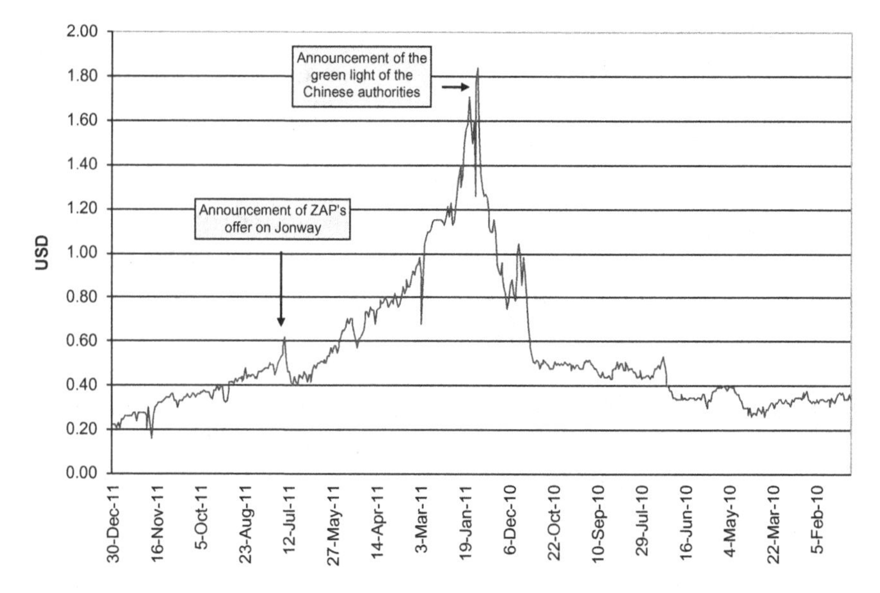

Figure CS3.2. Evolution of the ZAP Share Price.

The ZAP share price reacted well to this transaction and jumped to USD1.84 in January 2011, a record level since December 2005.

The payment of the first tranche of the transaction, USD19 million, was closed through Cathaya Capital in January 2011, a shareholder of the company since August 2009.

CS3.3. ZAP Jonway has the Ambition to Become an Electric Vehicle World Leader

The new entity's mission is to promote and develop the rich technological heritage of ZAP and access Asian markets with a new value proposition. Thanks to Jonway's logistics and reach, new customers can be reached through Jonway's distribution channels (about 80 exclusive resellers and about 100 non-exclusive ones). The merger seems to create the best conditions for the emergence of a strong player in this promising, but still risky, area.

Since 2011, the joint venture showed its capacities after the successful integration of ZAP technology in the Jonway vehicles. These

SUVs have been used as VIP shuttles during the Shanghai World Exhibition (Shanghai Expo).

The rationale for this acquisition emerged as ZAP realized that some critical components (long-range batteries) and infrastructure were not yet available to make the electrical vehicle a credible mass market substitute to the fossil fuel-powered cars. However, the corporate fleet vehicles dedicated to foreseeable tasks were ready. The choice of China was strengthened by the lack of interest of the American market, in general, for electric-powered cars.

ZAP considered the fact that Jonway had the capacity to annually manufacture up to 50,000 cars. Following the merger, ZAP was the only Asian manufacturer capable of producing for the needs of the corporate fleets: electrical vans, pick-up, delivery vehicles, and all electric SUVs in Asia.

CS3.4. The New International Ambitions of ZAP

In 2011, ZAP delivered its first batch of "Made in China" electric taxis to the Korean distributor, Samyang Optics, and stepped up on this promising market. Samyang will sell in Seoul the ZAP electric SUV based on the A380 design of Jonway. The firm is responding to the decision of the Korean Government to encourage the production of electric vehicles. ZAP has announced its ambition to capture 10% of the light commercial electric vehicle market in 2015, and also its ambition that electric vehicles (two or five seaters) represent about 10% of the cars in circulation in 2020.

Case Study Four

Temptative Acquisition of Huiyuan by Coca-Cola

Coca-Cola came back on the Chinese market in 1979. Two years later, the group was actively working on the opening of its first bottling factory in Beijing in 1982. Since then, Coca-Cola has built its presence all over China, and gets supplied from more than 30 self-owned or contract-controlled bottling companies.

Coca-Cola produces more than 35% of the carbonated drinks market in China and generates revenues over USD1.2 billion in this area. According to the information published by the group, the Chinese operations have been profitable since 1990.

The impact of the commercial success of the firm in China is shared between the 14,000 staff, the suppliers, the distributors, the wholesalers, and the retailers — representing about 400,000 jobs. Coca-Cola has renovated the old factories acquired in China, introduced international quality standards, and trained legions of managers in the non-alcoholic beverage segment in China. In the last 20 years, the firm's investment represented over USD1.6 billion. Under the Minute Maid brand name, Coca-Cola controlled an estimated 12% of the fruit juice market in China in 2008. The anticipated annual growth rate of this market was forecasted to 10% for the next 10 years.

Huiyuan Juice Group Ltd. (Huiyuan, 中国汇源果汁集团有限公司) is a privately-owned company created by a Chinese-born entrepreneur. Headquartered in Beijing, the company is listed on the Hong Kong stock market through its Cayman Island holding company. Huiyuan is ranked as the leader of the Chinese market, with a 52% market share in juice, 45.6% market share in nectars, and 8.5%

market share in fruits and vegetable cocktail juice — still a marginal segment. The global market is growing annually at 15% and the size of the market is estimated at USD2 billion. At this moment, the capital structure of Huiyuan is as follows: ABN Amro Holding 7%, Warburg Pincus 7%, Fidelity 7%, Danone 23%, market free float 15%, and founder and CEO, Zhu Xinli 41%.

CS4.1. The Coca-Cola Bid for Acquiring Huiyuan

As Coca-Cola wanted to strengthen its position on the Chinese juice market, the group informed the Hong Kong market authorities in September 2008 that it was contemplating a possible merger with Huiyuan. The target was valued at USD2.4 billion, HKD12.20/share, a level three times higher than the last closing share price, one month before the announcement. Huiyuan is "highly complementary to the Coca-Cola China business," Coca-Cola's president and chief executive officer, Muhtar Kent, said in a statement.

The motivation of the financial investors of Huiyuan was to exit and post a handsome return on their investment. For Danone, a long-term strategic investor in Huiyuan, well before it became a publicly listed company in Hong Kong, the motivation was to develop its partnership with the company over the long term and increase its presence in the capital of Huiyuan. ABN Amro was working for both Coca-Cola and Huiyuan and was acting as a facilitator in this transaction. The owner of the company explained that he has raised the company like a son but was planning to sell it as a "hog" (a graphic expression in Chinese meaning to maximize one's profit). The reaction by MOFCOM on the envisaged transaction was much awaited by investors in China and abroad. This bid was potentially the largest public bid on a Chinese listed company and the first launched since the adoption of the new Anti-Monopoly Law (AML) in August 2006.

The following share price graph clearly shows that the market was still sceptical on the outcome of the offer as the share price never reached the HKD12.20 offered by the bidder. The difference between the traded share price and the offer price showed the low probability put by investors on the likelihood of success of this operation.

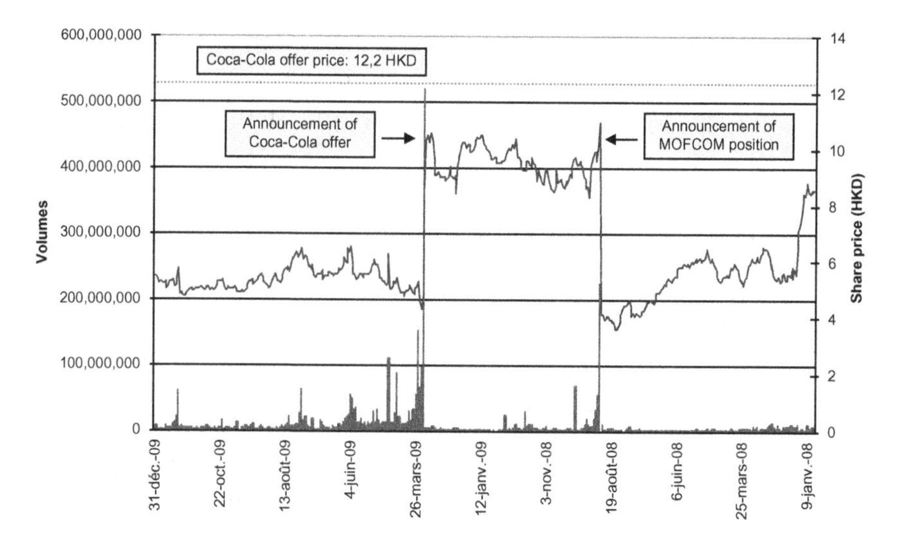

Figure CS4.1. Huiyuan Group Share Price (January 2, 2008–March 2, 2011).

MOFCOM requested Coca-Cola to complement four times its bid submission file before it was considered ready for review by the authorities. The review of the offer made by Coca-Cola started officially in November 2008. After an initial review of 30 days, MOFCOM decided to start a second review of 90 days to assess if the acquisition of Huiyuan was jeopardizing competition on the juice market, endangering consumer rights, and causing a threat to the possible technological development of this market segment.

The use of the 21-member AML committee of the State Council, established in 2008, was strengthened in mid-2014. It is expected that the enforcement of this law can serve as a good tool not only for creating a better market-based economy but also for reducing non-compliant or even corrupt behavior.[99]

[99]Lan Lan, "Antitrust Adviser Boosted off State Committee for Work Violations," *CHINADAILYUSA*, August 14, 2014; available online at usa.chinadaily.com.cn/epaper/2014-08/14/content_18310809.htm (accessed on October 10, 2014).

CS4.2. MOFCOM Bars the Coca-Cola Bid on the Basis of AML

In March 2009, MOFCOM announced its decision to stop the transaction on the basis of Article 28 of the newly adopted Anti-Monopoly Law (AML). MOFCOM then went into the details of its decision and highlighted:

- Coca-Cola would have a dominant position on the market of carbonated beverages and fruit juice; this will reduce competition and result in a reduced choice for the consumers.
- The presence of Coca-Cola on the Chinese juice market would be significantly increased by the control of both Minute Maid and Huiyuan. This will reduce the capacity of new companies to enter this market.
- The transaction will reduce the competitive space for medium- and small-sized players, thus reducing their capacity to grow and launch innovative products on this market.
- The transaction will have an adverse impact on the Chinese juice market competition structure in general and will not be positive for the market over the long term.

MOFCOM took good notice of the positive technological impact of the acquisition but considered that it was not likely to compensate for the negative consequence, and in particular, the possible impact on the consumer's interest. "Coca-Cola could use its market dominance in carbonated soft drinks to limit competition in the market for juice through tying, bundling, or other exclusive transactions, resulting in consumers being forced to accept to higher prices and reduced variety. [Moreover] because brands can restrict entry to the market, it would be hard for the threat of potential competition to remove the restrictive effect of competition," explained the regulator.[100]

[100]Lester Ross, Leon B. Greenfield, James W. Lowe, and Jeffrey D. Ayer, "Coca-Cola/Huiyan: China Prohibits Its First Merger under the AML," *WilmerHale*, March 20, 2009; available online at http://www.wilmerhale.com/pages/publicationsandNewsDetail.aspx?NewsPubId=91985 (accessed on December 22, 2014).

MOFCOM organized numerous informal meetings and working sessions with various actors on the market to gather information and form an opinion on the matter. The decision shows that MOFCOM had carefully structured its decision and visited many sites to get a clearer idea on the situation. The authorities also consulted with many Coca-Cola partners and academics specialists of law, economics, and agronomy.

Many were surprised by this decision; a competition specialist indicated in TIME magazine his opinion, which was that this transaction would have had no impact on the soft drinks market competition in China.[101] Before the decision was finally made by the authorities, some sources close to the acquirer indicated that the problem was obviously not so much about market competition, whatever the approach used to analyze the market impact was. The decision of MOFCOM led to a slightly negative reaction by international investors; the judgment was not considered very fair as many Chinese companies were granted the right to make acquisitions in many foreign countries.

CS4.3. A Defining Moment in the History of Huiyuan

The president and CEO of Coca-Cola, Muthar Kent, said in a press release, "We are disappointed, but we also respect the MOC's decision. [...] We put a tremendous effort into providing all the relevant materials to the MOC," he said, adding that Coca-Cola " [...] still holds a long-term view of the Chinese market and [is] committed to ensuring the Chinese consumers have a wide variety of top quality beverage options available to them."[102] The CEO of the group explained that the firm was going to concentrate all its energy and expertise to develop the existing brand, and that the group will continue innovating with new brands especially in the juice segment.

---

[101]Bill Powell, "China Says 'Keep Out' to Coca-Cola," *TIME*, March 18, 2009; available online at http://content.time.com/time/business/article/0,8599,1886024,00.html (accessed on December 22, 2014).

[102]Frederik Balfour, "Huiyan Juice: China Says Coke Isn't It," *Bloomberg Businessweek*; available online at http://www.businessweek.com/globalbiz/content/mar2009/gb20090318_570130.htm (accessed on December 22, 2014).

The group announced its intention to invest USD2 billion in the next three years to strengthen its production capacities, distribution, marketing, sales, and R&D.

In June 2009, Warburg Pincus sold its investment in Huiyuan and the capital fund dropped its option to exchange its convertible bonds for an additional 7% stake in Huiyuan. The firm announced that its USD66 million investment in Huiyuan convertible bonds was sold to a third party.

Danone, one of the food industry leaders committed to "bring health through food to as many people as possible", realized that it would not be able to develop more joint businesses with Huiyuan due to its minority holding and committed to sell its stake to the Asian capital fund, SAIF Partners. SAIF committed to buy the 22.98% stake of Danone in Huiyuan for HKD6 per share, about USD260 million in total. This price included a 10.7% premium on the share price. For the record, the same year, Danone sold the 51% owned in Wahaha after a 12-year partnership, which ended in a bitter spat between the partners in 2007.

Following the MOFCOM decision the share price collapsed, losing about 50%. Huiyuan announced a record profit of RMB234 million, a 162.5% increase compared to the previous year. Some time later, Huiyuan launched a new beverage named "Lemonme" to compete with Sprite (a Coca-Cola brand). At the beginning of 2011, Huiyuan acquired Hebei Rising Sun, an iced tead producer, one of the top 10 Chinese beverage companies and the market leader of iced tea drinks in China.

CS4.4. Some Final Thoughts

For the Chinese Government, the acquisition was in straight disagreement with the spirit of the 11th Plan of the National Congress of the Chinese Communist Party. The acquisition of Huiyuan would not have given much credibility to the decision of the Chinese Government to protect the Chinese brands. Maybe this transaction could have been a success at a different time with a different formulation more consistent with the political agenda.

Case Study Five

Acquisition of 51% of Guangdong Pharma by Nycomed

Nycomed is a mid-sized pharmaceutical group of Swedish origin based in Switzerland focusing on emerging markets. The group was initially known as Nyegaard & Co. until 1986, as it was named by its founder, a Swedish pharmacist. This company mostly grew by external growth in the last 10 years. The firm was created in 1874 to distribute foreign pharmaceutical products in Norway. During the 20th century, it gained international recognition after it started to sell generic products all over the world.

In 2000, the capital investment firm, Northern Capital, took control of Nycomed after acquiring 68.9% of its equity. At this time, Nycomed had only 2,372 staff and made €460 million revenues. Despite a small presence through representation offices in Japan, China, and Russia, Nycomed was generating most of its revenues from the North European markets. The company went through a radical transformation of its business, headquartered in Zurich, and in 2009, posted consolidated revenues of €3.2 billion.

At present, Nycomed is owned by four capital investment firms, Nordic Capital, still the controlling shareholder with 42.7%; Credit Suisse with 25.6%; Coller International Partners with 9.7%; and Avista with 8.9%. The firm is a mid-sized player in the industry and has 12,000 staff. Nycomed operates 17 facilities worldwide, including five competence centers in Europe and 12 production centers in emerging countries.

CS5.1. The Chinese Pharmaceutical Industry is under Transformation

Despite the size of its population, the Chinese pharmaceutical industry has a relatively small international footprint. In 2001, the year China joined WTO, there was no real, well-structured pharmaceutical industry in China and local players were relatively small compared to their international peers. Medical laboratories, manufacturers, wholesalers, and distributors were in the thousands, scattered all over China, most of them serving their local market. The government was traditionally not subsidizing R&D, FDA approvals were not very transparent and predictable, and the protection of intellectual property was problematic. Since then, significant progress has been made. The government created centralized supervision institutes, fostered industry consolidation, and funded the social security to provide better access to healthcare services. The local market has changed and great efforts are made to reach international standards. Governmental reforms, higher standards of living, and an aging population have transformed China into the world's largest emerging healthcare market, estimated at USD60 billion with an explosive annual growth rate of 20%.

CS5.2. The Techpool–Nycomed Transaction

In 2010, Nycomed was ranking 28th on the international industry scale; this performance resulted from the success of its external growth policy initiated in 2000. Despite strong growth in many markets, China only represented 5% of its total revenues: too weak a position compared to the potential of this market.

Guangdong Techpool Bio-Pharma Co., Ltd. (Techpool), created in 1993 in Guangzhou, specializes in the research, development, manufacturing, and distribution of bio-chemical medical products and drugs derived from natural extracts. Techpool posted a compounded average growth rate of 40% in the last five years.

Techpool has a partnership with one of the largest Chinese pharmaceutical companies headquartered in Shanghai — Shanghai

Pharmaceuticals Holding Co., Ltd. (SPH), specialized in R&D, manufacturing, and distribution of biological medical products. SPH is one of the leading pharmaceutical companies in the production and distribution of medical products including Rx, TCM, and OTC products. SPH has a strong position in China and exports its products to North America and Asia.

Techpool owns strong intellectual property (IP) including 35 patents filed and 17 registered, and one US registered patent including acute disease cures such as a treatment for Severe Acute Respiratory Syndrome (SARS). In addition, Techpool owns several state-of-the-art manufacturing facilities compliant with the European Drug Agency and the American FDA requirements.

After communicating in early 2009 its ambition to develop its business in China, Nycomed confirmed on November 1, 2010 the acquisition of the majority of Techpool's capital, together with the signing of a partnership with SPH. Nycomed acquired for USD234 million in cash, 51.34% of Techpool's equity, 28% from the Swiss capital investment firm, Starr International Finance, and the rest from Techpool's senior management. Starr International had previously acquired, in June 2008, its stake in Techpool for USD15 million and made a handsome eight times return, selling it with a USD101 million profit to Nycomed only 18 months later. This acquisition enabled Nycomed to take control of much needed production facilities in Asia including multiple sites all over China, and additional ones in Korea and Japan. Techpool's product pipeline and patent portfolio also quickly strengthened Nycomed.

The pharmaceutical specialization of Techpool, its experience of selling drugs on the Chinese market, and the strategic access to SPH's large distribution network mutually reinforced Nycomed's capacity to develop and launch new products in the Chinese market. Nycomed emphasizes that the main objective of the partnership is to enhance the competitive strengths of Techpool's key businesses to accelerate its growth and position in the Chinese market as a reference player.

Nycomed China and Techpool China will be managed as separate entities, and the value creation will be derived from well-targeted vertical and horizontal alliances between the two companies. Each company will continue to develop its own brand and sell its own products on the Chinese market.

The vice-president of Nycomed's commercial operations said: "This is a great opportunity for Nycomed and Techpool to build a strong player in the area of pharmaceuticals and biologics in China. Techpool's capabilities across the entire value chain were developed under the leadership of a formidable management team, headed by the founder and CEO Dr. Fu. This team will play a pivotal role for Nycomed's future expansion in China and the strong support of Techpool's existing shareholders, in particular Shanghai Pharmaceutical, makes us even more optimistic about our prospects in this exciting market," added Guido Oelkers, executive vice-president, Commercial Operations at Nycomed.[103] This successful acquisition will also have a positive impact on attracting new shareholders in the share capital of Nycomed and helping the firm to raise new funds to fund its international growth.

CS5.3. A Smooth Closing of the Techpool–Nycomed Deal

On January 1, 2011, Nycomed got the formal authorization to take control of Techpool, after some clauses prevented the company from assuming full control of its subsidiary. No additional payment was needed to clarify the matter. This acquisition contributed to help Nycomed double its revenues in China, and this take-over was fully consistent with the firm's strategy to focus on emerging markets. Nycomed positioned itself as one of the largest Western pharmaceutical companies operating in emerging markets and its performance continues to exceed the average industry growth in emerging markets. In 2010, Nycomed's total revenues increased by 30% compared to the previous year. The sales generated in emerging markets represented 39% of revenue, with the objective being to

[103]"Nycomed to Accelerate Expansion in China through Acquisition of Majority Stake in Guangdong Techpool Bio-Pharma," *Pharmaceutical Online*, November 2, 2002; available online at http://www.pharmaceuticalonline.com/doc/nycomed-to-accelerate-expansion-in-china-0001 (accessed on December 22, 2014).

reach 60% in 2015. At the beginning of 2010, Nycomed announced it was planning to invest USD300 million in Brazil over the next five years in acquisitions and partnerships. In Russia, the firm said it was willing to invest in new manufacturing facilities to strengthen its market footprint. The acquisition of Chinese companies seem not only attractive for foreign companies but also for local players, as it results in a positive infusion of know-how for the Chinese pharmaceutical industry. This series of ventures provided the Chinese pharmaceutical industry with a unique opportunity to catch up with the latest technologies and accelerate the industry learning curve.

CS5.4. Some Final Developments

Experts on predation have become increasingly convinced that ecosystems are run from the top. Mid-sized predators are always a game of choice for top ones. In May 2011, the Japanese pharmaceutical company, Takeda, announced the €9.6 billion acquisition of Nycomed to double its size in Europe and consolidate its presence on emerging markets.

Case Study Six

SEB Acquisition of the Majority of Supor on the Shenzhen Stock Exchange

In early 2006, SEB International, the small appliances French leader, whose brands include All Clads, Krups, Moulinex, and Tefal, was planning to acquire a majority stake in the Chinese company Supor, specialized in cookware and small appliances.

In 2003, when SEB started negotiations with the owner of Supor, the Chinese market leader for small appliances, the founding family replied that a foreign investor was not needed. SEB then started negotiations with China's number two player, and was prepared to bring a substantial portfolio of technologies to enhance the quality of the products sold on the Chinese market.

The Su family, owner of Supor, thought twice about the SEB proposal and finally decided to open negotiations with SEB.[104] The deal aroused strong and loud objections from other Chinese cookware firms before the Ministry of Commerce, which had launched an anti-monopoly investigation into the project, cleared the takeover in April 2007.

CS6.1. First Phase: Acquisition of a Controlling Stake in Supor

The deal allowed the French company to take a total stake of 52.74% in this Shenzhen listed cookware manufacturer. In August 31, 2007,

[104]Jean-Pierre Lac (2013), *MD Finance of SEB in Guide Chine,* Classe Export, pp. 66–67.

the French company had already acquired 30% of Supor's shares traded on the Shenzhen Stock Exchange before announcing that it would buy a maximum of 49,122,948 shares of the private cookware maker in East China's Zhejiang Province at RMB47 per share.

Previously the take-over price was RMB18 per share. The increased price had a premium of 16.2% against the average price of Supor shares in 30 trading days before November 15, and a premium of 17.6% against the closing price of Supor shares on the same day.

The SEB transaction was an unprecedented €327 million friendly public take-over on the PRC stock market. It was awarded the Merger & Acquisition Deal of the Year at the China Law & Practice Awards 2008.

This successful take-over has been an important milestone in the Chinese M&A history. This transaction was:

- The first direct acquisition by a foreign firm of a majority stake in a Chinese company listed on a regulated Chinese stock market (A-share).
- The first partial take-over bid on a Mainland China stock market.

CS6.2. Second Phase: Acquisition of an Additional Stake in Supor

In 2011, SEB received further approval to increase its stake from 51.31% to 71.31% of Supor's capital. This followed a formal approval from MOFCOM in July 2011 and a successful review carried out by the CSRC. Groupe SEB then purchased in December 115,450,400 shares of Supor, at RMB30 per share, for a total consideration of RMB3,464 million (approximately €400 million) and the Su family retained a 12.5% stake in the company. The remaining shares make up the free float and continue to be traded on the Shenzhen Stock Exchange. At the closing of this second transaction, the Supor revenues and valuation had tripled and the Su family, previous owner of Supor, made a substantial amount of money in this transaction.

Case Study Seven

The Airbus and Tianjin Free Trade Zone (TJFTZ) — AVIC Partnership

As far as 2005, China was poised to become over the next 20 years, the second largest aviation market in the world after the US. From 2000 to 2004, China's total aviation traffic grew at an average rate of 16.7%. Airbus forecasted that it might deliver a total of nearly 1,800 aircrafts to China over the next 20 years — an average of 90 aircrafts per year. And according to Airbus' forecast, the fast growing aviation market in China would need at least 200 large aircrafts like the A380 and China could likely become the first A380 customer in Asia.

The cooperation between the European and the China aerospace industry has been going on for a long time. China has extensive experience in aircraft manufacturing. China has been producing its own civil and military aircraft for decades and its state-owned manufacturing plants produce parts for almost all the Western manufacturers. In March 2014, Airbus president and CEO, Mr. Fabrice Brégier mentioned, "We are going to celebrate 30 years of successful cooperation with our Chinese partners in 2015 [...]. Our partnership with China, the mutual benefits we have explored, have been instrumental in furthering our global strategy [...]. We are looking forward to providing top performing aircraft from our Chinese assembly lines for many years to come."[105]

---

[105] "Airbus and China Take Their Partnership into the Future," *AIRBUS GROUP*, March 26, 2014; available online at http://www.airbusgroup.com/int/en/news-media/

CS7.1. Defining the Right Approach

China also had some other experiences in assembling Western aircraft, with Brazil's Embraer assembling ERJ-145s regional jets in Harbin city as part of a joint venture with China's Harbin Aircraft. However Harbin Embraer talks with Hainan Airlines for months, in 2008, concerning the 50 ERJ-145 delivery schedule resulted in a production slowdown of the Harbin JV and mixed feelings.

In the late '90s, McDonnell Douglas (MDD) assembled MD-90s in Shanghai with AVIC. The MDD's Chinese venture resulted in a failure as only two MD-90s were built. China Airbus sought to avoid the pitfalls that plagued the MDD experience by taking a different approach. While MDD relied heavily on AVIC to assemble the aircraft, with the Chinese partner producing the aircraft's main fuselage, wings, empennage, and nose, Airbus decided to perform only final assembly in China.

One of the lessons of the Airbus' successful partnership in China is that is was scaled in well-defined multiple steps over a very long period of time and gradually extended until the milestones were hit.

CS7.2. From Key Components to a Full Airbus Assembly Line in China

In 2005, AVIC 1 and Airbus signed a protocol to produce A320 family wing boxes in China. The protocol refers to the initial contract, with a projected total value of over USD500 million, signed in Beijing earlier this year between Airbus and AVIC 1, which committed the parties to the third phase of the A320 Family Wing Cooperation Programme, comprising the production of wing boxes and now also including the management of a second-tier supply chain. As wings are considered the most advanced part of an aircraft, it represents further significant progress in Airbus' overall programme of technology transfer to the Chinese aviation industry.

---

press-releases/Airbus-Group/Financial_Communication/2014/03/20140326_airbus_china.html (accessed on December 22, 2014).

"We have successfully kicked off the third phase of the programme in April this year. With joint efforts and close cooperation of the two sides, we are very confident that we can gradually undertake the production of whole wing box packages for the A320 Family," said Yang Yuzhong, AVIC I executive vice-president.[106]

"The A320 Wing Cooperation Programme has set an excellent example of mutually beneficial cooperation between Airbus and the major Chinese manufacturers. Airbus has no comparable project with any other country. We are looking forward to extending the scope and improving the levels of cooperation with our Chinese partners," said Iain Gray, Airbus general manager.[107]

In its industrial cooperation with China, Airbus is not only committed to technology transfer, but also committed to further increasing procurement volume to reach USD60 million per annum by 2007 and USD120 million by 2010. With regard to R&D, Airbus inaugurated the Airbus (Beijing) Engineering Centre in July 2015.

CS7.3. Launching a Final Assembly Line for the A320 in Tianjin

In October 2006, as a follow-up of the study initiated in late 2005, China Airbus signed a framework agreement with a Chinese Consortium comprising of Tianjin Free Trade Zone (TJFTZ), China Aviation Industry Corporation I (AVIC I), and China Aviation Industry Corporation II (AVIC II) in Beijing on the establishment of an A320 Family Final Assembly Line in China.

Airbus set up an A320 Family Final Assembly Line in Tianjin, and a joint venture was created between a Chinese Consortium led

---

[106] "Airbus and AVIC 1 Sign a Protocol Extending Cooperation on a $500 Million Contract for the A320 Family Wing Cooperation Programme," *Press Centre*, November 9, 2005; available online at http://www.airbus.com/presscentre/pressreleases/press-release-detail/detail/airbus-and-avic-1-sign-a-protocol-extending-cooperation-on-a-500-million-contract-for-the-a320-fami/ (accessed on December 22, 2014).

[107] *Ibid.*

by TJFTZ and Airbus. Airbus owns 51% of the joint venture, with the remaining 49% being held by a Chinese consortium comprising of AVIC and the Tianjin Free Trade Zone.

Aircraft assembly in China was planned to begin in early 2009, with the aim of ramping up production to reach four aircrafts per month by 2011. The factory will only be producing Airbus A319s and A320s, but it might later add A321s.

The aircraft sections will continue to be produced in Europe, and the assembly line delivers aircrafts to the same standards as those produced in Europe. Airbus' manufacturing partner, China's Xian Aircraft, already made the A320 wing box, which nevertheless had to be sent back and forth to the UK to be equipped. The long-term plan of Airbus was to have the wing boxes equipped locally and sent to the Tianjin assembly line. China is eager to do this work as the wings are recognized as one of the most technologically advanced sections of the aircraft.

On May 15, 2007, the site construction started in Tianjin after the approval by the State Council of the Feasibility Study Report for the project. The assembly line was opened in September 2008. All major parts of the plane were sent to Tianjin, China from Airbus' plant in Hamburg and Airbus China took the responsibility for recruiting and training all the people that will work on the assembly line dedicated to serve the Chinese market.

The first aircraft was completed and delivered on June 23, 2009 to Sichuan Airlines. By the end of the year, the assembly line had achieved its target, as the 11th A320 was delivered to Deer Air on December 16 in Tianjin.

CS7.4. Extending the China–Airbus Partnership Agreement in 2014

Three years later in 2012, the completion of the 100th A320 family aircraft by the Airbus Tianjin assembly line was a significant milestone for the cooperation between Airbus and China, as well as the Airbus strategy of internationalization. As a follow-up in

2014, Airbus strengthened its cooperation with the Chinese aviation industry in various fields, including Tianjin as an Asian Centre for Airbus and upgrading industrial cooperation in both scale and level.

Airbus and its Chinese partners, Tianjin Free Trade Zone and Aviation Industry Corporation of China (AVIC), have agreed to extend the successful joint venture to assemble A320 family aircraft in China for an additional 10 years. The "Phase II" will cover the period from 2016 to 2025, expand deliveries to the whole Asian region, and include final assembly of the A320neo family from 2017 onwards. During Phase II, capabilities of the Tianjin Final Assembly Line will be extended.

Two other areas of cooperation will be launched: (i) Supporting the CAAC with the latest state-of-the-art Air Traffic Management (ATM) in order to boost the capacity of Chinese airspace, and (ii) driving research into regional sustainable jetfuel and other initiatives in order to reduce the Chinese aviation environmental footprint.

The two parties plan to develop their cooperation on Airbus wide-body programmes. Airbus and relevant Chinese parties will work towards demonstrating the interest of setting up a wide-body aircraft completion center in China, which includes cooperation on wide-body cabin interiors with AVIC.

CS7.5. Key Lessons from the Partnership

The trusted and high level cooperation with the Chinese governmental authorities is probably the most important success factor for the project's success.

The assembly plant itself was being built not by Airbus but by the Tianjin FTZ to Airbus's requirements and leased to the European aircraft manufacturer. The plant's design is modelled after the Airbus Hamburg assembly plant, which is one the Airbus' group most advanced, in order to avoid mistakes and ensure maximum efficiency.

Producing aircrafts in China is cheaper than producing them in Europe, and the fact that the aircrafts are built locally means some significant delivery charges, import duties, and taxes can be avoided. However, the sale price of the aircraft is the same as in Europe[108] as it is the same aircraft.

[108]Leithen Francis, "Airbus China's Gamble", *Flightglobal*, October 28, 2008; available online at www.flightglobal.com/news/articles/airbus39-china-gamble-317890/ (accessed on December 22, 2014).

Appendix

PRC Laws about M&A and Partnerships

The presentation of the original laws from the People Republic of China is a good way to introduce the key Chinese legal framework for M&A. These texts provide the non-Chinese readers with the opportunity of having a better understanding and making a first opinion on the legal business environment of Mainland China. The authors also believe that gathering a consistent selection of key M&A related texts saves time for those who will be involved in the negotiations, as they can refer to them as needed.

These laws are written in a pragmatic business-minded style, in very clear and plain language. With the exception of the Circular of the Ministry of Commerce on Improvement of Foreign Investment's Verification and Administration —June 17, 2014 (only in Chinese for now), they have been directly published in a bilingual version (Chinese and English) and they originate from the Ministry of Commerce as the official source.

These laws are an excellent working base not only for legal practitioners but also for foreign businessmen in China. It is much recommended to read them to understand the key concerns of the Chinese lawmakers. Chinese negotiators usually do their homework well, meaning that they will be familiar with these texts: Even if they do not mention them explicitly during negotiations, they will leverage them.

The Chinese version prevails over the English one, and the nuances between the two may be important when negotiating a contract. A closer look at these texts shows that some wording remains relatively open for different interpretations, and one must be well aware of this specific feature of the Chinese legal framework.

Appendix 1. Laws of the People's Republic of China Applicable to M&A and Partnerships.

The original English version of these laws published by MOFCOM can be found and accessed on the PRC Ministry of Commerce website: http://english.mofcom.gov.cn/.

Circular of the Ministry of Commerce on Improvement of Foreign Investment's Verification and Administration — June 17, 2014.

Circular of the State Administration of Foreign Exchange on Issues Concerning Administration of Overseas Organizations' Foreign Exchange Accounts in China — July 13, 2009.

Anti-Monopoly Law of the People's Republic of China — June 22, 2009.

Circular of the Ministry of Commerce on Further Improving Examination and Approval of Foreign Investment — March 5, 2009.

The Catalogue of Advantaged Industries for Foreign Investment in the Central-Western Region (Amended in 2008) — January 1, 2009.

Circular of SAFE on Relevant Business Operations Issues Concerning Improving the Administration of the Payment and Settlement of Foreign Exchange Capital of Foreign-Funded Enterprises — August 28, 2008.

Circular of the National Development and Reform Commission on the Further Enhancement and Regulation of the Administration of Foreign Investment Projects — July 8, 2008.

Measures for Strategic Investment by Foreign Investors upon Listed Companies — April 30, 2008.

Labor Contract Law of the People's Republic of China — January 1, 2008.

Provisions on Mergers and Acquisitions of Domestic Enterprises by Foreign Investors — September 8, 2006.

Catalogue for the Guidance of Foreign Investment Industries (Amended in 2007) — December 1, 2007.

Appendix 2. Comparative Valuation of Chinese and European Car Manufacturers.[1]

Company	Country	Per	EV/EBITDA	EV/Sales
BYD Auto	China	15.1	12.4	2.0
SAIC Motor	China	21.2	23.3	1.7
Dongfeng Motor Group	China	14.3	11.1	1.3
Chongqing Changan Auto	China	24.5	12.2	1.6
JMC (Jiangting Motors)	China	29.1	19.2	2.8
PSA Peugeot Citroën	France	—	26.1	1.0
Volkswagen Group	Germany	47.2	15.7	1.6
FIAT Group	Italy	—	17.3	1.0
Daimler AG	Germany	—	78.3	1.7
Renault SA France	France	—	–23.2	1.5

Country of the Companies	PER Median	EV/EBITDA Median	EV/SALES Median
China	21.2	12.4	1.7
Europe	47.2	17.3	1.5

Company	Country	Market Cap (Billions, €)	Net Debt (Billions, €)	Company Value (Billions, €)
BYD Auto	China	6.6	2.0	8.6
SAIC Motor	China	18.4	7.0	25.5
Dongfeng Motor Group	China	10.3	2.7	13.1
Chongqing Changan Auto	China	2.9	1.3	4.2
JMC (Jiangting Motors)	China	3.1	–0.0	3.1
PSA Peugeot Citroën	France	6.4	42.6	49.0
Volkswagen Group	Germany	49.1	119.1	168.3
FIAT Group	Italy	7.6	44.7	52.3
Daimler AG	Germany	50.0	87.1	137.1
Renault SA France	France	11.4	39.4	50.8

(*Continued*)

[1] As of March 2011, based on the last published accounts in 2009.

Appendix 2. (*Continued*)

Company	Country	Net Result (Millions, €)	EBITDA (Millions, €)	Sales (Billions, €)
BYD Auto	China	438	699	4.2
SAIC Motor	China	871	1,097	15.0
Dongfeng Motor Group	China	724	1,183	9.8
Chongqing Changan Auto	China	118	344	2.7
JMC (Jiangting Motors)	China	108	161	1.1
PSA Peugeot Citroën	France	–1,274	1,875	48.4
Volkswagen Group	Germany	960	10,716	105.1
FIAT Group	Italy	–838	3,032	50.1
Daimler AG	Germany	–2,640	1,751	78.9
Renault SA	France	–3,068	–2,191	33.7

Appendix 3. Comparative Valuation of Chinese and European Food Companies.[2]

Company	Country	Per	EV/EBITDA	EV/Sales
Zhengzhou Sanquan Foods	China	53.8	37.8	3.4
Want Want China Holdings	China	28.2	21.2	4.7
Shunxin Agriculture Beijing	China	30	28.4	2.3
Tingyi Holding Corporation	Taiwan	17.4	16.4	2.5
Angel Yeast	China	31.4	9.9	5.6
Associated British Foods	UK	16.0	9.8	1.2
Parmalat	Italy	14.5	13.1	1.1
Danone	France	14.4	10.5	1.9
ConAgra	US	14.1	13.1	1.5
Nestlé	Switzerland	5.3	11.8	2.0

Country of the Companies	PER Median	EV/EBITDA Median	EV/SALES Median
China	30.6	24.3	3.4
Europe	14.4	10.2	1.5

Company	Country	Market Cap (Billions, €)	Net Debt (Billions, €)	Company Value (Billions, €)
Zhengzhou Sanquan Foods	China	0.7	0.03	0.7
Want Want China Holdings	China	7.2	0.2	7.5
Shunxin Agriculture Beijing	China	0.9	0.6	1.5

(*Continued*)

[2] As of March 2011, based on last published accounts in 2010.

Appendix 3. (*Continued*)

Company	Country	Market Cap (Billions, €)	Net Debt (Billions, €)	Company Value (Billions, €)
Tingyi Holding Corporation	Taiwan	10.6	1.1	11.7
Angel Yeast	China	1.1	0.1	1.2
Associated British Foods	UK	10.1	3.6	13.7
Parmalat	Italy	4.1	0.8	4.9
Danone	France	29.3	3.2	32.5
ConAgra	US	7.2	5.8	13.1
Nestlé	Switzerland	139.6	31.7	171.3

Company	Country	Net Result (Millions, €)	EBITDA (Millions, €)	Sales (Billions, €)
Zhengzhou Sanquan Foods	China	13	18.5	208
Want Want China Holdings	China	254	355	1,593
Shunxin Agriculture Beijing	China	28	55	679
Tingyi Holding Corporation	Taiwan	497	718	4,745
Angel Yeast	China	36	128	227
Associated British Foods	UK	646	1,399	11,545
Parmalat	Italy	285	377	4,301
Danone	France	2,034	3,092	17,010
ConAgra	US	515	1,002	8,578
Nestlé	Switzerland	26,492	14,507	84,913

Conclusion

There is a special providence in the fall of a sparrow.
If it be now, 'tis not to come.
If it be not to come, it will be now.
If it be not now, yet it will come — the readiness is all.[109]

The first objective of this book is to show the close interrelation between straight M&A transactions and partnerships (either joint ventures or shared shareholding in a Chinese domestic company). We tried to highlight two key success factors, (i) the necessary quality of relationships with the seller and its business ecosystem and (ii) the need to have a long-term perception of time. Usually, the closing of an M&A deal does not mean the end of the relationship. If the Chinese selling party is still a shareholder, then it is probably wiser to think of the acquisition as a *de facto* partnership. This means that the transaction should be replaced in a much wider time frame of continuous relationships. Sufficient time should be given to cultivate it in order to ensure that the parties keep a good understanding of each other. A mechanical processing of a transaction is likely to be possibly effective over the short term but very likely detrimental over the long term.

The second objective is to provide a practical and multifaceted vision on how to handle acquisitions and partnerships in China. We

[109]William Shakespeare. *Hamlet.* Act V, Scene 2.

try to emphasize China's specificities, and by extension, patterns that can be similar in other fast-growing, emerging countries. This means that possible acquisitions must be carefully planned. As soon as a decision is made to grow by acquisition, a reasonable budget must be allocated to identify possible partners, get to know them, and finally strike a transaction — either an acquisition or a partnership. Chinese businessmen expect foreigners to do their homework and prepare carefully to move on the rather complex Chinese market.

Cross-checking various sources show that more than half of the contemplated M&A deal failed before the signing of a Letter of Intent and only 20% would come to completion. The probability of success is correlated with the quality of preparation, which is rather good news when scratching behind the numbers. A rugged growth acceleration strategy must be designed, and various possible routes (options) must be defined and prioritized. This requires not only desktop analysis but, more importantly, on-the-field checks made by seasoned professionals and relationships.

As a rough guideline, the following briefly summarizes the key success factors of an acquisition or partnership in China, but then every detail is important when it comes to implementation.

Table C1. Key External Growth Success Factors.

Key Success Factors	What is Important to Pay Attention to
Relationships	Shared values, trust, and ethics. Business reputation and corporate responsibility.
Strategy	Analysis of market dynamics. Positioning of each target in this context.
Legal	Legal constraint must be well understood. There is always a certain degree of flexibility in the system.
Accounting	The books are not always very accurate. Numbers provided must always be reality checked.
Human ressources	Relationships and ethical behavior are important. HR management must be good and precise.
Valuation	Valuation must be based on international methodology. Specificities do apply for emerging markets.
Negotiation	Understand the Chinese culture and style. Be patient and flexible but very determined on objectives.

In China, the success of an acquisition or a partnership depends on the knowledge of the environment and the quality of relationships. It is also closely related to the quality of the advice received to select the best possible partner, to approach him, and to open and close the discussions in a smooth way.

Decisions must be taken under a clear leadership when needed. Nothing is more detrimental to a transaction than last-minute hesitations on the foreign side, and a perception on the Chinese side that the decision process is not understandable.

The third objective is to help decision makers realize that building quality partnerships or making smart and carefully planned acquisitions represent a bit of an upstream human and financial investment for a company. Just laying boots on the ground and cutting corners is certainly not a winning approach and one must be prepared to face the consequences of doing so. The Chinese will form a collective judgment and take their time to do so. Such opinions will be difficult to change afterwards: Corporate officers are replaceable assets, but no one is prepared to pay the price to replace a tainted brand name.

Given the size of the Chinese market, building a strong position represents a huge corporate achievement. Many foreign MNCs have excelled in doing so and continue to patiently strengthen their brand name by internal growth and carefully selected acquisitions. "Readiness is all", and it is important to put in the battle best resources and persistence, especially when headwinds will make navigation less comfortable. At the end of the journey, a series of successful hand-picked external growth operations will be a strong differentiating factor to accelerate one's growth and gain an even better competitive edge.

Bibliography

Ambler, Tim, Morgen Witzel, and Chao Xi (2008). *Doing Business in China.* 3rd edition. London, UK: Routledge.

Bessière, Véronique and Olivier Coispeau (1996). *L'évaluation des entreprises* (Corporate Valuation). 3rd edition. France: SEFI.

Brahm, Laurence J. (2007). *The Art of the Deal in China: A Practical Guide to Business Etiquette and the 36 Martial Strategies Employed by Chinese Businessmen and Officials in China.* Vermont, US: Turtle Publishing.

Chakravarty, Vikram and Soon Ghee Chua (2012). *Asian Mergers and Acquisitions: Riding the Wave.* New Jersey, US: Wiley.

Charles Wolf, Jr. *et al.* (2011). *China's Expanding Role in Global Mergers and Acquisitions Markets.* California, US: RAND Corporation.

Chen, Chien-Hsun and Hui-Tzu Shih (2008). *Mergers and Acquisitions in China: Impacts of WTO Accession (Advances in Chinese Economic Studies).* Cheltenham, UK: Edward Elgar Publishing.

Chong, Seung (2007). *The Law and Practice of Mergers and Acquisitions in China.* Oxford, UK: Oxford University Press.

Coispeau, Olivier, Stéphane Luo, Thierry Labarre, Joséphine Chow, and Steven Yu (2012). *Partenariats, Fusions & Acquisitions en Chine* (Partnerships and Mergers & Acquisitions in China). France: SEFI.

Devonshire-Ellis, Chris, Andy Scott and Sam Woollard (eds.) (2011). *Mergers & Acquisitions in China.* New York, US: Springer.

Doing Business in Emerging Markets. Harvard Business Review, Collectif. Massachusetts, US: Harvard Business School Press, 2008.

Etaix, Sylvain and Nicole Hoffmeister (2013). *Guide Chine, Tome 1. Réussir en Chine 70 témoignages* (China Business Guide, Volume 1. How to Be Successful in China, 70 Interviews). France: Classe Export.

Fei, Yiwen (2009). *The Institutional Approach to Mergers and Acquisitions: A Case Study in China.* Saarbrücken, Germany: VDM Verlag Dr. Müller.

Giard, Jacques and Jean Vincensini (2014). *M&A in Fast Growing Countries: Traps and Structuring Opportunities.* (A study encompassing the BRICS and next 10 emerging or emerged countries). France: Marccus Group and Mazars.

Harvard Business Review on Doing Business in China. Massachusetts, US: Harvard Business Review Press, 2004.

Ho, C. K. and C. S. Koh (2012). *HR Due Diligence: Mergers and Acquisitions in China.* Oxford, UK: Chandos Publishing.

Huang, Song (2008). *Mergers and Acquisitions* (Chinese edition). Beijing China: China Development Press.

Kenna, Peggy and Sondra Lacy (1994). *Business China: A Practical Guide to Understanding Chinese Business Culture.* New York, US: McGraw Hill Professional.

Khanna, Tarun and Krishna G. Palepu (2010). *Winning in Emerging Markets: A Road Map for Strategy and Execution.* New York, US: Harvard Business Review Press.

Kwek, Ping Yong (2013). *Due Diligence in China: Beyond the Checklists.* New Jersey, US: Wiley.

Lehman, Edward *et al.* (2011). *Best Practices for Mergers and Acquisitions in China.* Boston, MA, US: Aspatore Books.

Li, Guo, Christiano Rizzi, and Joseph Christian (2012). *Mergers, Acquisitions and Take-overs in China: A Legal Cultural Guide to New Forms of Investment.* Alphen aan den Rjin, Netherlands: Kluwer Law International.

Li, Jerry Z. (2007). *Invest in China: A Practical Legal Guide to Mergers and Acquisitions.* Beijing, China: Law Press China.

Li, Shu Feng (2012). *Corporate Mergers and Acquisition Restructuring in China Capital Market.* China: Economic Management Press.

Liu, Chengwei (2008). *Chinese Company and Securities Law: Investment Vehicles, Mergers and Acquisitions, and Corporate Finance in China.* Alphen aan den Rjin, Netherlands: Kluwer Law International.

Louapre, Emile and Aldo Salvador (1997). *L'incroyable métamorphose de la Chine* (The Incredible Metamorphosis of China). Paris, France: Editions L'Harmattan.

Marr, Julian and Cherry Reynard (2010). *Investing in Emerging Markets: The BRIC Economies and Beyond.* New Jersey, US: Wiley.

Marx, Mischa (2011). *Cross-border Mergers & Acquisitions in China: Implikationen und Handlungsempfehlungen für ein Modifiziertes Phasenmodell*

(Consequences and Recommendations for a Dedicated Acquisition Model). Hamburg, Germany: Diplomica Verlag.

Meinl, Matthias (2011). *Mergers & Acquisitions in China — Lessons from a Mid-Cap Transaction: A Description of the Take-over Proceedings and Negotiations with a Chinese Mid-Cap Company by an International Investor.* Saarbrücken Germany: VDM Verlag Dr. Müller.

Meril Emmanuel (2007). *Chine — Juridiqve, Fiscal, Social* (China — Legal, Fiscal, Social). 2nd edition. Dossiers Internationaux, Francis Lefebvre.

Mungenast, Hannes (2013). *Mergers and Acquisitions in China (with Special Focus on the Financial Industry)*. Munich, Germany: GRIN Publishing.

Orientation China Guidebook. Leading You to Business Success. China: The American Chamber of Commerce in Shanghai, 2013.

Pacek, Nemad and Daniel Thorniley (2007). *Emerging Markets: Lessons for Business Success and the Outlook for Different Markets.* New Jersey, US: Wiley.

Pereiro, Luis E. (2002). *Valuation of Companies in Emerging Markets: A Practical Approach.* New Jersey, US: Wiley.

S'implanter en Chine (Starting a Business in China). Missions économiques Pékin (French Missions Economiques (Beijing)). Paris, France: Ubifrance, 2010.

Tang, Robert Y. W. and Ali M. Metwalli (2006). *Mergers and Acquisitions in Asia: A Global Perspective.* London, UK: Routledge.

The Economist, 2006; available online at graphics.eiu.com/files/ad_pdfs/eiu_M_n_A_inChinaWP.pdf (accessed on October 14, 2014).

Vermander, Benoit (2013). *Corporate Social Responsibility in China.* Singapore: World Scientific Publishing.

Weber, Yaakov, Christina Oberg, and Shlomo Tarba (2013). *A Comprehensive Guide to Mergers & Acquisitions: Managing the Critical Success Factors across Every Stage of the M&A Process.* New Jersey, US: FT Press.

Wolf, Lutz-Christian (2007). *Mergers and Acquisitions in China: Law and Practice.* Hong Kong: CCH Hong Kong Limited.

Xiaoye, Wang (2014). *The Evolution of China's Anti-Monopoly Law.* Cheltenham, UK: Edward Elgar Publishing.

Yang, Guilian (2012). *International Merger and Acquisition in China: From Legal Perspective.* Saarbrücken, Germany: LAP Lambert Academic Publishing.

Yi, He (2009). *Post-Acquisition Management in China.* Oxford, UK: Chandos Publishing.

Zhang, Lusong (2007). *Regulation of Foreign Mergers and Acquisitions Involving Companies Listed in China.* Alphen aan den Rjin, Netherlands: Kluver Law International.

Zhou, Huiping (2012). *China's Mergers & Acquisitions: A Comparison with United States.* Saarbrücken, Germany: LAP Lambert Academic Publishing.

References

Agrawal, Ankur, Christina Ferrer, and Andy West (2011, May). "When Big Acquisitions Pay off." McKinsey & Company.

Aguiar, M. and G. Gopinath (2007). "Emerging Market Business Cycles: The Cycle Is the Trend." *Journal of Political Economy,* 115(1), 69–102.

Altman, E. (1984). "A Further Empirical Examination of the Bankruptcy Cost Question." *Journal of Finance,* 39(4), 1067–1089.

Authers, J. (2006). "The Long View: How Adventurous are Emerging Markets?" *Financial Times,* October 20, 2006; available online at http://www.ft.com/s/o/be77c600-605f-11db-a716-0000779e2340.html#axzz3QOEenlme (accessed on February 4, 2015).

Bao, B. and L. Chow (1999). "The Usefulness of Earnings and Book for Equity Valuation in Emerging Capital Markets: Evidence from Listed Companies in the People's Republic of China." *Journal of International Financial Management and Accounting,* 10(2), 85–104.

Barrow, C. *et al.* (2001). "Valuing High Growth Potential Companies: An International Comparison of Practices by Leading Venture Capitalists and Underwriters." *International Management,* 6(2), 55–73.

Bekaert, G. and C. R. Harvey (2002). "Research in Emerging Markets Finance: Looking to the Future." *Emerging Markets Review,* 3(4), 429–448.

———, C. Harvey, and C. Lundblad (2007). "Liquidity and Expected Returns: Lessons from Emerging Markets." *The Review of Financial Studies,* 20(5), 1783–1831.

——— *et al.* (1997). "What Matters for Emerging Equity Market Investments?" *Emerging Markets Quarterly,* 1, 17–46.

Black, B. S., H. Jang, and W. Kim (2006). "Does Corporate Governance Predict Firms' Market Values? Evidence from Korea." *Journal of Law, Economics and Organization,* 22(2), 366–413.

Bruner, R. *et al.* (1998). "Best Practices in Estimating the Cost of Capital: Survey and Synthesis." *Financial Practice and Education,* 8(1), 13–28.

——— *et al.* (2002). "Valuation in Emerging Markets"; available online at SSRN: http://ssrn.com/abstract=354241 (accessed on October 14, 2014).

——— and J. Chan (2002). "The Risk Premium for Investing in Emerging Markets: What Is It? Where Is It?" Working Paper, Darden Graduate School of Business Administration, University of Virginia.

Chen, C. *et al.* (2001). "Is Accounting Information Value Relevant in the Emerging Chinese Stock Market?" *Journal of International Accounting, Auditing and Taxation,* 10(1), 1–22.

Chen, Zhiwu and Peng Xiong (2001). "Discounts on Illiquid Stocks: Evidence from China." Working Paper, Stern University.

——— and ——— (2002). "The Illiquidity Discount in China." Working Paper, International Center for Financial Research, Yale University.

China Mergers & Acquisitions Playbook. New York, US: Deloitte Touche Tohmatsu, 2011.

Chong, James, Yanbo Jin, and G. Michael Phillips (2013, April 29). "The Entrepreneur's Cost of Capital: Incorporating Downside Risk in the Buildup Method." MacroRisk Analytics Working Paper Series.

Cogman, David and Gordon Orr (2013, December). "How They Fell: The Collapse of Chinese Cross-Border Listings." McKinsey & Company.

Copeland, T. E. (2002). "What do Practitioners Want?" *Journal of Applied Finance,* 12(1), 5–11.

Cruces, J. J., M. Buscaglia, and J. Alonso (2002). "The Term Structure of Country Risk and Valuation in Emerging Markets." Working Paper Series, No. 46, Universidad de San Andres, Argentina.

Damodaran, Aswath (2013, March 23). "Equity Risk Premiums (ERP): Determinants, Estimation and Implications — The 2013 Edition"; available online at SSRN: http://ssrn.com/abstract=2238064 (accessed on October 14, 2014).

Erb, C. *et al.* (1995). "Country Risk and Global Equity Selection." *The Journal of Portfolio Management,* 21(2), 74–83.

Estrada, J. (2000). "The Cost of Equity in Emerging Markets: A Downside Risk Approach." *Emerging Markets Quarterly,* Fall, 19–30.

Estrada, J. (2001). "The Cost of Equity in Emerging Markets: A Downside Risk Approach (II)." *Emerging Markets Quarterly,* Spring, 63–72.

Fama, E. and K. French (1992). "The Cross-Section of Expected Stock Returns." *Journal of Finance,* 47(2), 427–465.

Ferrer, Christina, Robert Uhlaner, and Andy West (2013, August). "M&A as Competitive Advantage." McKinsey & Company.

Godfrey, S. and R. Espinosa (1996). "A Practical Approach to Calculating Cost of Equity for Investments in Emerging Markets." *Journal of Applied Corporate Finance,* 9(3), 80–90.

Harding, David, Satish Shankar and Richard Jackson (2013, January 16). "The Renaissance in Mergers and Acquisitions: The Surprising Lessons of the 2000s." Bain & Company.

Harvey, C. R. (2001). "The International Cost of Captial and Risk Calculator (ICCRC). Duke University, North Carolina, US, July 25, 2001; available online at https://faculty.fuqua.duke.edu/~charvey/Research/Working_Papers/W35_The international_cost.pdf (accessed February 4, 2015).

James, M. and T. Koller (2000). "Valuation in Emerging Markets." *The McKinsey Quarterly,* 4, 78–85.

Kohers, G., N. Kohers, and T. Kohers (2004). "A Comparison of the Risk and Return Characteristics of Developed and Emerging Stock Markets." *Journal of International Business Research,* 3(1), 59–67.

Lee, C. (1987). "Accounting Infrastructure and Economic Development." *Journal of Accounting and Public Policy,* 6(2), 75–85.

"Les clés du marché chinois (The Key to the Chinese Market)." Minutes of an M&A conference organized by Mazars, Paris, February 13, 2014.

Lesmond, D. (2005). "Liquidity of Emerging Markets." *Journal of Financial Economics,* 77(2), 411–452.

Lessard, D. (1996). "Incorporating Country Risk in the Valuation of Offshore Projects." *Journal of Applied Corporate Finance,* 9(3), 52–63.

Lourdes, Alers (2002). "Cost of Capital: The Downside Risk Approach." Working Paper, University of Virginia, Darden School of Business.

Luehrman, T. (1997). "Using APV: A Better Tool for Valuing Operations." *Harvard Business Review,* 75(3), 145–154.

Mariscal, J. and K. Hargis (1999). "A Long-Term Perspective on Short-Term Risk: Long-Term Discount Rates for Emerging Markets." Goldman Sachs Investment Research; available online at people.sterm.nyu.edu/jmei/hargis.pdf (accessed on October 14, 2014).

Mehra, R. and E. C. Prescott (1985). "The Equity Premium: A Puzzle." *Journal of Monetary Economics,* 15, 145–161.

Mirza, N. (2005). "The Death of CAPM: A Critical Review." *The Lahore Journal of Economics,* 10(2), 35–54.

Oetzel, J. *et al.* (2001). "Country Risk Measures: How Risky Are They?" *Journal of World Business,* 36(2), 128–145.

Oyerinde, D. T. "Value Relevance of Accounting Information in Emerging Stock Market: The Case of Nigeria." In Simon P Sigue (ed.), *Repositioning African Business and Development for the 21st Century*, 8–14. Proceedings of the 10th Annual Conference, May 19–23, 2009, Volume 10. International Academy of African Business and Development (IAABD), Uganda.

Pereiro, L. (2001). "The Valuation of Closely-held Companies in Latin America." *Emerging Markets Review*, 2(4), 330–370.

——— (2006). "The Practice of Investment Valuation in Emerging Markets: Evidence from Argentina." *Journal of Multinational Financial Management*, 16(2), 160–183.

Rehm, Werner, Robert Uhlaner, and Andy West (2012, January). "Taking a Longer-Term Look at M&A Value Creation." McKinsey & Company.

Sabal, J. (2007). "WACC or APV? The Case of Emerging Markets." *Journal of Business Valuation and Economic Loss Analysis*, 2(2), 1–15.

Schoenberg, R. (2006). "Measuring the Performance of the Corporate Acquisitions: An Empirical Comparison of Alternative Metrics." *British Journal of Management*, 17(4), 361–370.

Stulz, R. (1999). "Globalization, Corporate Finance and the Cost of Capital." *Journal of Applied Corporate Finance*, 12(3), 8–25.

Thurner, M. (2003). "Valuation of MNC Subsidiaries in Emerging Markets: The Case of China." Working Paper, University of St. Gallen.

Villarreal, Julio E. and Maria J. Córdoba (2010, July 30). "A Consistent Methodology for the Calculation of the Cost of Capital in Emerging Markets"; available online at SSRN: http://ssrn.com/abstract=1663845 (accessed on October 14, 2014).

Wang Xing and Ding Qingfen (2011). "Foreign M&A Given Oversight: Panel will Review Proposed Overseas Purchases of Domestic Companies." *The Marketplace of Life*, February 14, 2011; available online at themarketplaceoflife.blogspot.fr/2011/02/foreign-m-given-oversight-in-china.html (accessed on December 22, 2014).

Worthington, A. C. and H. Higgs (2006). "Evaluating Financial Development in Emerging Capital Markets with Efficiency Benchmarks." *Journal of Economic Development*, 31(1), 1–27.

Zenner, M. and E. Akaydin (2002). "A Practical Approach to the International Valuation & Capital Allocation Puzzle." Global Corporate Finance Papers, Salomon Smith Barney Financial Strategy Group.

Index